CHRISTIAN WORSHIP

SOME MEANINGS AND MEANS

BY GEORGE HEDLEY

The Symbol of the Faith
  a study of the apostles' creed
The Christian Heritage in America
The Superstitions of the Irreligious
Christian Worship
  some meanings and means

CHRISTIAN WORSHIP

SOME MEANINGS AND MEANS

GEORGE HEDLEY

NEW YORK   THE MACMILLAN COMPANY   1953

PREFACE

SEVERAL YEARS AGO the chairman of the Student Chapel Committee at Mills College, herself the daughter of a Lutheran pastor, suggested that we might work out a service more generally representative of our varying traditions than was the form we had come to use. I put in her hands a number of official service books—Lutheran, Anglican, Presbyterian, Methodist, Congregational, Unitarian—and asked her to see what she could do with them. Ere long she brought them back. "It's no use," she said. "They're all alike anyway." They are, and of right ought to be. But most of us still have much to learn about their significance and their proper using.

The major premise of this book is that the Lord is great, and greatly to be praised. The minor premise is that members of the Christian fellowship have praised him well, and will praise him best, in the usages that through the centuries have grown up within that fellowship. The conclusion is that if we are to worship aright, we first must know and understand our heritage of worship, and then must employ it to declare God's glory and our own devotion.

Most of the chapters therefore are constructed on a what-why-how plan. "What" and "why" both are historical, and both are interpretive too. "How" is practical; but its practicality is inseparable from knowledge and understanding of the "why" and the "what." In terms of the general title, "what" refers both to meanings and to

v

means, "why" to meanings, and "how" to means and to meanings as well.

The historical sections are integral to the discussion. They include considerable reference to technical detail, though (I hope) they are not stated in difficult technical language. Perhaps the chief weakness of the current attempt to resume the use of historic forms has been its too common lack of acquaintance with the development of those forms, and with their original and ever changing implications. The clergy, having special professional responsibility, need most to know the backgrounds and to consider the procedures; and a few of the paragraphs are rather specially for them. The laymen too, however, will worship better as they become more familiar with that heritage of worship which is rightly theirs. Some of the story is told here; and the works listed in Appendix A will tell much more to those who wish to pursue the enquiry.

At the same time I have tried to keep in mind the actual situations of our own day, physical and psychological and social. Much that is suggested about specific practice in the services of the Church has been tried and tested in a ministry of thirty years; and most recently and most completely in the Chapel of Mills College. Now and then I must fall back on the sound injunction, "Do as I say, not as I do," for even at Mills there are problems occasioned by physical setting, and a few by cultural lag. Thus (as will be seen below) I regard kneeling as the proper posture for prayer, and for receiving the Communion; but the surviving strength of Puritan tradition among our Presbyterian and Congregational constituents requires that we shall make here no positive requirement.

The will of Cyrus Taggart Mills specified that the trustees should "keep the College for ever thoroughly Christian, but not sectarian." Some have somewhere supposed that the way to have a "nonsectarian" service is to leave out of it everything any particular sect doesn't use, and so to move nearer and nearer to an absolute zero. At Mills we have tried rather to make our services interdenominational on the positive side, by drawing from every source which can contribute materials of value; and so we have found ourselves not negatively sectless, but more and more affirmatively Christian. It is such a quest, not for a lowest common denominator but for highest common factors, that is represented in the pages which follow.

Those highest common factors, for more than three-fourths of the history of Christianity, and for seven-eighths of that of the total Hebrew-Christian tradition, belong equally to every Western Christian, Roman and non-Roman alike; and the divergences of Eastern Orthodoxy are much less than are the agreements. The main stream of Christian worship did split, four hundred years ago, into a number of delta rivulets, and some of them ran quite shallow. Now it is evident that many of them are flowing together again, and that for the reason that the old river bed has proved to be the broadest and deepest after all. There are those who hope and believe (and the present writer is one) that this renewed sharing of our Christian heritage in worship points toward a true reuniting in fellowship.

To catalogue my indebtedness I must begin with the historic and universal Christian Church, and all it has given to me as one of the latest and least of its members. More immediately and specifically, I would pay tribute to my father, the late Reverend John Hedley, who as an English Methodist transplanted to America stood stubbornly for the authentic position of that stubborn high churchman John Wesley. My thanks are due also to Dr. H. Augustine Smith, long ago my teacher in hymnology, whose vital concern with worship won my heart even more than his specific opinions dismayed my judgment.

In the nearer past I am deeply indebted to three men, of three major denominations but of one Christian faith, who have been kind enough to look over the manuscript and to overlook many of its shortcomings. These are the former chaplain of Columbia University, now the Right Reverend Stephen F. Bayne, Jr., Protestant Episcopal Bishop of Olympia; my former student on two campuses, today Bishop Gerald Hamilton Kennedy of the Los Angeles Area of the Methodist Church; and that great Presbyterian the late Reverend Dr. Lynn Townsend White, professor emeritus in San Francisco Theological Seminary, whose thoughtful letter to the publishers about the manuscript was one of the last things he wrote. These learned and reverend gentlemen helped me with the book long before I thought of writing it, and their generous aid continued through the final revisings. They are not to be charged, however, with any errors, either of fact or of judgment, that may be present.

My thanks are due to clergy, architects, and photographers, as indicated below, for providing or allowing me to secure the pictures from which the plates have been made; and to numberless friends, lay and clerical, who have contributed specific information and sound judgment in informal discussions through the years.

Finally I record my deep and perduring debt to the successive Student Chapel Committees at Mills College, whose creative imagination has helped so much to develop the forms of divine service on this campus, and whose devoted activity has made the services beautiful as forms of art and real as worship of God. To them their chaplain dedicates this book, as to them and to all their fellow students he would seek to dedicate himself in the service of God in Christ Jesus.

G. H.

RUDDIGORE, MILLS COLLEGE
Easter Tuesday, 1953

CONTENTS

ix

ILLUSTRATIONS

LINE DRAWINGS

PLATES

GRANT, O LORD, that the ears which have heard the voice of thy songs may be closed to the voice of clamour and dispute; that the eyes which have seen thy great love may also behold thy blessed hope; that the tongues which have sung thy praise may speak thy truth; that the feet which have walked thy courts may walk evermore in the way of light; and that the bodies which have tasted thy living Body may be restored in newness of life. On this congregation let thine aids be multiplied, and let thy great love remain with us; and by thee may we abound in the manifestation of thy glory.

—LITURGY OF MALABAR

I

WHY WORSHIP?

"WHY," ASKED A Mills College sophomore, "should worship be a part of religion? In other words, why don't we go to Church just for the sermon?" She sent in her question on a post card, asking that it be used as the basis for a Sunday sermon in the Chapel. It was her own question; but it was and is the question of very many others in our American churches of today.

It did take a sermon, of course, to offer any sort of explicit reply. Yet that sermon was embedded in a matrix of praise and prayer, and of congregational activity as well as clerical utterance. This book is an attempt to enlarge the explicit reply of that Sunday morning. Like the sermon, however, it can serve its purpose aright only if it is linked with the implicit and much more important answer of personal experience in worship. Here will be discussed some of the usages of worship, in the hope that somewhat more detailed knowledge will issue in deeper understanding. But let us keep it in mind that understanding will grow not nearly so much by knowledge and discussion as it will by earnest experiment.

WHAT IS WORSHIP?

"Worship" itself needs at least a preliminary definition as we start our enquiry. Our own word is Anglo-Saxon, by way of Middle English, and it signifies "worth-ship." Thus when we worship we are declaring worth. "Worthy is the Lamb that was slain," sang the

1

angels who numbered "ten thousand times ten thousand, and thousands of thousands." And every creature answered, setting forth the divine worthiness,

Blessing, and honour, and glory, and power, be unto him that sitteth upon the throne, and unto the Lamb for ever and ever.

The account of this part of St. John's vision therefore rightly ends, "The four and twenty elders fell down and worshipped him that liveth for ever and ever."

The Greek in the book of Revelation uses the standard New Testament word for "worship": *proskuneo*, literally "I kiss toward," implying "I kiss the hand toward." The force is that of doing homage, and thus the term is employed from the classical Greek dramatists down. The corresponding word in the Hebrew is *shachah*, "to bow down," or to prostrate one's self. *Shachah* is used of Abraham when he thought to offer Isaac, of Solomon in the new Jerusalem Temple, and in such Psalm verses as "O worship the Lord in the beauty of holiness." *Proskuneo* appears in the account of Jesus' temptation, in the Fourth Gospel's "worship him in spirit and in truth," and no less than twenty-four times in the New Testament Apocalypse. Our total tradition thus sees worshiping man as one who declares, by his own humble acts of homage, the worth-ship of his Lord and Maker.

Some related words ought to be examined here. "Service" is our casual term for a period of worship in a church or elsewhere, and "divine service" often a formal designation. There are many ways of serving God, in the church and outside it; and our usage has insisted that one important way is that of asserting together our intent to serve God by proclaiming together his worthiness to be served.

"Minister," it should be noted, once was a term precisely equivalent as verb to "serve," and as noun to "servant." The lord was the *magister*, the greater one, the master to whom service was rendered. The lesser person, the *minister*, served his lord in the lower state that was his. He who served at the altar came to be called the "minister" in a special sense, the servant of the servants of God; but all who serve are ministers in truth, as all are called to serve both God and his people.

Yet another word, which had just about the same original force, is "liturgy." This has come to be understood to refer to ritual in general. The Greek *leitourgia*, however, meant first "working for the people," and thus was applied to secular duties performed for the Athenian state, even before it became attached particularly to religious observances. Strictly, in historic Christian terminology, a liturgy is a specific form used in the celebrating of the Holy Communion, or Mass, as the supreme form of Christian divine service. Thus the common expression "liturgical Churches" is inexact; for the only nonliturgical Christian groups, in the precise sense, are those who, like the Society of Friends, do not include the Communion in their practice.

"Ritual," from the Latin *ritus*, "ceremony," is a more fitting word for general application to prescribed or traditional modes of worship. Unfortunately the history of dispute from the Reformation onward has given "ritual" an unfavorable coloring in many Protestant circles, so that to speak of "ritualistic Churches" is almost to pronounce a negative opinion of them. Yet ritual, as soon we shall observe, scarcely is to be avoided even by those who most enthusiastically decry it.

Divine service then is the declaring of God's worth-ship in the united voice of his people. Ministry is service, whether rendered by clergy or by laymen. Liturgy is to be understood as a particular procedure in the serving of God in the supreme Christian symbol of sacrifice and fellowship, the Holy Communion. Ritual is the special manner of rendering service which has developed within a given tradition, and which has taken a relatively fixed form. All of these are involved in our sophomore's question.

THE BEGINNINGS OF WORSHIP

"Why should worship be a part of religion?" The first reply is that it always has been. All definitions of religion make some reference to worship, verbal or implied. Even a definition in terms of loyalty to a scheme of values, which would not necessarily include a God, involves the worthiness of those values to which one's loyalty is pledged.

Historically considered, the overt declaring of that worthiness seems to have been inescapable. They who saw divine power in a tree, a rock, a spring, or a storm pronounced their respect for that power in words and in actions: words of prayer and praise, actions of humility or sacrifice. As man's sophistication grew, and as he looked beyond the immediate phenomenon toward its more distant cause, he sought for better words to express his praise, and more significant actions in the performing of his service.

Inevitably in each culture such words and actions came increasingly to be repeated and standardized. Those who most had pondered the problems of worth-ship led their fellows to join in what seemed to them the proper modes of expression. These leading individuals became thus a kind of clergy, and their once experimental practices a settled ritual.

It is no more possible to dogmatize about single or multiple origins of worship than it is about single or multiple origins of Homo sapiens. We know man throughout the world; and we find him, in all his variety, so definitely one that we classify him as a single species. Even so, in all the multiplicity of the forms of religion, there is an essential identity at these points of recognized leadership and regularized observance: and so in the ways of worship of all mankind.

THEY WHO DO NOT WORSHIP

But that something has been done in the past is not to the modern mind a compelling reason that it must be done hereafter. Man has worshiped. That we know; and we know that worship has been included in his religion wherever we can trace it in time or in geography. It does not necessarily follow, from this single datum, that religion without worship is quite unthinkable.

The question is whether the historical development we have noticed really was inevitable in the make-up of the human individual and of human society. Superficially a negative reply seems quite possible. Certainly today there are countless millions, in this country and elsewhere, who never consciously worship at all. Even of those who are nominal adherents of religious systems, a very high proportion take no part, or a minimum one, in the formal practices of their respective faiths. Yet many of these would claim to be religious people.

Again, there are those who say explicitly, as did John Burroughs, that their religion as scientists is the love of truth. There are also those whose first loyalty is to a politico-economic system, such as Marxism. Both these groups of secularists would deny that they worship at all, or that they have any need for worship as a factor in their living.

In many ways akin to these are those extreme Protestants who have inherited and maintained so great a fear of formalism, and therefore of ritual, that they discount worship both by their statements and in their practice. It is a reasonable guess that our sophomore had been influenced from this direction. The sermon, as a sort of lecture, she could appreciate. The remainder of the service, sometimes described as the "preliminaries," seemed to her quite pointless.

If we add together these groups of people: those whose religion thus openly deprecates the uses of worship, those others who altogether deprecate religion in their thinking, and those who more casually deprecate both worship and religion by their behavior, we probably have a majority of the American community of today. It might seem, then, that neither is worship integral to religion, nor religion to human life. The one question that must be raised is whether the testimony of these groups is to be received as valid evidence.

OR DON'T THEY?

The first of them, that vast company which professes religion without thinking seriously to practise it, obviously has the lowest standing in the court. That to a large extent these people get along without worship may be true; but this is because in some measure they succeed in getting along without religion. They have no certain scale of values to which personally they are committed, and so they have no worth-ship that they are properly qualified to proclaim. Their witness therefore is not to the irrelevance of worship to a complete life, but rather to the irrelevance of themselves to any meaningful living.

It is a notable fact that many of these unreflective ones turn, it would seem automatically, to the traditional practices of religion when crisis comes upon them. "There were no atheists in the foxholes," and there were prayers and conversions on life rafts in the Pacific. Desperate illness and personal bereavement, as every clergyman knows, bring sudden calls for the ministries of the Church. Men and women often do turn to God when they find they need him; and when thus they conclude at last that God is worthy of their attention they worship him whether they know it or not.

The case of the articulately nonreligious is a more difficult one to estimate and argue. So far as Marxist atheism is concerned, there are substantial grounds for the view that an authentic equivalent to religious worship has grown up within the Soviet system despite all its atheistic pronouncements. The singing of the *Internationale*, the raising of the clenched fist, the maintenance of the shrine of Lenin, the blown-up pictures of Stalin: these may seem to us to be horrible caricatures of singing the *Te Deum*, and kneeling in prayer, and commemorating the saints, and making the Stations of the Cross. They appear nevertheless to be psychologically identical with the Christian uses, springing from the same kind of psychological needs, and producing the same kind of psychological satisfactions.

Some years ago the Soviet film agency distributed throughout the United States a picture called *Three Songs about Lenin*. Suddenly the film was withdrawn, one suspects because it demonstrated so conclusively that the avowedly irreligious Leninists had created an intensely devout and extremely naïve religion of their own. One of the three songs seemed to be a direct borrowing from the Fourth Gospel, including as it did such professions of faith as that "Lenin gives us bread," "Lenin gives us light," "Lenin gives us life," and even that "Lenin is dead and is alive for evermore." Whatever may be our opinion of the object of this honoring, we can not fail to recognize that this sort of thing is worship indeed.

The avowedly secular scientist is less readily to be identified as a religious and worshiping person. Yet when he announces that his personal devotion is to truth, he certainly is religious and surely is not far from worshiping. "Sit down before fact as a little child," urged Thomas Huxley. Fact, then, to him, and to all who share his views, is worthy of absolute respect. The more deeply a scientist penetrates into the mysteries of the universe, the more profoundly he recognizes that he never can be sure of all the answers. Is not this then to declare his own ministry, his own lesserness and his obligation to serve the greater than himself? He may not call it worship; but he would be hard put to it to disclaim the reality of his reverence for what he knows best and cares for most.

WORSHIP AND RITUAL

There remain to be considered those people who count themselves to be religious, but who consider worship unimportant and ritual undesirable. Their thinking stems from historic Protestantism, particularly by way of those Reformed and Separatist groups who played so large and determinative a part in the history of the North American colonies. Distaste for Rome and all her works was a major positive factor in producing this negative mood. Separation from the sources of tradition and from the interplay of further debate, along with the necessarily informal life of the pioneer, served to fix the negativity in general American practice.

On the other hand, those who had broken away from Rome, and subsequently from the Church of England, felt compelled to state their reasons for the faith that was in them. Preaching therefore became the focal point of the gatherings of these dissident Christians. No little of the preaching, dwelling on the faults of those institutions from which the preachers and their hearers had withdrawn, emphasized in particular the dangers of priestcraft and the emptiness of standard forms. Thus both in example and by precept the typical American church long placed much more weight upon discussing God than on praising him.

Did it then abandon worship altogether? By no means. Geneva rewrote the Psalms in ballad meters, and sang them to sturdy, forthright tunes. The very first book published in the American colonies was *The Whole Book of Psalms,* the famous "Bay Psalm Book" printed in Cambridge, Massachusetts, in 1640. Prayer was not offered in the historic words of Gregory or of Cranmer, but praying continued in full intensity of desire and of faith. Perhaps most significantly of all, the rejection of the traditional liturgies did not mean giving up the practice of the Holy Communion. Indeed, the one authentically American denomination among our major Churches of today, the Disciples of Christ, restored the practice of an administration of the Communion as the center of its standard Sunday morning service.

The one notable exception in the matter of the Communion of course was that of the Quakers. Seeking to gain the inner light by direct revelation from God, the Society of Friends ruled out all fixed forms and all symbolic objects, the Communion included. What happened, however, was that the silence of the Quaker meeting became a ritual in its own right, and the very absence of symbols a symbol of intense significance.

Less happily, because with less of conscious purpose, the average Protestant church, declaring its hatred of ritual, usually developed an *ad hoc* ritual of its own: a ritual which scarcely was less rigid than the older ones, but which differed from them in its being less considered, and therefore less beautiful and less effective. Every Protestant minister, however "anti-liturgical" he may think himself, has his own ritual phrases with which he passes from one part of the service to another; and the less he is conscious of them, the more likely he is to use them without variation. They who have attended Wednesday evening prayer meetings know how regularly the same people have prayed in the same words: words in part their own, in part borrowed from other sources written or oral, but no less fixed than is any formula in *The Book of Common Prayer*.

Singing, too, persisted in American Protestantism, and singing can not but follow form. The dominant form in many cases became that of the Gospel song: in its words an accurate enough reflection of the faith as commonly it was preached and held on the frontier, in its tune a product of the musical habits of midwestern America in the nineteenth century. Again there was no more flexibility in its use than there had been with the forgotten Gregorian chant. Indeed there usually was less, since the lack of attention to the Christian calendar led commonly to the repetition of a few favorites without any thought of varying the pattern.

What all this seems to mean is that no one quite escapes worship if he is conscious at all of values; and further that no one quite avoids ritual however much he may proclaim his dislike of it. We do worship, and we worship in regular, habitual forms. The issue that remains is that of what form or forms we shall choose, and of how thoughtfully and creatively we may use them.

There can be no absolute unanimity here. Our own personal heritages in language, in music, in behavior, condition all our judgments and reactions. There will be always those who find delight in the intricate, and those who actively prefer the sparse. This indeed is one of the difficulties that must be faced by those who seek the organic union of our Churches as well as functional unity among them. Is it possible to find one way of worshiping God, even within the Christian tradition, that will satisfy equally all those who would worship him in spirit and in truth? The answer has to be No.

Yet the Christian tradition itself, built up and enriched through these nineteen centuries, carries the weight of long experience and the authority of glad acceptance by millions of men and women. We have developed our ways of worshiping, and in some of them many of us together have found meaning and inspiration enough to demand their continuation. It may be that if we examine our tradition more carefully, and on our own part experiment with it more diligently, we shall gain even more than we have known hitherto.

We who believe in God do worship him, and we can do no other. The more consciously we seek to perform our ministry aright, to carry out our service truly, the greater is our hope of entering verily into the presence of God in our prayer and our praise. The means we use are those of considered form, and so of ritual. The meaning is that God's worth-ship ever is to be proclaimed by his children.

II

BACKGROUNDS OF OUR USAGES

ADHERENTS OF THE Orthodox tradition of Judaism, arguing from the late priestly writings in the Old Testament, hold that the ritual of the Israelite tabernacle, and so that of the later Jewish Temple, was specified in every particular by the revelation of God to Moses. No Christian group ever has been quite so categorical in claiming divine authority for the full detail of its procedures in worship, though most Christians have assumed that at least the sacraments of Baptism and the Lord's Supper were established by divine direction. In many cases, however, precedent and custom have served to make a given ceremonial system seem absolute to those who have grown up in it, to create in them an intense devotion to its every word and movement, and so to produce the same effect as if these usages were understood to have been specified by direct instruction from God himself.

History will support neither the view of specific revelation set forth by Jewish Orthodoxy, nor the common Christian assumption that one or another set of habits in worship is from everlasting. Both in Judaism and in Christianity the record is one of long and continuous development, moving from simple beginnings through many varying complexities, and never wholly static even when conservatism has sought most to resist change. The story of our usages therefore is one that has to be traced from the desert days of Israel, and from the Galilean origins of Christianity, through new settings and amid alien cultures one after another, to the practices we know today and the changes we may find ourselves making tomorrow.

JUDAISM: THE BEGINNINGS

Sir Leonard Woolley, working from evidence found in his excavation of Ur of the Chaldees, has suggested that the Lord God of Israel first is to be found in the character of the family God of Abraham. An earlier theory, and one more widely held, is that Moses was introduced to the worship of Jahveh (whom sometimes, and less accurately, we call "Jehovah") when he was keeping the flock of his father-in-law Jethro, "the priest of Midian." In either case, whether Jahveh was originally a Chaldean or a Midianite deity, it is clear that he invariably was worshiped in those ways that before the dawn of history had become standard in the religious life of the Middle East.

These standard procedures involved sacrifice as their essential element. The earlier of our two tellers of the flood story, writing perhaps in the middle of the ninth century B.C., takes it for granted that Noah knew already not only the usages of sacrifice, but also the rules for distinguishing between "clean" and "unclean" creatures; that is, between those that were considered suitable for sacrifice and those that were not. (This is shown, of course, by the seven pairs of each "clean" species mentioned in his account; the extras, beyond the pair needed for reproduction, being provided for sacrifices to be offered en route.) The North Israelite narrator of perhaps a century later, whose hand first appears in Genesis 20, records the episode of Abraham thinking to sacrifice his son Isaac, but learning that he may substitute the ram caught in the thicket. He speaks also of Jacob's offering sacrifice when he parted from Laban, and of his erecting altars (necessarily sacrificial in purpose) at Shechem and at Bethel. It is only the priestly strand in the "books of Moses," dating from not earlier than the fifth century, which avoids making any reference to sacrifice in the patriarchal days, and which declares that the sacrificial system was revealed en bloc to Moses himself.

This last view is flatly denied by some of the greatest of the early prophets. The herdsman Amos vigorously repudiates "feast days," "solemn assemblies," "burnt offerings and . . . meat offerings," and questions whether Israel indeed had offered "sacrifices and offerings in the wilderness." Only a few years later Hosea declares, for his Lord, "I desired mercy, and not sacrifice; and the knowledge of God more than burnt offerings." The famous lines in the book of Micah carry the same negative implication about sacrificial practices:

Wherewith shall I come before the Lord, and bow myself before the high God? Shall I come before him with burnt offerings, with calves of a year old? Will the Lord be pleased with thousands of rams, or with ten thousands of rivers of oil? Shall I give my firstborn for my transgression, the fruit of my body for the sin of my soul? He hath shewed thee, O man, what is good; and what doth the Lord require of thee, but to do justly, and to love mercy, and to walk humbly with thy God?

Jeremiah, himself a priest by heredity and training, makes the denial outright in his speech at the Temple's gate:

I spake not unto your fathers, nor commanded them in the day that I brought them out of the land of Egypt, concerning burnt offerings or sacrifices.

The likelihood is that sacrifice in Israel was both older and newer than the priestly documents maintained: older in that it had been practised in the desert long before Moses, since the memory of man ran not to the contrary; and newer in that most of the elaboration of the system, and the crystallizing of its details, occurred after the settlement in Palestine and largely under Canaanite influence. Thus the early tales seem to be right in speaking of sacrifice as having been known in high antiquity, and the prophets right in maintaining that the intricate practices of the priesthood of their times were not a part of the original religious heritage of their people.

What seems unquestionably to be true is that at the beginning, and far into the period of recorded history, sacrifice was understood to be a necessary condition of effective prayer. "Thou shalt not take the name of the Lord thy God in vain" seems to have meant at the outset neither the taboo on pronouncing the sacred Name which Judaism developed, nor the rule against profanity which we have thought it to be. Rather it should be read, "Thou shalt not call upon Jahveh thy God when thou art empty-handed." Sacrifice thus appears to have been integral to Israelite worship from the earliest days, even as it was to continue central so long as Jewish nationality was maintained.

THE CENTRAL TEMPLE

The ritual specified in the books of Exodus and Leviticus, while ostensibly belonging to the portable tabernacle in the wilderness, actually is a late reading back of the practices which were followed in Jerusalem in the second Temple, in about the fifth century B.C. Accordingly it takes for granted a single place of legitimate sacrifice, in line with the unification which had been demanded in the book of Deuteronomy, and enforced by the young king Josiah, in the latter half of the seventh century. It should be remembered that it was only in 621 B.C. that there occurred this actual centralizing of worship at Jerusalem, and the correlative outlawing of sacrificial observance at any provincial shrine; and that the first Temple was destroyed by the Babylonians just thirty-five years later.

This means that only one generation in Judah, before the exile of the sixth century, actually lived under the restrictions of Deuteronomy and Josiah. The test of a king who "did that which was right in the sight of the Lord," according to the Deuteronomic editors of the books of the Kings, was whether he enforced the centralization required by this ex post facto law. Therefore no king of North Israel, whatever his personal moral character, is admitted to have done right; for Jerusalem never was in North Israelite territory, and so no worship at all could have been carried on by the people of that nation except by their doing what they did; namely, establishing their own major shrines at Bethel and Gilgal, and doubtless many minor ones throughout the kingdom.

Southern Judah, in point of fact, had done exactly the same. Early in his career Jeremiah, "of the priests that were in Anathoth in the land of Benjamin," daringly undercut his own professional status by appearing as a campaigner for the Deuteronomic reformation: "According to the number of thy cities were thy gods, O Judah." Jeremiah's remark is supported in detail by the report of Josiah's activity in II Kings 23:8:

And he brought all the priests out of the cities of Judah, and defiled the high places where the priests had burned incense, from Geba to Beersheba.

Later Jeremiah concluded that even the concentration of the worship of the one Lord in one sanctuary had not solved the problem: "Trust ye not in lying words, saying, The temple of the Lord, the temple of the Lord, are these." Very shortly afterward any trust in the temple became indeed impossible, with its raiding by the Babylonian army in 597 and its total destruction in 586.

So strong, however, was the effect of the change that Deuteronomy and Josiah had brought about, that Judaism seems never again to have thought it possible to maintain the sacrifices anywhere but at the one sacred center in the one holy city. Ezekiel devotes much space to an ideal temple of the future, but he locates it as a matter of course in a restored and purified Jerusalem. The rebuilding of the Temple in 520 B.C., under the leadership of Zerubbabel and the urging of Haggai and Zechariah, produced a revival of the earlier usages, and their definite fixing in those forms which are set forth in the priestly codes of Exodus and Leviticus.

From 19 B.C. onward Herod the Great devoted himself to building a new Temple, though without interrupting at any time the continuity of the services. The Jewish revolt against Rome, begun in A.D. 66 by Eleazar the Zealot, ended in the year 70 with the fall of the city to Titus, the destruction of the Temple, and the abolition of the high priesthood and the council of the Sanhedrin. Not since then has the sacrificial worship of Judaism been conducted anywhere; nor will it be, until and unless the Jews regain possession and control of the sacred site which still (1953) remains in Muslim hands.

RISE OF THE SYNAGOGUES

Thus for the two generations of the Babylonian exile, in the sixth century B.C., and for these almost nineteen centuries leading up to the present time, the sacrifices of Israel and Judah have been impossible for the inheritors of the Mosaic tradition. Under the assumptions of the law of Deuteronomy, this would have meant that all worship of Jahveh would have ceased, for until the exile worship and sacrifice had been assumed to be inseparable. The new situation, creating a new demand, created also a new way to meet it.

The most casual reader of the Bible will realize that he has seen many references to "synagogues" in the New Testament, but none at all in the Old. It happens also that the Old Testament Apocrypha contain no allusion to these now familiar and typical Jewish institutions. The word "synagogue" is the Greek term for "assembly," and in the Greek version of the Old Testament it is used to render the Hebrew *edah*, "congregation." It is generally thought that meetings of local groups of the Jewish people for purposes of worship, apart from the Temple cultus, began during the Babylonian captivity as a direct response to the breakdown of the former ritual practices. Something of this sort seems to be suggested in Ezekiel 11:16:

Thus saith the Lord God; Although I have cast them far off among the heathen, and although I have scattered them among the countries, yet will I be to them as a little sanctuary in the countries where they shall come.

By the time of Jesus the "little sanctuary" of the synagogue was a widespread and characteristic expression of Jewish community life. We are told that, just before the final destruction of the Temple by Titus, there were some four hundred synagogues in Jerusalem itself; which suggests that group expressions of faith and devotion, quite distinct from the official ceremonies at the central shrine, had approved themselves even among those who could get to the shrine most easily. Jesus is recorded as having taught in the synagogues of Nazareth and Capernaum, and St. Paul in many scattered through the eastern Mediterranean regions. Synagogues of great fame, and synagogue buildings of no little splendor, arose in Babylonia and in Alexandria, the two great centers of Jewish settlement outside Palestine; and in recent years archaeologists have uncovered many early synagogue structures in almost all parts of the Mediterranean world.

The synagogue service, which by definition excluded sacrifice and which by necessity sought to inculcate knowledge of the Jewish religious heritage, made use of what had been the secondary elements accompanying the Temple sacrifices: that is to say, Psalms, readings from the Scriptures, and prayers; and added to them impromptu oral instruction which approximated what we would call a sermon. Late in the first century after Christ, the Rabbi Gamaliel II set forth the order of worship that has been the basis of synagogue practice ever since: Psalms, the *Shema* ("Hear, O Israel: the Lord our God, the Lord is one"), the "Eighteen Benedictions" or prayers, and reading (always) from the Law and (often) from the Prophets.

It is evident that here we have the basic structure of "morning worship" as modern Christians know it in practically every Protestant denomination. Praise, prayer, and instruction are the integral parts. When therefore we follow the familiar routines of hymns and responsive readings, of "pastoral" and congregational prayers, of Bible reading and sermon, we are reproducing the customs of the dispersed Jewish community as they have been carried on for more than two thousand years.

Every Christian will find it highly instructive to attend a Jewish service in his own vicinity, or, better, a number of Jewish services. The Orthodox congregations have much the longest ritual, and use almost wholly the ancient Hebrew text. Reform Judaism holds services which are shorter, and which include from a little Hebrew to almost none. On both points Conservative Jewish practice occupies a middle ground. In all three, however, the essential structure is that which has been mentioned: the sequence of praise, prayer, and instruction which Gamaliel so long ago set forth and which Christians as well as Jews so long have followed.

We may note in passing that the Orthodox Jewry of our time is careful to maintain the historic distinctions of terminology. It calls its buildings "synagogues," which they are. The Reform Jews, on the other hand, perhaps because they are less keenly interested in restoring the sacrifices in Jerusalem, commonly refer to their houses of worship as "temples," which in the strict sense they are not. ("Do you mean the synagogue," said a testy old Orthodox gentleman who was being asked for a contribution, "or that other —— place?") "Congregation," representing the Hebrew *edah*, still is the common term for a Jewish community which has organized itself for religious purposes, and which finds in the synagogue's historic type of worship its central and unifying factor.

CHRISTIAN BEGINNINGS

When Christianity came into being as a Jewish sect, it found in operation both Temple and synagogues, and therefore the services both of sacrifice and instruction. As we shall see, the Christians have maintained both types of service ever since. Jesus and his followers worshiped in the Temple in Jerusalem, and they attended synagogue services in the villages and towns that they visited in their journeyings. As it became increasingly clear that Christianity was destined to be an autonomous religion rather than a cult within Judaism, the Christians separated themselves from the Jewish groups and held gatherings of their own; and so most commonly on Sunday, the day of the Resurrection, rather than on the Jewish Sabbath of Friday to Saturday evenings. Necessarily, however, they devised their practices in imitation of the Jewish models they knew so well; and Christian worship thus springs directly and unmistakably from Jewish origins.

The Temple soon was out of reach for both communities, and at once geographically and historically. Judaism did maintain its one non-Temple sacrifice, that of the Passover, which always had been primarily a family festival; and also the *Kiddush*, a quasi-religious meal on the eves of Sabbaths and festival days. The association of the Last Supper with one or the other of these (there is dispute as to which) inevitably led the early Christians to develop a rite of their own, and with their own special meanings. The Lord's Supper appears already as the principal Christian service in the time of St. Paul, who discusses its conduct at some length in his letters to his rather difficult friends in Corinth.

At the same time the service for instruction, as it had grown up in the synagogues, was almost exactly reproduced in Christian practice. The familiar Psalms were sung, and no doubt such Christian hymns as the *Magnificat* and the *Nunc Dimittis*, which early were transcribed into St. Luke's Gospel. The famous letter of the Roman governor Pliny, written to the Emperor Trajan in A.D. 112, speaks of the Christians in Bithynia as engaging in the practice of antiphonal singing. Prayer clearly was included, as witness St. Paul's insistence that praying should have meaningful content both for him who prayed and for those who heard. The apostle's own letters were read in the assembled groups, and certainly sections of the Old Testament also. By the time of St. Justin the Martyr, about the year 150, "the memoirs of the apostles," presumably our Gospels, were read regularly as part of the service. Spontaneous preaching, described as "prophecy," completed the usual pattern of procedure.

Apparently the Lord's Supper was from the beginning a separate observance, held commonly in the evening and associated with the *Agape*, or "love feast." The basic elements here were the thanksgiving (*Eucharist*), the breaking of the bread, and the distribution of the bread and wine to the congregation. While anyone was welcome to attend the services for instruction, the Eucharist early was restricted to those whose initiation into the faith was regarded as complete.

(This probably is the origin of the term "Mass," in the dismissal, *missa*, of the catechumens, or probationers, from the assembled company of believers before the most sacred rites began.)

THE MASS

As early as the middle of the second century, precise formulae for the eucharistic prayer were being worked out. The *Didache*, "The Teaching of the Twelve Apostles," sets forth the approved phrasing:

As to the Eucharist, give thanks thus: First for the cup: We thank thee, our Father, for the holy vine of David, thy son, which thou hast revealed to us through Jesus thy son. To thee be glory for ever.

For the bread: We thank thee, our Father, for the life and knowledge which thou hast revealed to us through Jesus thy son. To thee be glory for ever. As this broken bread, scattered on the mountains, is brought together and become one, so bring thou together the church from the ends of the earth into thy kingdom; for thine is the glory and the power, through Jesus Christ, for ever.

It cautions then,

Do not let anyone eat or drink of your Eucharist, except those baptized into the name of the Lord. For it was of this the Lord said, Give not the holy thing to the dogs.

Finally it supplies a thanksgiving prayer very similar to those which, with varying details, conclude the Holy Communion in our several Christian usages of today.

The Mass became the basic Christian form of worship, and the elaboration of its accepted procedure continued apace. Each major jurisdiction of the Church worked out its own variations of the basic plan, so that by the fourth century we find already in existence the distinct types of Christian liturgy known as Syrian, Alexandrian, Roman, and Gallican, with a number of subtypes of each. Ultimately "The Divine Liturgy of St. John Chrysostom," a Byzantine version of the Syrian usage, became dominant in the Eastern Churches, and that of Rome in all the West.

When we come to our specific study of the Holy Communion, we shall see that not only the Lutheran and Anglican liturgies, but also those of practically all our Western denominations, are derived from the primitive Christian Eucharist by way of the standardized liturgy of Rome. It is enough here to note that fact, along with the observation that the break from Rome led in most Protestant circles (with the notable exception of the Lutheran) to the subordination of this service, as one primarily of sacrifice, to the service of edification which medieval Christian custom had relegated to a secondary place.

MORNING AND EVENING PRAYER

Since in practical terms the layman could not attend services very often, normally not more than once a week, he naturally went to that service which was regarded as the most important. For the early Christians, and for those of the Middle Ages, the solemn commemoration of the sacrifice on Calvary manifestly held that place. Thus the Mass became the one service for general lay attendance, and consequently the most frequent service in the ordinary parish church. The other type of Christian worship, that for instruction and devotion without the sacrifice at the altar, was left chiefly to those who had more time to give to specific religious observance; that is to say, the monastic orders.

It is possible that the "offices," the sequence of daily services in the monastic system, are to be traced to the ancient Jewish hours of prayer. In any event, their content was noticeably similar to that of the customary worship of the synagogue. By the end of the fourth century the monks of the East were instructed by St. Basil the Great to gather for prayer eight times in each twenty-four hours. Rome seems at that time to have had six such daily services; and in the sixth century St. Benedict of Nursia added two more. Typically all these offices included specified Psalms, canticles, lessons, and prayers, with the monkish choirs developing more and more stylized modes of chanting. Laymen were allowed to attend as they had opportunity; but in practice few did, and probably fewer as the years went by.

The Reformation in England, under the leadership of Archbishop Cranmer, worked a number of positive, if not critical, changes in the worship usages of the English Church. All services were required to be said in English, a revolutionary departure from medieval custom. The Mass, now described as "The Lord's Supper, or Holy Communion," was much shortened and simplified. The most far-reaching change of all, however, resulted from Cranmer's creation of the offices of Morning and Evening Prayer, by combining for the former the materials of the older services of Mattins, Lauds, and Prime, and for the latter Vespers and Compline. What happened was that these services, rather than the Holy Communion, became in time the regular ones for general lay attendance; and so they set the pattern for the standard Sunday worship of the English-speaking world.

Again it is evident that the tradition of the synagogue, reproduced (though variously modified) in monastic practice, controls the unified services as Cranmer worked them out. Psalms, lessons, and prayers provide the framework of the structure; and sermons (or authorized homilies) commonly were added after the completion of the specified ritual. The two services, morning and evening, were deliberately made almost identical in the sequence of their materials, so as to encourage ready following by the laity.

THE REACTION AGAINST RITUAL

Cranmer did not go nearly far enough to satisfy many of the more extreme Protestant groups. The Prayer Book of 1552 represented the views of many who had thought that of 1549 still "too papist"; but even the later work was disapproved by most Puritans, and detested by all Separatists. The Communion was by these still further shortened, and much of the fixed text of the service was dropped in favor of extempore utterance. The services of instruction also were simplified and deformalized, with chanting replaced by the singing of metrical Psalm paraphrases, and in some groups also of hymns, and with written prayers giving way to spontaneous petition.

It was at this point in history, and largely by those who held most sharply the antiritualistic position, that the Atlantic seaboard of North America first was settled. New England was Separatist (Plymouth), Puritan (Massachusetts Bay), and Baptist (Rhode Island). Pennsylvania was Quaker, Presbyterian, and German Pietist. New York, Virginia, the Carolinas, and Georgia indeed were dominantly Anglican; but the ties of the English Church to the British Crown were a decided handicap to that Church as tension grew between Britain and her colonies. In Virginia, Patrick Henry first gained fame by challenging the financial prerogatives of the established clergy, and in many cases throughout the South revolutionary enthusiasm was symbolized by leaving the Church of England to join the Baptists.

The Revolution itself, and the securing of colonial independence, served further to trouble the Church which had seemed to belong to the tyrant state, and so to discredit the usages which that Church had maintained. The great migration to the West, again, began before the new Protestant Episcopal Church really had recovered from the shock of formal separation from its English roots. Thus the standard Christianity of the American Midwest was the dissident, minority Protestantism of England, antipathetic to almost everything in the old traditions, and particularly conscious of its dislike of regularized ceremony.

John Wesley, ever a high churchman even in a Church which came near to disowning him, did his best to stem the tide. Wesley was revolutionary indeed in his laying of hands on Thomas Coke to set him apart as a "general superintendent" for North America, with power to ordain. (It was to be long years yet before the Methodists thought to refer to their general superintendents as "Bishops.") Wesley was at the same time extremely conservative about the services of the Church, whether sacramental or not. Declaring that "I believe there is no liturgy in the world, either in ancient or modern language, which breathes more of a solid, Scriptural, rational piety than the Common Prayer of the Church of England," he prepared in 1784, for the embryonic Methodist Episcopal Church in the United States, a prayer book "little differing from that of the Church of England (I think the best constituted national church in the world)." Wesley's Sunday service was a practically unchanged transcript of Morning and Evening Prayer, save that for the Declaration of Absolution he substituted the Collect for the Twenty-fourth Sunday after Trinity, with its first-person-plural petition "that we may all be delivered from the bands of those sins, which by our frailty we have committed." This, let us observe, does not necessarily mean that Wesley disapproved the priestly absolution. What he clearly did disapprove was the possibility of any of his lay preachers pronouncing it.

Just as the British Methodists, immediately upon Mr. Wesley's death, disregarded his injunction not to separate themselves from the Church of England, so those in America became more and more indifferent to the ritual he had prescribed. The Holy Communion was to a large extent used in the form which Wesley had copied from the

1552–1662 Book of Common Prayer; but it was celebrated very infrequently—in most local churches not more than once in three months—as compared with Wesley's advice that the elders should "administer the Supper of the Lord on every Lord's day." The "Sunday service" dropped out of official Methodist publications for many years, and a single sparse "Order of Worship" was printed opposite the title page of *The Methodist Hymnal.* On the prairies and along the frontier Methodist enthusiasm attached itself to the Puritan values of the dominant surrounding culture, so that in many American minds Methodism became identified as a chief representative of rigidity in personal conduct and complete informality in worship.

Through the nineteenth century, and well into the twentieth, Protestant services in the United States were standardized in terms of extreme simplicity and often of deliberate casualness. All historic symbolism remained suspect, so that the cross seldom was seen on the church or in it, and candles were the subject of heated dispute when anyone tried to use them, or even suggested the possibility. Church music was regarded either from the point of view of concert performance, or as a means to jovial good fellowship, without concern for its fitness and without interest in its meaning as worship. The old synagogue and Morning Prayer items of hymns, scripture, prayer, and sermon were retained, as if by force of habit; but chanting, written prayers, and in many cases the reciting of the Creed, were forgotten, and the sermon was regarded as central. This is where we came in: with the sophomore's question as to why the sermon isn't enough without the rest of the service.

THE RETURN TO RITUAL

It proved not to be enough; and the leaders of the great American denominations came gradually to realize that much had been lost in making the pulpit a lecture platform, and the service an unconsidered and perfunctory setting for an oratorical display piece. The Lutherans and Episcopalians of course had preserved their traditions of worship, and their service patterns, essentially as they had been adapted from the Roman uses in the sixteenth century: Lutheranism holding to the Communion type of service as primary, whether or not the Communion itself was celebrated, and Anglicanism using both the Communion and the "choir offices" of Morning and Evening Prayer.

Within these Churches, however, there has been recently a resurgence of active interest in liturgics, and much attention has been given to the history, nature, and meaning of the historic rites. In the remainder of American Protestantism, the past half-century has seen more than a resurgence: in fact almost a total revolution.

Just fifty years ago, in 1903, the Presbyterians (North) appointed a committee to prepare "a book of simple forms and services," and in 1906 published the product as *The Book of Common Worship*. There have been two major revisions since, in 1932 and 1946. The sequence of the morning service here is almost exactly that of the Anglican Morning Prayer: opening sentences, confession, "assurance of pardon," Psalm, *Gloria*, two lessons, creed, and prayers. Canticles were mentioned as optional in 1932, but disappeared in 1946. Nevertheless they are generously provided in an appendix to *The Hymnal* (Presbyterian). The Communion in its 1932 form, as was to be expected in the Reformed tradition, diverged much more largely from the Anglican liturgy; but it did include the long avoided *Sursum Corda*, Preface, and *Sanctus*. The 1946 revision has restored much else of Anglican and even of Roman use. This book of worship, while set forth with the approval of the General Assembly, was marked on the 1932 title page as being "For Voluntary Use." That phrase now has been dropped; but one gathers that voluntary disuse of the book still prevails in many local Presbyterian churches.

The Pilgrim Hymnal of the Congregationalists, published in 1931, provided a total of fifteen detailed orders of worship, two of them being for the Communion, and all following to a large extent the Morning Prayer pattern. Apparently there must have been some dissatisfaction with the 1931 work; for a new edition appeared as early as 1935, containing but three orders for general worship, but with the addition of a great wealth of litanies and prayers. The total bulk of this worship section was increased from fifty-one to fifty-five pages, with somewhat smaller type providing a still greater proportional increase in material. The responsive readings were reorganized, with a greater use of the Psalms and a return to their original biblical order.

In 1948 the Congregational Christian Churches completed a ten-year project by publishing *A Book of Worship for Free Churches*. This, which at many points resembles the Presbyterian *Book of Common Worship*, provides five orders for morning worship, the latter three closely patterned on the traditional Morning Prayer, one for

Evening Worship, a considerable number for special festivals and seasons, three orders each for Communion, Baptism, Confirmation (thus headed), and Marriage, a variety of other services for particular occasions, 122 pages of prayers, a two-year lectionary, and a calendar. An introductory treatment of "Symbolism in Worship" explains many traditional symbols and usages, and hints gently that they well might be adopted by churches of the Congregational fellowship.

Methodism, reexamining its own history and reappraising its values, became recognizably more "Episcopal" in practice even while it was dropping that word from the name of the reunited Methodist Church. A principal pioneer had been Bishop Wilbur Patterson Thirkield, whose *Service and Prayers for Church and Home* (1918) introduced Wesley's Sunday service to thousands of Methodists who never before had heard of it. That service, somewhat shortened and omitting reference to the "collect of the day," appeared as "Order of Worship III" in *The Ritual* of 1932, and is numbered "IV" in that of 1944.

In 1940 the first General Conference of the Methodist Church, following the union of 1939, appointed a Commission on Ritual and Orders of Worship, and instructed it to draw up forms and orders drawing "upon richer and wider sources than those that have been available up to the present time." This commission's work issued in a revised and considerably enlarged *Ritual*, officially promulgated, and in *The Book of Worship for Church and Home*, approved by the 1944 General Conference for publication but marked "for voluntary and optional use." This latter book provided a total of eleven general orders for morning and/or evening worship, seventeen for special subjects and occasions, a section of sixty-three pages of materials for the Christian year, including a lectionary, and 183 pages of other worship materials, plus the full text of the *Ritual*. *The Book of Worship*, however, no longer is in print, presumably because of lack of interest and appreciation.

Those fellowships whose strength is principally in the South and the Midwest, such as the Baptists and Disciples, are at once less closely organized and more suspicious of established forms, and so have done less in the direction of establishing uniform ritual practice than have the Presbyterians, Congregationalists, and Methodists. Many local Baptist and Christian churches, however, especially in urban areas and on the two coasts, have developed quite deliberately ritualistic services of their own. The Riverside Church in New York, with its magnificent building so largely modeled on the Cathedral of Chartres, is a notable case but is far from being the only one.

Since the writing of the original script of this chapter, there has been issued by the Christian Board of Publication a volume of 598 pages titled *Christian Worship: A Service Book*, and edited by Professor G. Edwin Osborn of Phillips University. This, which is designed as a companion to the Baptist-Disciples *Christian Worship: A Hymnal*, is highly flexible and is described as being for "voluntary use." It would be possible to use it, however, for the development of a definitely traditional pattern of worship on practically all occasions. Calendar and lectionary include the major historic festivals, and also a number of observances which are American or belong specifically to the Disciples' own usage.

Unitarianism long has had orders of service set forth in its official books, and provides a striking (though not at all a new) specimen of a "high" type of service in King's Chapel in Boston. A comparison of the Unitarian hymnal of 1914 with that of 1937 shows that the latter includes more services (sixteen to ten), longer ones (sixty-nine pages to thirty-seven), and in all of them a much closer approximation to the traditional order of Morning Prayer. At the other extreme from historic Unitarian dignity and scholarship, even the "store front" groups of the Southwest, once transplanted into new urban settings, seem to catch something of the current mood. Only a few hundred feet from the Mills College gates, for example, is a Pentecostal Church which now has placed a large cross on its steeple, and has a vested choir leading its music. (Our students naturally are speculating as to how long it will be before the minister appears in robes.)

Mention should be made of recent work done toward the enrichment of worship apart from the official authority of any single denomination. A typical book of a generation ago is Milton S. Littlefield's *Hymns of the Christian Life* (1925). This contains, in addition to sixty selections for responsive reading, the Apostles' Creed, the Ten Commandments, the Beatitudes, and thirty-eight prayers, of which not less than fourteen are from *The Book of Common Prayer*. Also in 1925, not as representing the Disciples of Christ, but quite evidently working largely within their tradition, Charles Clayton Morrison and Herbert L. Willett issued their *Hymns of the United Church*, with two suggested orders for general worship and two for the Communion, along with many pages of prayers, chants, choral responses, and responsive readings.

H. Augustine Smith, the present writer's teacher of hymnology many years ago, has edited a number of hymnals with worship materials. In *The New Church Hymnal* (1937) he has supplied a series of brief rituals for various purposes, accompanied by a large number of prayers, litanies, and responsive selections. The *Inter-Church Hymnal*, compiled by Frank A. Morgan in 1938, includes an "Aids to Worship" section edited by Albert W. Palmer, the distinguished Congregationalist who until his retirement was president of Chicago Theological Seminary. The Morgan-Palmer work contains six orders of worship with varying amounts of detail in specification, and many prayers, responsive readings, confessions of faith, and selections for devotional meditation. It is to be assumed that such books as these will be used chiefly in those churches which are not closely tied to a central denominational authority; and here again it is evident that historic ritual usages are coming newly into the focus of interest and use.

Anyone who has attended services at any appreciable number of Protestant churches in recent years will have recognized this trend to restore much that once was rejected: not only a fixed order of worship following closely the ancient forms, but also crosses, candles, vestments, and the divided chancel with a central altar. Some odd things happen in such a period of transition, for assimilation of change never can be wholly uniform and smooth. In one large Methodist church the writer found, placed below the central pulpit, an altar complete with candles and cross; but then, just before the service was to begin, he saw the janitor stroll down the (necessarily side) aisle, nonchalantly strike a match on the seat of his trousers, and proceed to light the candles. For some reason the minister, when told about this, didn't think it was funny.

It is funny, but it is also perfectly human. In four centuries of repudiating beauty and order, we have forgotten many of the procedures that were familiar and natural to our fathers. We have gone in for Gothic, and then we have put into the Gothic shell a concert hall platform rather than a sanctuary. We have built an altar, but we have treated it often as mere wall decoration rather than as the Lord's table. We have vested the minor ministry of music in the choir, while leaving the first minister in secular garb. We have thought academic robes (which long ago became secular too) permissible for our clergy, while still the specifically Christian vestments are abjured.

Much in detail thus is illogical, and much could be done better. The important thing is that man's need for worship has risen again to the level of our consciousness, and that therefore the historic practices of worship once more are being tested, even if sometimes with less than full knowledge and understanding. It remains for us to study our heritage even more closely, and to experiment within it even more thoughtfully and earnestly. Not all at once, but increasingly as we pursue the quest, we may hope to worship in that decency and order which will aid us most to realize and to express the worthship of our eternal God.

III

THE HOUSE OF GOD

"BEHOLD THE HEAVEN and heaven of heavens cannot contain thee; how much less this house that I have builded." Thus, according to the first book of the Kings, Solomon prayed at the dedication of the Temple; and thus must say every one who longs to find the infinite God in the world of finite man. Where shall we seek for God? Where shall we worship him?

The inclusive answer is "everywhere." Man's experience, however, long ago taught him that a vague everywhere is all too likely to become an actual nowhere. From his earliest days he set aside particular places as particular shrines; and as his skill in building grew he gave of his best skills in his planning and erecting of the house of God. Leaving aside the temples of ancient Babylonia and Egypt, we stand now at the end of three thousand years of specifically religious architecture within the Hebrew-Christian tradition.

Our church buildings of today reflect those three millennia of experiment and achievement in varying degrees, but all to a very large degree. They reflect also the general cultural settings within which the successive planners and builders have lived, planned, and built, down through history: Palestinian, Greco-Roman, medieval, Renaissance, modern; Mediterranean, North European, British, American. Not always do our churches reflect the actual faith and the actual needs of those who worship in them. We need continuingly to clarify our faith, and to be sure of the real nature of our needs. We need also to consider very carefully how best we may express and satisfy them

28

in the devising of our structures for divine service. What should church buildings be like? It is important to ask first what they have been like from the beginning until now.

TENT AND TABERNACLE

"This is none other but the house of God," cried waking Jacob, "and this is the gate of heaven." Thereupon he set up a stone as a ceremonial pillar, poured upon it a libation of oil, and named the place *Beth-el*, "God's house." It was to be many years, however, before the people of Israel were able to roof the house and fully to adorn it.

Unquestionably temporary outdoor altars long preceded any enclosed shrine. In the earliest strand of narrative in the book of Genesis, Noah is represented as building an altar for his sacrifice after his landing, and offering on it a veritable holocaust "of every clean beast, and of every clean fowl." Abr(ah)am builds an altar eastward of the later Bethel, and returns afterward to call upon the Lord at the same place. He erects another in the plain of Mamre, and (now according to the North Israelite narrator) one on Mount Moriah, in tradition identified with the Temple site in Jerusalem. We find Isaac setting up an altar at Beersheba, and Jacob doing likewise at Shechem and finally at his own beloved Bethel.

This practice of worshiping at various sites, each of them as it were consecrated *ad hoc*, was inevitable in the nomadic life of the early tribes. Moses (again as reported in the most primitive tradition) seems to follow the usage after Joshua's battle with the Amalekites in Rephidim. To a member of the later official priesthood, however, it was unthinkable that the worship of the Lord ever should have been thus occasional, casual, and uncontrolled. Accordingly the priestly writers worked out a theoretical reconstruction which sought to ascribe to Israel the possession of a permanent shrine even while the nation was on the move from Egypt to Canaan.

Our earliest teller of the Israelite story, writing in Judah in the ninth century B.C., has nothing to say of any structures at all to enclose the various altars which he mentions. In the so-called "E" document, the Northern cycle of the eighth century, there appears a "tent of meeting" pitched outside the Israelite camp. It is important to observe that the word here, *ohel*, is an altogether different one from "tabernacle," *mishkan*, which is used consistently in the later priestly account. According to "E" the *ohel* sheltered the ark of the covenant, and was marked by the cloudy pillar standing before its door. Thither Moses went to receive divine instruction; and thither also, it seems, resorted "every one which sought the Lord" for a specific personal purpose.

This representation is altogether distinct from that of the priestly narratives. In these latter the tabernacle is placed in the mathematical center of the whole encampment, and it is much too elaborate to be

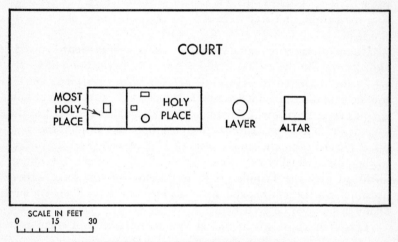

THE PRIESTLY TABERNACLE (EXODUS 35-38)

regarded as a mere "tent." The building itself, consisting of vertical boards of acacia wood each 15 feet by 2 feet 3 inches, is 45 feet long and 15 wide. It is covered and roofed by elaborately colored fabrics in pieces 42 feet in length, and these in their turn are covered by goats' hair curtains. The assembled structure is set in a court measuring 150 feet by 75 feet. This court too is enclosed by hangings, 7½ feet in depth, evidently cutting off any vision from the ground outside. In the court is placed an altar of burnt offering 7½ feet square and 4½ feet high, made of wood with a thin covering of bronze. There is also a bronze laver for priestly ablutions.

The roofed shrine is divided into a "holy place" 30 feet by 15, and a "most holy place," 15 feet square, at the western end. In the former are the golden lampstand and the table of shewbread on either side, and an incense altar just before the veil which encloses the inner sanctuary. That sanctuary contains "the ark of the testimony," described as a chest of acacia wood overlaid with gold both inside and out, and measuring 45 by 27 by 27 inches. Upon it is placed the "mercy seat," a slab of solid gold equal in area to the top of the ark itself, but of a thickness not specified.

It scarcely needs a more detailed study of the specifications (such as the question of how many pillars actually would have been required to hang the curtains) to make it evident that here we are dealing not with an actual shrine, but with an abstracted idealization. Not only would there be inconceivable difficulty in moving, setting up, and striking this elaborate structure, but also the availability of so many such precious materials to wandering desert tribes would seem to be out of the question. What the priestly description of the tabernacle witnesses is not how Israel worshiped in the wilderness, but how intensely the priests of the fifth century believed that such surroundings as these were essential to valid worship. The priestly tabernacle thus is simply the second Jerusalem Temple read back into primitive times, and arbitrarily made portable to fit the ancient nomadic situation.

THE TEMPLES IN JERUSALEM

History, as distinct from loving legend, finds the "tent of meeting" first localized at Shiloh, between Bethel and Shechem in South Central Palestine, after the Israelites have gained a foothold in Canaan. Presumably the actual tent now was replaced by a more substantial building, for the account speaks of a "temple" and of its having doors and door posts. We are told nothing about the ground plan or the furnishings, save that a lamp was kept burning before the ark. From later references we gather that some terrible catastrophe befell Shiloh, perhaps during the Philistine wars, so that its destruction became a byword in Israelite speech.

The sacred ark, taken into battle against the Philistines, was lost to them and for a time was sequestered in a Philistine temple of Dagon. Thence it was returned to Israel, and for twenty years remained at Kirjath-jearim, about halfway between Jerusalem and the cities of the Philistine confederacy. David at last, after his capture of Jerusalem and his enthronement as king of a united Israel, brought the ark to his new capital, with a three-month delay, however, en route. Finally it seems that the ark was placed in a new tent (*ohel*, not the more elaborate *mishkan*) which David had pitched for it. Not until long afterward do we hear of David's buying the threshing floor of Araunah, traditionally identified with the later Temple site, and building an altar there.

Our knowledge of the architecture of the Temple of Solomon is gravely limited both by the rather slight description provided in the earlier narrative in I Kings, and by the dubious accuracy of the much

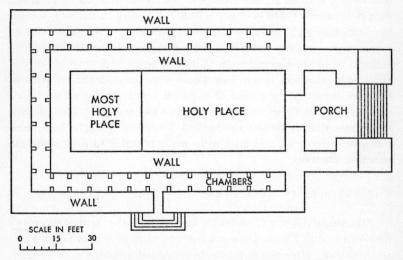

SOLOMON'S TEMPLE (I KINGS, EZEKIEL)

later account in II Chronicles. This latter, indeed, was written at about the same time as the priestly description of the tabernacle, and, like it, almost certainly paints the past largely in the colors of a new present. A little more light may be thrown upon the first Temple by the specifications for an idealized shrine in the book of Ezekiel, if we date that prophet early in the sixth century and assume that he was remembering the sacred building he had known before he was carried off into exile.

In general the Temple proper as built by Solomon seems to have been twice as long and twice as broad as the theoretical tabernacle: that is, 90 by 30 feet, and with the most holy place a perfect 30-foot cube. The sacred chambers, however, were enclosed by heavy walls of native limestone, with a series of cells for the priests running around three sides. Inside the shrine the stone walls were overlaid with cedar planks from Lebanon. There is no decisive indication as to where the great altar (30 by 30 by 16 feet) stood, except that it was outside the house. The "brazen sea," possibly but not certainly corresponding to the tabernacle laver, and said to have been 15 feet in diameter, was placed to the southward, somewhat off the direct line between the altar and the enclosed building. There were also ten smaller, movable lavers grouped about the altar. The table of shewbread appears again in the holy place, along with ten golden lampstands, but there is no mention of an altar of incense. The ark, of course, remains the sacred center of the most holy place.

Ezekiel's Temple (which we must remember existed only in the prophet's vision) is larger still than Solomon's. The outer court is 750 feet square, and the principal building 150 feet long in outside dimension, though with the inner rooms only 60 by 30 and 30 by 30 feet respectively, as in Solomon's structure. There are also three other buildings, designed to house the priests, and so arranged as to provide a partly enclosed central space for the altar of burnt offerings. This altar, appreciably more elaborate than Solomon's, is a kind of step pyramid, 27 feet square at the base and 18 at the top, and altogether 18 feet high. (This can readily be visualized if one thinks of the fairly standard 28 by 18 living room; and it is to be remembered that Solomon's altar is said to have been even larger, though of slightly lower elevation.)

The second actual Temple, that of Zerubbabel, is described in no such detail as is the imagined one of Ezekiel. Cyrus of Persia is said to have authorized a building 90 feet square, but there is no clear statement that anything so large was erected. The furnishings of the holy place are those we have found already in the priestly tabernacle: table, incense altar, and lampstand. The ark had been lost in the time of the Babylonian conquest of Judah, and was not replaced; so that in the most holy place there was only a bare foundation stone as a symbolic reminder of glory departed. In general it seems, from the difficult history of the Jews in this period, and from the reticence of the contemporary recorders, that the restored Temple must have been much poorer and less impressive than its predecessor.

Antiochus Epiphanes of Syria plundered whatever was in the building in 168 B.C., and Crassus of Rome in the year 54. The building enterprise of Herod, at first supposed to be a repair job, became a total reconstruction which required more than eighty years for its completion (19 B.C. to about A.D. 63). The Temple area now was twice that of Zerubbabel's day, and corresponded roughly with the present *Haram-esh-Sherif* as modern tourists see it: approximately six hundred feet each way, though slightly asymmetric. The inner court, set crosswise within the great enclosure and well to the northward, in-

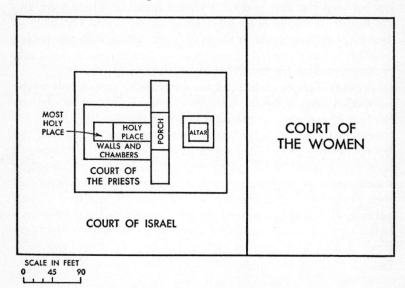

HEROD'S TEMPLE: SIMPLIFIED GROUND PLAN
OF THE INNER COURTS

cluded a women's court, a narrower space open only to Jewish men, and a rectangular "court of the priests" within which were the altar and the Temple buildings. The dimensions of the holy place and the most holy place were the same as those of Solomon's time: another indication that Zerubbabel scarcely can have built on a larger scale.

Only six to eight years after this last of the Temples was completed, it was destroyed by Titus. Oddly enough, much of our knowledge of the appearance of its furnishings comes to us from their depiction on Titus' triumphal arch in Rome. We do not know what became of them later. We do know that the loss of the Temple did not destroy Jewish identity or Jewish faith. Judaism continued and reorganized its worship in the synagogues, and its Christian offshoot soon was to begin the building of its churches.

HOUSE, BASILICA, AND CHURCH

Before this, however, the Christians used buildings which already were in existence. These were first of all the Jerusalem Temple and the various local synagogues in Palestine, Syria, Asia Minor, and Greece, in which the Christians shared in the worship of the local Jewish communities. The exclusively Christian gatherings were held

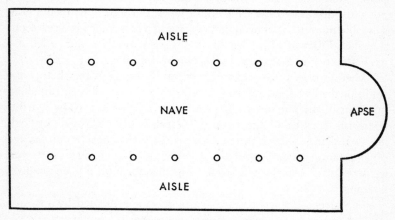

BASILICA WITH APSE

in private homes, from the time of the household of John Mark and his mother onward. St. Paul sends his greetings through Philemon to "the church in thy house" in Colossae, and the epistle to the Hebrews is thought to have been directed to a house-church organized in Rome. In Ephesus, St. Paul appears to have lectured regularly in a philosophical school managed by one Tyrannus; but this is the unique case of its type in the early days, and probably it is irrelevant to worship services as such.

The famous catacombs of Rome were places not primarily of worship but of burial. Created by further excavation of the ancient quarries, they provided for unobtrusive disposal of the entire body of the departed believer, in hope of the Resurrection at the last day, as against the Greco-Roman practice of cremation. Sacred symbols marked the graves, and small altars of devotion came to be erected beside them. But the narrow passageways were not suitable, and they certainly were not planned, for the use of large worshiping congregations. The catacomb thus is not to be thought of as a church, but at the most as a mortuary chapel.

Here and there, from the beginning of the third century onward, new buildings began to be erected specifically for the services of Christian worship. Clement of Alexandria speaks of "the structure raised in God's honor," though he insists that "it is not the place, but the company of the elect, that I call the Church." Diocletian (emperor from 284 to 305), the last imperial persecutor of the Church, not only desecrated the catacomb graves, but also destroyed a considerable number of church edifices. Eight years after his death Constantine's Edict of Milan legalized Christian worship, and so led immediately to the first great era of church building.

There is dispute among architectural historians as to whether the traditional church structure had its origin in the Roman dwelling house or in the public building known as the basilica. (The word is one naturalized into Latin from the Greek *basilikos*, "royal" or "ruling.") It is indisputable, however, that the great churches of the age of Constantine were essentially basilicas in their basic design; and the word itself remains the standard Roman term for a major church building.

The Greco-Roman basilica was a rectangle divided by rows of interior pillars into side aisles and a central space known as the nave (from *navis*, "ship"). Commonly, though not necessarily, it ended in an apse, a semicircular projection surmounted by a half-dome. The basilicas of the pagan world were places of judgment, of assembly, and also of trade. It was only natural that now the priests should take the former seats of the judges in the apse, while the congregation filled the area long occupied by the populace. The increasing importance of the Mass was conveniently served by placing the altar in the apse or immediately before it. (There was pagan precedent for this too, as the apse of the secular basilica often had contained an altar or the statue of a tutelary deity.)

Old St. Peter's in Rome, the great church commissioned by Constantine himself, and dedicated in A.D. 326, was a basilica with a nave and four aisles, projecting transepts which made the ground plan that of a T-cross, and a relatively small apse. The basic rectangle measured 330 feet by 200, and the interior of the nave rose to a central height of 136 feet. The roof was a wooden one of relatively simple construction, supported by four parallel rows of twenty-five pillars each. This church was demolished by Pope Nicholas V in the fifteenth century; and the St. Peter's we know, whose dome was the magnificent achievement of Michelangelo, was in process of construction from 1450 to 1626.

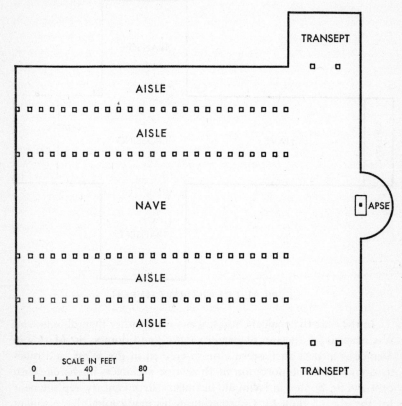

OLD ST. PETER'S BASILICA, ROME

The cruciform church, a simple adaptation of the plain basilica by the adding of two transepts, had originally a practical rather than a symbolic significance. The special privileges accorded to the clergy, from Constantine's time on, greatly increased their number; and the cross-like building, whether T-shaped as in Old St. Peter's, or in the more familiar form of the Latin cross with the crossing further down from the apse, probably had its beginning in the effort to provide more space for the ministers near the altar, while the laity occupied the body of the church. It was only much later, and after the cross could be regarded as a symbol of faith rather than of fear, that the concept of the ground plan as a reminder of Calvary began to arise.

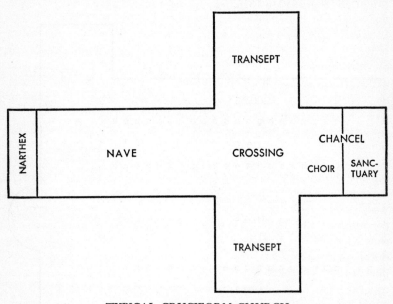

TYPICAL CRUCIFORM CHURCH

In the East the typical church was square rather than oblong, and was marked by the use of barrel vaulting and domes. St. Mark's in Venice is in part an Eastern church erected in the West, and owes its domes to the importation of Byzantine architects in the eleventh century. St. Sophia in Istanbul, Justinian's sixth century replacement for the church built by Constantine in his new capital, has a square central area under the main dome, but is extended to a length of 265 feet (by 107) by semicircular spaces added at the east and west ends. The Muslim conquest required a change in orientation, from due east to the southeasterly direction of Mecca, and so the church become a mosque has its prayer rugs laid slantwise to the main axis.

FROM EGYPT TO AKRON

Little has been said as yet about "styles" of church architecture. The obvious thing to say, and the true one, is that the churches of each region and each time reflected, in their structure and their decoration, the total cultural heritage of their people. Solomon's Temple no doubt was dominantly Egyptian in its appearance, and Herod's Greco-Roman. The Byzantine dome became familiar in the West only with the Renaissance, which was basically a Greek revival. In Slavic countries the lightweight outer covering of the dome, made necessary for protection from the frosts of winter, was set free from its nucleus to swell into the familiar bulbous dome of the Russian churches. Meanwhile the West was working out its own structural problems seriatim, first with the rounded arch and then with the pointed.

We laymen in architecture can get along fairly well by identifying the round arch as "Romanesque" and the pointed as "Gothic." As stone vaulting replaced the early and dangerously inflammable wooden roof, naves became at once narrower and higher: narrower for strength, and higher then to permit of better lighting. "Gothic," thus named by a Renaissance which regarded all medieval art as purely barbarous, developed out of the Romanesque in order to decrease the lateral thrust of the walls. By transferring the stresses to a skeleton frame of buttresses, to which relatively thin walls now could be attached, it produced that effect of soaring lightness which everyone recognizes as typical of the Gothic structure. The flying buttress, appearing first in the twelfth century, was necessary to receive the pressure of the upper parts of the wall; and in the hands of the late medieval designers it became a thing of rare beauty as well as of essential utility.

The Renaissance returned to Greece and Rome for its models. Hence the new St. Peter's in Rome, and the host of English churches built by Sir Christopher Wren and under his influence. Now the dome and the pillared portico became standard, and the spire was turned into a series of diminishing stages only slightly reminiscent of the upward thrust of the Gothic. Wren had intended to add flanking spires to his great church of St. Paul in London, as well as the western towers, but the spires never have been constructed.

The "New England" church so familiar to us is a product of the Renaissance pattern, though extremely simplified in harmony with the mood of Puritanism. Its proportions usually are good, and its effect is one of sobriety and dignity if not of soaring imagination. The very lack of decoration, while motivated theologically rather than aesthetically, is a signal merit especially when we compare it with what came after.

The nineteenth century was guilty of much bad art, and in no area worse than in its church building. Europe was on the whole fortunate in that already she had built most of her great churches, and her smaller ones as well: in England some Norman, many Gothic and Renaissance, not a few which in themselves were museums of the history of ecclesiastical architecture through the successive periods. Latin America too, where European civilization had been naturalized into this hemisphere in the sixteenth and seventeenth centuries, had done the greater part of her important church building. It was therefore in the United States that Victorian bad taste had its greatest opportunity. Let none suppose that the opportunity was missed.

Part of the difficulty was that cultural tradition and cultural leadership long remained centered in Europe, as definitely in architecture as in painting, music, and literature. Part of it was that Victorianism everywhere encouraged romanticism to run riot in an uninformed and undisciplined individuality. But the most effective cause of thoughtless and tasteless church building in America was the simple fact of America's deep-rooted distrust of worship, expressed in popular antipathy to ritual.

As the service was subordinated to the sermon, so the church ceased to be a holy place and was turned into an auditorium. The altar was abandoned, and the pulpit, now become a desk set on a high platform, took its central place. The ministers' seats faced those of the congregation, so that the clergy could look over the crowd and in their turn be in full view of the people. The choir, regarded as a performing unit, was placed on a still higher level, immediately behind the pulpit, where it might be seen and duly admired. Then why not let the people have a lovely view of gilded organ pipes behind the choir; and what did it matter that the visible pipes were fakes?

To give the preacher an even greater centrality for his audience, the central aisle was replaced by two or more side aisles, with a centered block of "orchestra" seating; and curved pews, or curving rows of orchestra chairs, served still more to bring the focus upon the orator of the day. Theater construction, concerned first of all with the visibility of the stage, next suggested a sharply sloping floor; and since kneeling had been pretty much given up anyway, no one saw any disadvantage in this. The entire structure, of course, was covered with the gingerbread decoration with which the tycoons of the days after the Civil War loved to embellish their homes; and if the churches were less egregiously bad at this point it was only because they had less money to spend.

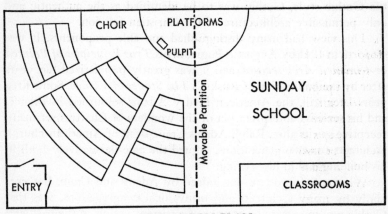

THE AKRON PLAN

The nadir of unchurchly churches was touched with the epidemic spread of the "Akron plan." This invention of the Central West, taking for granted the church as auditorium, sought to provide maximum capacity for sell-out occasions. Accordingly it set the pulpit platform across one corner, oriented the pews diagonally to face it, and made one entire side wall movable so that the Sunday-school space beyond it could be thrown into one enlarged hall seating now twice as many people as normally came to the services. (This happened on Easter Sunday, and sometimes when the local church was host for a conference or convention; but this seemed enough to justify the design to many building committees.) The Akron plan was born in 1867. Happily it seems now to be dead, or at least not to be spawning its kind; but its creaking skeletons (anAkronisms?) still dot and blot the American Christian landscape here and there.

REVIVAL AND ADVENTURE

The gradually reviving concern for worship led to new enquiries and experiments as to the kind of house in which God truly might be sought and rightly might be praised. Now that the Renaissance had spent its creative force, and Victorianism was beginning to lose its deadly power, the spectacular, ethereal beauty of medieval Gothic attracted attention first and most. To many it seemed that, since the most famous and most lovely cathedrals of Western Europe were of the Gothic style, Gothic was to be identified as the authentic and only permissible architecture of the Christian religion.

This view had many distinguished and able proponents. It was set forth in 1841 by Augustus Pugin, in his *True Principles of Pointed or Christian Architecture*, and it was greatly popularized ten years after by the publication of Ruskin's *The Stones of Venice*. Some fifty years later still, the American Henry Adams sojourned in France, and his sensitive interpretation of the wonders of Chartres set many receptive spirits afire. Ralph Adams Cram, dean of American church architects for two generations, argued the case persuasively both in his building and in his writing.

What was forgotten, not indeed by Adams and Cram, but certainly by many architects and many local congregations, was that Gothic was an expression at once of a particular time in the past, and of a particular building material. The designing and erection of Chartres and Amiens had been a creative adventure for the believing communities in whose midst and by whose hands they rose. The copying of those buildings in the American scene was neither a creative achievement in itself, nor a valid expression of the mood and mind of the American people. The arches and the flying buttresses had solved problems in the handling of stone masonry. They had no kind of meaning when they were reproduced slavishly, and without functional purpose, in concrete or even (save the mark) in wood.

> No item in this day's anomalies,
> No psychopathic modern's weird intent,
> Not stucco's virulent monstrosities
> So brutally reveal the age's bent:
> The Time Ghost's final jibe consists in these
> Gothic cathedrals molded of cement.

That was a reaction to a long and unhappy ride up a fashionable street in an American city, where one after another there were displayed the meaningless copies of a beauty real in its own character, but truly at home only in its native surroundings of time and place. Gothic remains undeniably beautiful; but a nostalgic medievalism is not the distinguishing mark of a living Christianity, and contentment with the medieval triumph will not give us a living answer as we seek to build today's temples for the everliving God.

It was not only Gothic that was imitated. With varying degrees of success we have followed also Romanesque, Byzantine, Renaissance, and colonial models. Only very recently has it become possible to persuade modern American churchmen that their faith, living in this day as well as in the past, can be reflected not only with the use of modern building materials (which had been accepted readily enough), but also in contemporary design (which had been welcomed only for theaters, department stores, and apartment houses).

Once more Europe has led the way. Wide publicity has been given in this country to the Matisse Chapel of the Rosary at Vence in France, both by magazine articles and illustrations and by the model included in the traveling Matisse exhibition. A look through Edward Maufe's little work called *Modern Church Architecture* will provide an introduction to twenty-nine European churches of contemporary design, scattered from Rome to Helsinki: churches which are startling perhaps at first glance, but challenging too; and, what matters most, declaring in their very structure that the worship of the eternal God is a legitimate and lively concern of people who are at home in the world of today.

Little by little we are daring to launch out into the deep for ourselves, and in our own manner. The great churches of America mostly are committed, and most of them to Gothic. The smaller ones have a remarkable opportunity to provide visible expressions of continuing, vital Christianity in the twentieth century scene. It is possible now, in almost every region, to find a number of examples of church buildings planned first of all for worship rather than for public speaking, yet unashamedly using the clean lines and clear surfaces and crisp angles which reflect man's newly realized effort to create beauty in following the simple patterns of use. A few illustrations from the San Francisco Bay area are provided herewith, and with warm thanks to the several architects not only for their supplying the photographs but still more for their daring to do the buildings. The reader will do well to engage in his own quest, alike among the churches that exist in his neighborhood, and among the possibilities that challenge the creative imagination everywhere.

Whatever may be the style of church building on which congregation and architect agree, integrity of structure is of the essence. Shortly after the Santa Barbara earthquake of 1925, I visited the ruins of the Mission church. To the young friar who was showing me around I remarked that the walls had fallen inward, and the buttresses outward. "Oh," he said reassuringly, "we're going to fix that when we rebuild. We're going to bolt the buttresses to the walls." A buttress that leans away from the thrust, a pillar that does not support a weight commensurate with its size, a beam that is decorative rather than functional: all of these are dishonest, and they ill become the house of the God of truth. One of the great virtues of good contemporary architecture is its high standard of structural honesty; and this is another reason for considering the use of contemporary modes in the building of an honest contemporary church.

CHANCEL, CHOIR, AND SANCTUARY

While styles of building have varied from generation to generation, the essence of Christian worship has remained the same; and so the ground plan of the church is less subject to continuing and justifiable change than are the details of walls, arches, and decoration. We have seen how the pagan basilica first lent its design to Christian use, and a little of how that design has been modified through the years. We need now to enquire, for the sake of our highest achievement in worship, into the arrangement and proportions of a truly usable place of worship.

If we are thinking of worship as primary, it is evident that the pulpit never should provide the focus of attention. This means that some sort of chancel must take the place of the pulpit platform, with all the lines of vision drawn compellingly to an altar which is dedicated to the glory of God, and whose cross is the perduring reminder of the sacrifice of the Christ. But there are great varieties in the planning of chancels: varieties of which some depend upon the particular usages of the given Christian group, and some are purely adventitious.

The chancel may be defined as that part of the church which is beyond the front of the congregational seating: in a cruciform church, the part immediately above the crossing of nave and transepts. It may or may not include a choir; but always it includes the sanctuary. The prevalent usage of referring to the whole church as "the sanctuary" is an unfortunate blunder, arising probably from the fact that so many people loosely have used "church" to describe a complex including offices, Sunday-school rooms, dining halls, kitchens, gymnasiums, and all manner of other secular appendages. The church proper is the place of worship; and the sanctuary is that most sacred part of it where the ministers of Christ perform their most sacred duties.

In the typical Anglican chancel one sees choir, communion rail, and then the sanctuary. In most Roman churches the sanctuary occupies the whole chancel, with the communion rail therefore much nearer to the congregation, and the choir withdrawn to a rear gallery. The chancel choir actually is an inheritance from the monastic chapel, in which the monks sang the offices in their daily sequence, and the stalls were set in facing rows to facilitate antiphonal singing. Cathedral churches, withdrawing the clergy from the transepts which originally had been created for their use, reproduced the chapel of the monks to provide seating for the numerous ministers. The total effect now was not only to separate the clergy further from the laity, but also to withdraw the altar much farther from the congregation.

Rome has done the most to correct the error. The usual Roman chancel is wide and open, so that all who are present can see what transpires before and at the altar. All too many of the great churches of Anglicanism, including some of the newer American ones, have in effect prevented congregational sharing in the service by affording only a distant view of the altar to anyone in the nave, and no view at all to many. The rood screen between nave and chancel, however intricately it may be carved and however proud of it its wealthy donor may be, serves also to separate the worshipers from the center of worship, and to that extent to deny the fellowship of the faithful.

There is no compelling reason why the singers of the church, professional or amateur, should be made into yet another screen between the people and the sanctuary. The most common argument for this arrangement, nowadays frequently and thoughtlessly imitated by many non-Anglican churches, is that it provides opportunity for an impressive processional. Against it may be pointed out not only the factors of space and distance, but also the fact that a choir's business is to be heard to advantage, and not necessarily to be seen at all. Choir seating in the chancel also means that choir members must hear lessons and sermon from behind reader and preacher, which often leads to their scarcely listening at all. The antiphonal effect of choral responses, again, is practically lost if the minister's voice and those of the choir reach the people from a single direction. Finally, the removal of the choir from the chancel will take away also the cumber-

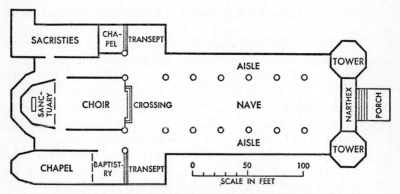

SIMPLIFIED GROUND PLAN OF GRACE CATHEDRAL,
SAN FRANCISCO, CALIFORNIA (THREE BAYS OF
THE NAVE, AND ONE TOWER, YET TO BE
COMPLETED)

ing organ console, and well may transfer the organ itself to a more convenient place.

If there must be a processional to satisfy the desire for pageantry, it can be provided for very simply by putting the choir into one of the transepts: or better, for antiphonal purposes, into both of them. This indeed is one of the few sensible reasons for adding transepts to the plan for a small or medium-sized church. (In a larger one, of course, the transepts may be serviceable as side chapels.) The transept choir, formerly much more usual than it is today, seems to be regaining favor here and there. In Laurel Methodist Church in Oakland the problem has been solved by the choir's entering the chancel in a conventional procession, and then turning through a side door and back into a transept whose floor is on a level with that of the chancel itself.

The chancel without choir seating need be no deeper than will provide full freedom of movement for the ministrants at the altar, plus space for a reasonable number of other clergy. It should be almost, if not quite, as wide as the nave, so that those latecomers who are forced into the front corners of the congregational area will not be denied full vision of the service they have come (however tardily) to share. Only those churches which call the communicants to kneel before the altar will require the communion rail; and in a small chapel a low outer step, without a railing, will serve the purpose perfectly

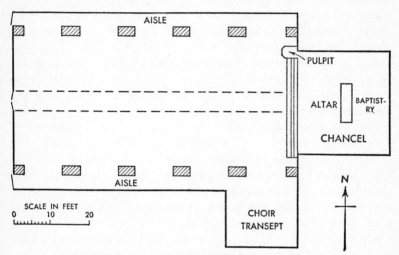

SKETCH OF THE GROUND PLAN OF UNIVERSITY
CHRISTIAN CHURCH, BERKELEY, CALIFORNIA

well. If there is a rail, it should of course have a center opening. One of the oddities of our time is that so many Methodist churches, whose dominant theory has denied any sharp separation between clergy and people, have given exactly the contrary impression by building a completely closed rail, and thus seeming to assert the existence of an immovable barrier between congregation and minister.

The appearance of the altar, and its precise planning, will depend necessarily upon the theological presuppositions of the given church. The altar set against the end wall of the sanctuary is appropriate, though not inevitably necessary, for those churches where the priest or minister performs the service alone or with none but clerical assistance. In churches of the congregational tradition, where lay deacons play an important role in the celebration of the Communion, the altar well may be brought forward some distance into the chancel, so as to allow room for movement behind it. In this case, of course, any dorsal or reredos can not be attached to the altar, but must be affixed to the wall. University Christian Church in Berkeley, California, affords an admirable example of the Lord's table made truly central, yet still available for use in accordance with the historic customs of the Disciples of Christ.

Pulpit and lectern normally belong at the two sides of the chancel entry, affording the fullest possible sight and hearing both for what occurs at them and for what transpires at the altar beyond them. Because of the bulk of the pulpit it should be, strictly speaking, just outside the chancel rather than within it. There is no uniform tradition, let alone any rule, as to whether the pulpit should be set at the right or at the left. It need not be so high as it is in some Gothic (and perhaps more neo-Gothic, quasi-Gothic, and pseudo-Gothic) churches; but it should be elevated sufficiently so that the preacher can see the faces of all those to whom he is speaking.

The chancel then, considered functionally, is a part of the whole church rather than a separate chamber. It culminates in sanctuary and altar, but it keeps the most holy place close enough to the people so that they will know it is theirs, and not the minister's only. True Christian worship requires that all the people shall hear and see, and shall fully share in, the entire divine service of song and prayer and instruction and adoration. With a chancel that is open, and an altar that is near, they can do this, as scarcely they can with the too common narrow arcade which the cathedral churches borrowed from the monasteries.

PEWS AND PEOPLE

The essential consideration in providing and furnishing the space for the congregation is that the people shall be encouraged to worship. Anything that serves this purpose is legitimate. Anything that defeats it is improper. This means, as has been said, the fullest possible visibility and audibility for everyone present. The first implication here is that the church should not be larger than will provide sufficient room for its normal congregation. It is far better to have a medium-sized church crowded, or even overcrowded, than to have vast empty areas Sunday after Sunday, and to spend large sums for space used only to house the Easter fashion show of that day's secular invaders.

A second principle is that every congregational seat shall be placed where there is an unrestricted view of the service being conducted in the sanctuary or before it. Modern construction does not require the rows of columns that were inevitable in the ancient basilica; and there is no reason why they should be imitated for tradition's sole sake. Seats placed behind pillars are conducive neither to peace of mind nor to elevation of spirit; and the competent architect can plan so that nothing of the sort is necessary.

The main aisle should be in the center, leading directly toward the central altar and the central cross. For convenience there should be side aisles also, though there is no need that there should be seats beyond them except in the very largest churches. The center aisle takes for granted the side pulpit, so that the preacher can speak directly to the people and not to emptiness. It happens that the widest center aisle I ever have seen, outside a major cathedral, is in a church with a centered pulpit; with the consequence that I found myself preaching to physical vacuity immediately before me, and wondering about an equivalent spiritual vacuity out on the edges of my vision.

The congregation's seating, whether pews or chairs, should be neither so uncomfortable as to cause annoyance, nor so soft as to be soporific. If the service is properly planned, the people will have not more than twenty minutes (the sermon time) in which continuously to remain seated; and for this they do not need plush cushions. In a church where kneeling is customary, the space between pews: that is, from the back of one to the back of the next: should be from 33 to 36 inches. In those where it is not customary, there still is the consideration of courtesy for those who may prefer to worship God in the historic attitude of reverence. The money saved in not buying needless seat cushions well might be spent in providing kneeling benches for those who care to use them. (The Methodists used to kneel, and not so long ago. Is it the saving of six inches per pew, or a loss of the sense of devotion, that has led them into the habit of sitting down to seek God?)

If the transepts are to be used not for a choir, but for added congregational space, the pews or chairs should by all means face the altar rather than the crossing. ("I'm so glad our pew is in the nave," remarked an elderly English cousin of mine. "'It saves my having to meet the issue of turning for the creed.") Very deep transepts are worse than useless for the congregation, since they condemn those sitting in them to seeing very little and often (acoustics being what they are) to hearing scarcely more. The trend today happily is toward building no transepts, or extremely shallow ones, for the church of average size. Whatever violence this may do to the retrospective symbolism of the Latin cross, it does much less harm to the opportunity of all the people truly to worship together.

A PLACE OF PRAYER

The church seen as lecture hall became almost inevitably a place of informal chitchat among members of a congregation that thought of itself as an audience. There is, curiously enough, some precedent in the Jewish tradition for casualness of behavior in the place of worship. Particularly in Orthodox synagogues there is no expectation that the worshipers shall even maintain silence, let alone pay close attention to what is going on. They come and go at various times, move about, greet their friends gaily, talk things over with their neighbors. One young European Jew said to me, anent a Reform service he had attended, "It was much too Christian for me: they all just sat like mummies."

These paragraphs are no plea that Christians shall sit like mummies. They are, however, a definite plea that we shall regard God's house as a very special place, and the act of worship as a very special experience. Whatever may be the rationale of Orthodox Jewish informality on the part of the congregation, it does not belong to the Christian estimate of our holy mysteries. The church, built to the glory of God, is not rightly to be used for any of the trivialities of secular life. When we Christian men and women enter the church, we are God's guests in his dwelling, and it is God only with whom we ought to concern ourselves.

The conversational hubbub heard in many an American church before the service, and even during the organ prelude, is that of a theater audience rather than of a worshiping congregation. Probably it is true that there is more of this clatter in the churches that are built like theaters than in those which are planned for worship; and this for immediate psychological reasons as well as because of inherited habits. The objective existence of sanctuary and altar, however, does not guarantee automatically the subjective attitude of reverence. In the retraining of modern Christians to the worship of God, there needs to be specific reminder that worship is the Christian's only proper occupation in the place prepared for worship. Note might be made also of the factor of courtesy to those who themselves wish to worship, but who are interrupted and confused by noise and confusion around them.

The service for each worshiper begins as he enters the church, and it ought not to end before he leaves it. Indeed the service, if it has been a real one, will not end for him even with his departure; for the experience of the presence of God scarce can be cut off so sharply at a point in time. The Roman and Anglican practices of private devotional prayer on first entry, and of a quiet moment after the final blessing has been pronounced, well might be emulated by other Christian believers. These usages will do much to establish an atmosphere in which the service as a congregational experience will have a genuinely reverent beginning, and which the individual worshiper will find still about him as he takes his homeward way.

This leads to the comment that the church ought to be available as a place of worship all of the time, and not only when scheduled public services are being held. The custom of locking up the church at other than service times is an unconscious assertion that this is an auditorium for meetings rather than a place for personal consecration. At least during the daylight hours, and preferably for twenty-four hours of every day, the house of God should be ready to welcome everyone who would seek God's presence. Commercially-minded trustees and fussy janitors may object; but their measures of worth are not the important ones, and their primary concern for physical property is not a Christian position. In point of fact the incidence of theft or vandalism is no greater in open churches than in locked ones; but even if it were, this would have no relevance. The incidence of personal respite and restoration is the only consideration here worthy of our notice.

We have come a long way from Noah's altar and Jacob's pillar, but still we would worship the one God whom Noah and Jacob and we have sought, if haply we might feel after him and find him. Men and women have worshiped at the tent of meeting, and before the

Jerusalem Temples, and in Christian churches oblong, square, and round. They have not ceased in their effort to build temples worthy of the Lord's glory; and the best of their experiments, though glorious, have been something less than perfect.

It is a long tradition that is ours, and an informing and enriching one. It is not a closed tradition yet, nor will it be while human beings live on this earth. Our goal still is that of our drawing near to God in our offering to him of the worship that is his by right. We can do this anywhere. We shall do it most readily in those places which we have designed in intelligence, and have built in devotion, and enter in humble faith. "The glory of Jehovah filled the house of God." It will do so again, and as often as we come to him in a house where fittingly he and we can meet.

IV

FOR GLORY AND FOR BEAUTY

THE CAPTION IS from the priestly account of the "holy garments" prescribed for Aaron, the first high priest of Israel. We shall come to the question of vestments in the course of a few pages; but there are other items of beauty and glory, and some principles relating to their design and use, that ask for our attention first.

Even as man has built the house of God in various patterns and in various styles, so also he has sought to record visually within that house the values which he cherishes and the faith which he holds. No doubt it was in reaction against the naïve idolatry of the surrounding peoples that Israel first established the second commandment's taboo upon the representation of living creatures. But this self-imposed limitation was not absolutely obeyed in the earlier centuries, and it never has denied to Judaism genuine artistic achievement in its religious life.

The cherubim, though not denizens of the natural world, certainly were thought of as being "in the heavens above"; yet they were also "within the oracle" of Solomon's temple, and their fifteen-foot wing spreads joined to span the entire space from one wall to the other. The molten sea rested upon the backs of twelve oxen, which evidently were altogether naturalistic in appearance. The bases of the ten lavers, too, were decorated with lions, oxen, and cherubim. Centuries afterward there was built at Jerash in Transjordan a synagogue, excavated only in our time, whose mosaic floor portrayed not only the whole menagerie of Noah's ark, but also Noah and his sons and their respective wives.

53

When in later years Judaism began to take with greater literalness the prohibition of making "any likeness of any thing," it concentrated instead upon symbols derived from the inorganic world. Chief among these were the two tables of the Law, the six-pointed star of David, and the seven-branched candlestick. These continue to be leading motifs of Jewish art, and may be seen in practically every synagogue of today.

Impelled by the same human desire to reflect the intangible in the objective, the invisible by the thing that could be seen, the early Christians soon began to create new symbols of their own. In nineteen hundred years Christianity has developed many such; and in them it has known continuingly the satisfaction that comes when man finds the object of his aspirations placed before him in a form that he can see, and rejoice in, and reproduce for himself. Our present enquiry is into the nature and meaning of some of the visual art forms that through the centuries have adorned the church, and have played an important part in Christian worship.

A symbol, properly defined and understood, is not a portrait. It stands for something other than that which externally it seems to reproduce. Thus the altar cross, of whatever material it may be made, represents physically only two beams of wood. Spiritually it reflects something quite other, the sacrifice of the Son of God on our behalf. Similarly the vestments of the priest imitate in fact the daily apparel of an upper-class citizen of many centuries ago, but in meaning announce the special responsibilities which the Church has laid upon its ministers. Church art includes both the symbolic and the directly representational. Sometimes it is not quite easy to be sure which is which, and confusion here has led now and then to unfortunate results in religious thought and life. In this chapter we shall be considering both symbols and representations; but we need always to remember that the two types of expression are distinct one from the other.

SYMBOLS OF DESIGN

The best known of all the Christian symbols is the cross, but it was by no means the first one. At the time when Jesus was crucified, and for three centuries after, the cross was a token not of glory but of shame. (St. Paul indeed had written otherwise to the Galatians and Corinthians; but few were able to share the brave paradox which he discerned.) Long before the cross, and recently publicized in the cinema version of *Quo Vadis*, the fish was the chief symbol in Christian use. This was in essence a code sign based upon an acrostic. The Greek word for "fish," *ichthus*, early was seen in the initial letters of the phrase *Iesous CHristos THeou Uios Soter:* "Jesus Christ, God's Son, Saviour." When a believer guessed that a new acquaintance might be of the Christian faith, he used the simple test of drawing the fish sign. If it was recognized, the brotherhood in Christ was established forthwith. If its meaning was missed, no harm had been done.

The fish, commonly a dolphin, appears on the earliest Christian tombs, declaring the Christian witness that Jesus is the Son of God and the Saviour of men. In common use, scratched in the dust, it was drawn in two curved lines which met at one end and crossed at the other. Ultimately this was stylized into the pointed oval, which still encloses many of the other visible tokens of Christianity as we use them in the decoration of our churches; and which thus attests our inheritance from those who ventured to mark themselves as Christian when such marking was perilous indeed.

Akin to the fish symbol in being alphabetic in origin, but retaining their primary alphabetic form, are several combinations of letters often seen, but not always identified with accuracy. What looks like IHS does not represent the schoolboy's guess of "In His Service," nor even the fourteenth century Latin supposition, *Iesus hominum salvator*, "Jesus the Saviour of men." The characters are the Greek *iota*, *eta*, and *sigma*, the first two and the last letters of *IEsouS*, Jesus. Akin to this is the *chi rho*, which looks to us like XP, but actually reproduces the two first letters of the Greek *CHRistos*, Christ. The *alpha-omega* monogram, an *A* coupled with a circle which is truncated at the bottom, derives directly from the words of the Lord in the final chapter of the book of Revelation: "I am Alpha and Omega, the beginning and the end." NIKH and NIKA, less frequently used, are the Greek words *nike*, "victory," and *nika(i)*, "he conquers." INRI, seen at the top of many Roman crucifixes, represents Pilate's sardonic inscription over the cross of Calvary, *Iesus Nazarenus Rex Iudaeorum*, 'Jesus the Nazarene, King of the Jews.'

The Empress St. Helena, mother of Constantine I, found what she announced to be the true cross of Christ in Jerusalem in 327. It was much later, however, before the cross became at all familiar or popular as an emblem of Christianity: not indeed till after the barbarian invasions had wiped out that empire which had made crucifixion the death of utter shamefulness. The crucifixion scene seems not to have been represented in Christian art before the fifth century; and one of its earliest examples, on the door of St. Sabina's in Rome, portrays our Lord flanked by the two thieves, but with the three crosses conspicuous by their absence. It seems that the pictured cross finally became standard as an orthodox reply to those heretics who were denying that the Christ really had suffered and died. It appeared with

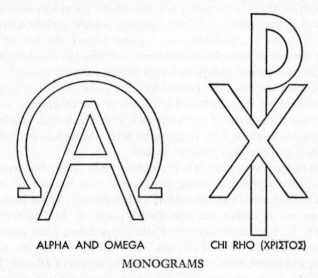

ALPHA AND OMEGA   CHI RHO (ΧΡΙΣΤΟΣ)

MONOGRAMS

growing frequency from the sixth century on, and had gained general acceptance as the primary Christian symbol by about the tenth century.

Regional traditions and designers' ingenuity produced numerous varieties of the cross form. The Latin cross is the most familiar one, with the crosspiece placed well toward the top of the vertical beam. The Greek cross has four arms of equal length, the Maltese is a square with wedges cut out from the corners, and the St. Andrew's cross is an X-shaped reminder of the legend of that apostle's martyrdom. The Russian cross has three crossbeams, adding a small one at the top for the inscription, and a slightly larger and slanting one near the bottom, to provide for nailing the feet of the crucified. The Celtic cross, with an attending "circle of eternity," often is interpreted as symbolizing the continuity of life victorious over the instrument of death.

The crucifix, which began to appear in the sixth century, added to the symbolism of the cross a direct representation of our Lord's body, technically known as the "corpus." In the West the corpus at first was fully robed, while from the beginning the East used the more naturalistic depiction of the unclothed body. This was adopted in the

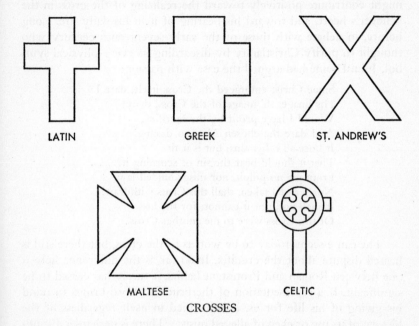

LATIN   GREEK   ST. ANDREW'S

MALTESE   CELTIC

CROSSES

West from the ninth century on. A striking modern return to the earlier Roman usage may be seen in the hanging rood in St. John's Church in Woodbury, New Jersey, which portrays the Prophet, Priest, and King wearing a prophetic robe, the priestly chasuble and stole, and a royal crown.

The extreme Protestants of Reformation days, disturbed by what they regarded as idolatry in the use of both crucifix and cross, rejected in its visible form the Christian symbol of which yet they spoke and sang. Majority American Protestantism followed this negative fashion practically up to our time; and a generation ago the cross scarcely was to be found in the typical church building. "This ain't no church," said a Portuguese workman looking around a Methodist Church in western Massachusetts. "You ain't got no cross." His hearer wondered perforce whether this might refer also to a lack among us other than that of a physical object.

Little by little it began to dawn on American Christians that the visible presence of the cross of Christ in the church, and on the altar, might contribute positively toward the realizing of the cross in the believer's heart, and toward his bearing of it in his daily life. Long before, in debate with those of the early seventeenth century who thought to purify Christianity by discarding its every physical symbol, John Donne had argued the case with passion:

> Since Christ embraced the Cross itself, dare I
> His image, th' image of the Cross, deny?
> Would I have profit by the sacrifice,
> And dare the chosen Altar to despise?
> It bore all other sins; but is it fit
> That it should bear the sin of scorning it? . . .
> From me no pulpit, nor misgrounded law,
> Nor scandal taken, shall this Cross withdraw.
> It shall not, nor it cannot; for the loss
> Of this Cross were to me another Cross.

The cause seems today to be won as to the cross, but there still is heated dispute about the crucifix. In so far as the difference here is one between Roman and Protestant habits, it surely has ceased to be significant. If a representation of the crucified Lord brings to mind his giving of his life for us, it is justified in itself regardless of the history of its use or even of alleged misuse. There is perhaps a distinction of meaning implied, in that the crucifix speaks to us of the dying Christ, and the empty cross of his glorious Resurrection. This would seem to argue, however, that rather than choosing between the two we ought always to make use of both. (Incidentally, it may be remarked that the almost universal symbol IHS, placed at the center of the altar cross, obviously is an adumbration of the corpus as it appears on the crucifix.) The question for us is not one of distinguishing Protestant from Roman Christians. It is rather one of aiding all of us to be Christian in truth; and in so far as cross and crucifix may serve toward this end they are rightfully to be used by every member of the one body of Christ.

IMAGES AND PICTURES

Once early Christianity had broken away from its Jewish matrix, it readily accepted the pagan rather than the Jewish attitude toward the graphic arts. The original symbol of the fish certainly violated the second commandment as late Judaism had understood it. On the catacomb tombs and walls were portrayals both Greco-Roman and Hebrew-Christian in their origins: Orpheus, Odysseus, Castor and Pollux, on the one hand; Noah, the three Hebrew children, and the Good Shepherd, on the other. The Christ was represented often as the Lamb of God, and in highly naturalistic form. The phoenix also, betokening life out of death, was an early and popular symbol of the Resurrection. Even the statues of pagan deities were drafted into Christian use, with Isis transformed into the Blessed Virgin and a head of Aesculapius recut to present the visage of the Man of Sorrows.

For centuries no one seems to have thought of any moral or theological distinction between one form of graphic art and another. Statuary, bas-reliefs, and paintings all were used, and all accepted as legitimate means for conveying the Christian story and the Christian faith to those who saw them. No doubt abuses arose, as simple people confused the immediate with the ultimate, and therefore fell to worshiping the physical artifact rather than the spiritual reality.

Nevertheless the great dispute about images which developed in the eighth and ninth centuries, known as the iconoclastic controversy, had other and less valid roots than distaste for idolatry as such. The leader of the campaign against the use of images, the Eastern Emperor Leo III, was seeking to establish peace with his Saracen neighbors. The Saracens, being Muslim in faith, held firmly to the antirepresentational rules which Muhammad had borrowed from the Jews; and one of their principal propaganda points against the Christians had been the existence of alleged idols and idolatrous practices in the Christian churches.

In 725 Leo forbade the use of images in his domains, and in 727 Pope Gregory II countered by declaring iconoclasm (image breaking) a heresy. The second Council of Nicea, in 787, attempted to distinguish between veneration, which was permitted, and adoration, which was proscribed. Ultimately the East settled down to the com-

promise of permitting flat paintings and mosaics, and from the ninth
century on the Orthodox churches have made use of these ikons as
major features in their devotional life. The West continued to use
both pictures and statuary, as does Rome to this day.

A new iconoclasm arose with John Calvin, who regarded the religious employment of art works as being at once theologically improper (a Jewish judgment) and economically unsound (a middle-
class attitude). The English Church, ever resolving issues by
compromise, held to a middle ground between the Roman and Calvinist positions. It had taken over the Roman churches and cathedrals,
and despite the efforts of the Puritans it preserved much of the art
treasure of the earlier days. Painting had been a lesser factor in Britain
than on the Continent, but stonework and pictorial windows in many
cases were magnificent, and in most cathedrals and parish churches
were not destroyed. There was a different and a less happy story in
the seizure of the monastic establishments under Henry VIII, as witness the ruins of Tintern and Fountains abbeys. Crucifixes and statues
of the saints were removed from the churches (and occasionally destroyed by violence within them), though memorial statuary of a
secular kind seems not to have come under either official or popular
ban.

The first churches built by the nonconformists had bare walls and
plain glass windows. Little by little the austerity was modified. In
America the religious picture first appeared, significantly enough, not
in the church proper but in the Sunday-school rooms. This perfect
equivalent of the early Christian practice of using pictures for the
religious instruction of the simple seems to have occasioned little protest, though there still is some reluctance to allow the picture to be
hung or painted on the walls of the church itself. ("Mills Chapel is
a high church, isn't it?" remarked a visitor. And the evidence was that
"You have pictures of angels on the walls.") Pictorial windows often
have been accepted, and greatly admired even when they have been
rather feeble art, in churches where a fresco would not yet be tol-
erated.

Again the only relevant issue is that of actual worth, at once religious and artistic. It is absurd to suppose that glass is morally superior to paint, or paint to stone. If the art work occasions idolatry,
it is a menace. If it provides inspiration, it is a blessing. The danger
of idolatry today surely is less than the danger of spiritual dullness

and sterility. We need to have our memories refreshed, our imaginations stirred, our devotion deepened. To these ends the use of worthy religious art will contribute greatly; and we but rob ourselves if we are afraid to use it.

SYMBOLS OF LIGHT

"The Lord said that he would dwell in thick darkness." This concept of the withdrawn and hidden God was implemented in the inner structure of all the successive Temples in Jerusalem. No natural light at all could penetrate the veil of the most holy place, and only the occasional gleam from an opening door entered even the outer part of the sanctuary. The sole interior lighting was that of the golden lampstand, or, in Solomon's shrine, of the ten lampstands. The lamps were shallow containers for olive oil, not at all the candles we are likely to associate with the traditional mistranslation "candlestick."

The use of that word in the version of 1611 does reflect the fact that the candles of Christian usage long have been thought of as a direct inheritance from the lamps of the Jewish Temple. Light and fire are well-nigh universal symbols of the divine power and presence, and almost always and everywhere man has used them as instruments of his worship. God's own darkness was relieved by man's votive offering of light in Jerusalem, and God's house ever has been brightened for the Christian by the ceremonial use of lamps, rushlights, and candles.

From the fifth century onward the Feast of the Purification was observed with a procession of lights, and on the same date (2 February) as a much older pagan rite of the same kind. The practice seems to have been attached to this particular Christian celebration because of the reference to the giving of "light to them that sit in darkness" in the *Benedictus,* or song of Zacharias; and in medieval times the festival became known as Candlemas. Those who have attended the Eastern Orthodox services of Easter Even, and especially those who have witnessed the annual ceremony of the Holy Fire at the Church of the Holy Sepulchre in Jerusalem, know the joy with which the light is passed first from the central shrine, and then from one believer's candle to another's, until each has secured for himself a personal share of that light which constantly divides itself without ever growing less.

Lights on the altar, and about it, once practically necessary for illumination, always have been regarded also as symbols of spiritual light. It is difficult to see why the living flame of the candle ever should have been so detested and feared by those who were satisfied with kerosene lamps, by those who in the nineteenth century welcomed the introduction of gas and the installation of its ugly fixtures, or by those who in our time are perfectly content with the hard glare of electricity, and some of whom even decorate their churches with neon. There are some wonderful stories about controversies on this point, and some of them of not many years ago. One is that of the major church in New York City which was left a large bequest on the sole condition that "There shall be no Roman candles on the altar." It is said that the vestry took legal advice, was confirmed in its opinion that Roman candles are fireworks, and so kept its candles and the legacy as well. How silly can we Christians get?

Current Roman practice provides for a straight row of six candles across the altar, and two Eucharistic candles which are lighted only during the celebration of the Mass. There is also a Paschal candle, on a standard at the Gospel side of the altar, which is kept lighted from Easter Even to Ascension Day. The Roman usage is imitated today in many Anglican churches, though without official authority. There is ancient English precedent for the use of only two altar candles, and for the lighting of these at all services rather than reserving them for use at the Holy Communion only. Side candles have been used in many varieties of arrangement, commonly with larger numbers lit for the greater festival occasions.

The reverent lighting of the church candles when the service is about to begin, and their orderly extinguishing as it closes, may contribute much toward marking the time of worship as one of special import. The traditional order of lighting the side candles in the sanctuary is to start from the altar outward, first on the epistle side (the congregation's right), and then on the gospel side. Extinguishing is done in reverse order, beginning on the gospel side and from the outside inward. If only the two altar candles are used, they should be lit and extinguished in the same sequence: epistle, gospel, and gospel, epistle. Needless to say the use of properly constructed lighters, which can be secured at very little cost from any church supply house, will provide a dignity that is impossible with the striking of matches.

Votive lights, while undeniably effective as they gleam in the far recesses of a darkened church, should be used with great caution. A white light on the altar at other than service times betokens the presence of the reserved Sacrament, and has no meaning otherwise. Before a side altar, a statue, or a picture, the votive light stands for a personal act of devotion on the part of the one who has lit it. Even Rome has not defined clearly the significance and validity of this usage, though it encourages the practice as providing some kind of satisfaction to the devotees. Recently a new Roman church in California has installed electric votives with coin slots. To mention this is to say enough about the taste of those who invented it, and of those who allowed its invasion of the church.

The natural light entering the church by the windows early was modified by filtering it through many-colored glass. The Gothic churches, lacking the flat wall spaces of the Romanesque, began to use their windows, instead of paintings, as the illustrated Bible for the unlettered. Stained glass as we know it dates from the tenth century, when for the first time leaden strips replaced wood for separating the panes, and so made possible the substitution of a great variety of shapes for the early rectilinear sections. Once begun, the art of stained-glass making rose rapidly to such climactic glories as those of the windows of Chartres.

The Protestant flight from church art, accompanied by the general debasement of taste in the nineteenth century, robbed many architects and churchmen of any sound criteria for the planning, execution, and evaluation of windows. The worst windows of all were those which consisted of plain glass with colored paper pasted over it: horrible phenomena even before they started to crack and peel. Not much better were the copies, painted on flat sheets of glass, of works by such naturalistic artists as Hans Hofmann and Bernhard Plockhorst: sentimental in concept, second rate in performance, and sad indeed as adornments of the house of God. It is better far to have altogether plain glass, or the most simple of geometric designs, than such crudities as these.

Stained glass is not veneer or lamination, nor is it superimposed paint. Only if the color is genuinely that of the piece of glass itself can there be secured the vivid translucence which makes a window beautiful. Since a window in the nature of things does not provide photographic reproduction (even in technicolor), it should not attempt it. The design ought always to be symbolic rather than directly representational, and the leaded sections should be small enough to give real variety of intense color pattern rather than the great dull areas of feeble coloring that are seen in so many churches of our time.

There is good glass being made today, and much of it in America, but not nearly enough of it is being used. Even those communions which have maintained a continuing artistic heritage often have been led astray here. The windows of a new church building should be planned from the outset, in consultation with the architect and with the best available technicians. They need not be completed all at once, but they should be kept in the considered pattern of relationships without impromptu revisions, so as to present finally a coherent scheme of design, meaning, and value. A donor who wishes to pay for a memorial window is by precedent entitled to a small credit line; but he never should be allowed to contravene the canons of taste, and the established window plans of the given church, by intruding his own notions of what would be pretty.

SYMBOLS OF COLOR

The use of color in paintings and windows led naturally to the idea that colors in themselves might be employed to symbolize particular values in the Christian life, and to mark the corresponding days and seasons in the Church year. The standard Roman color sequence is the most orderly and the best known, and it is widely used today outside the Roman communion. Each of the liturgical colors appears in its turn in the altar frontal, in pulpit and lectern hangings (antependia), in the burse and veil for the Communion, in the stole of the officiating minister or priest, and in the Eucharistic chasuble and maniple when these are worn.

White, reflecting light and joy, is assigned to festivals of the Christ and the Blessed Virgin, and of saints who were not martyrs or who are commemorated in connection with an event other than their deaths. Thus St. John Evangelist, who according to tradition died a natural death at a great age, is honored with white materials. Thus also, though certainly St. John Baptist died a martyr's death, and St. Paul almost certainly, the feasts of the Nativity of St. John Baptist and of the Conversion of St. Paul make use of white. White is the correct color also for baptisms and marriages.

Red is used for the feasts of martyrs, and for Whitsuntide (the feast of Pentecost and six days thereafter). This latter probably reflects the "tongues of fire" which, according to the book of Acts, appeared upon the disciples at the coming of the Holy Ghost. A corollary of this is that red is the normal color for confirmations, ordinations, and consecrations, though sometimes white is used on these occasions.

Purple (or violet) is assigned to seasons of penitence and preparation: Advent, Lent, and the Rogation Days and Ember Days. Black belongs to Good Friday and, in Roman practice, to All Souls' Day; and it is used also for the burial office. Roman custom permits the use of rose-colored materials on two Sundays of the year: Gaudete, the third in Advent, and Laetare, the fourth in Lent, both of these days providing deliberate breaks in the austerities of the penitential periods. Rome also allows the substitution of gold (not yellow or orange) for any color except purple. Days and seasons which do not fall into any of the preceding categories employ green, interpreted as the color of continuing life and growth.

There are elaborate rules of precedence governing cases in which, through the shifting relationships of the solar and the ecclesiastical years, two special observances would fall on the same day, and a choice has to be made between them and therefore between their respective colors. The regulations are too elaborate to be detailed here; but they may be followed easily by making use of the standard Church Calendars which are published every year. From the Sarum (Salisbury) tradition of the Church of England there is derived a plan of color changes which is quite different from the Roman, and which is preferred by a number of Anglican purists. It is, however, much less clearly organized than is the Roman sequence, and permits of such great variety of option as to make it scarcely a regular pattern.

The frequent changing of colors involved in following either the Roman or the Sarum scheme will mean that someone will have to do a good deal of extra work, and also that the church will be involved in some added expense for the necessary materials. The assignment of making the changes, however, is one both pleasant and educative for the person who receives it; and a women's or young people's society, or a specially organized altar guild, well may assume the responsibility. Nor need the financial outlay be very great. Good brocades with churchly patterns, in all the standard liturgical colors, are available at reasonable prices; and the making of the sets of frontals, antependia, and stoles is another enterprise that should enlist the ready interest and skillful work of church women. Elaborate embroidery is not necessary. If there is to be embroidery at all, however, it should be done entirely by hand. Machine-made work looks like what it is.

The variety provided by the seasonal and festal changes in color is itself an emotional and intellectual stimulus to the congregation. Instead of one uniform scheme of decoration maintained throughout the year, and after a time scarcely noticed, there are recurring and happy surprises when fresh new colors meet the eye, and there is a direct challenge to the beholder to think in terms of the special day or season thus emphasized. A minor practical advantage is that while hangings left permanently in place become inevitably dusty, and more and more drab, the release of one set after another from duty provides convenient opportunity for cleaning and for any needed repairs.

Flowers long have been used in the churches, and naturally enough. Ideally, since they are decorations rather than instruments of worship, they should stand not on the altar itself, but on a ledge (gradine or retable) at its back. If there is no retable the flowers may be set on the altar as long as they do not obscure the cross or impede the celebration of the Sacrament; but on the whole they are better placed at either side, leaving the altar's surface clear except for the cross, the two lights, and the service book. The flowers need not be of the particular color of the day, though manifestly they should not clash with it. Most churches without liturgical tradition tend to use too many flowers. They never should be so numerous, or the bouquets so large, as to deflect attention from the central cross; and their total elimination in Lent, except on Laetare Sunday, will help to stress the solemnity of that season.

GARMENTS OF PRAISE

All clothing tends to have symbolic overtones as well as practical utility. The sport shirt speaks of casual summer afternoons, and the white tie and tails of diplomatic dignity. The furious controversies over the use of clerical vestments in early Reformation times attested not only Roman, but quite as clearly Protestant, recognition that the garments worn by the clergy in the service stood for recognized emphases and values. Denying so many of the values and emphases of sixteenth century Rome, the Protestants to a large extent repudiated the garb that seemed to speak of them.

They did not thereby escape sartorial symbolism. The Geneva gown asserted the austerity of Calvinist doctrine quite as clearly as the embroidered chasuble denoted the performing of the priestly office. The Quaker distaste for expensive frippery produced a thoroughly stylized costume by which the members of the Society of Friends immediately could be identified. The Prince Albert coat, marking in an earlier day two types of public orators, political and religious, became in time as definitely a nonconformist clerical uniform as ever the cassock had been a Catholic one. The difference between the ancient vestments and the more recent habiliments was one of their specific references only, and not (as some have supposed) of the symbolic as contrasted with the simply practical.

In general all clerical attire, whether old or relatively new in form, stems from the standard secular apparel of former days. The historic vestments of the Roman and Anglican traditions reproduce ancient Roman and early medieval clothing, only slightly modified with the passing of the centuries. In just the same way the frock coat remained a ministerial property when it had ceased to be fashionable elsewhere. The morning coat succeeded it in a similar sequence; and some clerics of today, who never would deign to put on a clerical collar, persistently mark themselves by the white piping on their waistcoats.

The basic argument for special ministerial garb, in the church or outside it, is not that the minister as an individual should be dressed up, but precisely that his personal identity should be subordinated to the claims and the dignity of his high calling. Vestments thus glorify the office, not the man; and seen thus they become real and useful factors in the worship both of the ministrant and of the laity who worship with him and with his help. "For glory and for beauty" Aaron was assigned his priestly robes: not that Aaron was to be glorified, nor that he individually was to appear beautiful, but that the glory of God might be proclaimed in the beauty accorded to his first minister in Israel.

One of the most unfortunate vagaries of the Protestant reaction was that black became standard for the clergy, and black only. This custom is often attributed to the decision of Martin Luther, though the Scandinavian Lutherans use white and colored vestments freely. Surely of all the choices that could have been made to mark the joyous proclaiming of the Christian gospel, and the glad sharing in the ministries of the Church, black was quite the least fitting. The prejudice in favor of black seems still to be dominant in many Protestant circles, where the Prince Albert or the business suit at last has yielded indeed to a robe, but only to one of lugubrious, funereal appearance. Increasingly the black is being relieved by the use of academic hoods, whose bright bits of colored velvet and silk do improve the situation somewhat. The next necessary step is to go beyond this left-handed, half apologetic procedure, and frankly to adorn the ministers of Christ with evident symbols of the light and hope and beauty that belong to the Christian life.

Academic and quasi-academic robes can not provide the lasting answer, helpful as they may have been in breaking through distaste for any robes at all. The church is not a university, and the minister in its services should wear not professorial but churchly garments. When he does so he will better reflect his true office, and incidentally he will be much easier to look at.

The basic clerical garment, the cassock, is black indeed. This is a more comfortable and a more satisfactory piece of clothing than is the academic gown, or any of the currently popular variants of it. It can be worn at least about the church and church grounds, even if not on the street; and on such occasions as wedding rehearsals it does much to remind the participants that they are engaged in a serious religious matter rather than in family gaiety or secular nonsense.

The surplice, a loosely fitting overgarment of white linen (and always it should be generously cut), is worn over the cassock during service times, and only then. Nylon and orlon surplices now are available, and will save the altar guild or the minister's wife many hours of pressing. For the "choir offices," those services which are primarily for instruction, it is correct for the minister to wear the hood of his degree, and with it a black tippet which may be embroidered at the ends with an appropriate crest or coat of arms. The hood should not be worn at sacramental services, and for these the tippet is replaced by a stole in the color of the day. All outer vestments should be taken off as soon as the service is ended, and the plain cassock worn while the minister greets the departing congregation.

In our time not many clergy of the typical Protestant denominations will be ready to wear the historic Eucharistic vestments, and in Anglicanism there still is much controversy about them. Irish bishops of the Anglican communion, for example, are forbidden by law to wear anything of the kind. The opposition to these vestments, in Ireland and elsewhere, is largely a matter of surviving prejudice against anything Roman. Surely the marking of the supreme Christian service by the use of special garments, reserved to it only, can not be held to be improper in itself.

A more practical objection is that good Eucharistic vestments, in all the variety of seasonal colors, are very costly indeed. Few ministerial salaries would allow their purchase, and not many churches would want to use so much money for this purpose. That they will spend more for a gymnasium directly across the street from the local high school, or for a fully equipped kitchen that will be used perhaps once or twice a month, may be true; but that's the way they are, and arguing the point with them will do little good for some time to come.

For the record, the Western Eucharistic vestments include alb, girdle, stole, amice, maniple, and chasuble. The alb is a white linen robe worn over the cassock, and reaching all the way down to its hem. The girdle is a white rope or band, whose ends are allowed to hang loosely. The stole, when worn with these, is crossed in front, and its ends are tucked through the girdle. The amice, originally a hood, is an oblong piece of linen resting upon the shoulders and forming a high collar at the back; and the maniple, perhaps once a napkin or handkerchief, is a narrow strip of silk or linen placed over the left arm, just above the wrist. The chasuble, made of silk or brocade, is the Eucharistic garment par excellence. It is a mantle with a single circular opening, and is decorated front and back with a Y-shaped cross. Stole, maniple, and chasuble are in the color of the given day. The remaining Eucharistic vestments are uniformly white, and made of linen. (A current Anglican compromise is an all-purpose chasuble in white, worn with a stole of the seasonal color. Aside from economy, this seems to be a gentle way of introducing some congregations to the celebrant's using other vestments than cassock, surplice, and stole.)

Not strictly vestments, but historic items of clerical attire, are the cope and various types of headdress. The cope is an outer cloak, made of silk, and with shield-shaped embroidery on the back. It is worn for solemn processions, and in the Roman use at the benediction of the blessed Sacrament and for the absolution of the dead. The miter is the bishop's ceremonial hat, used in the Roman Church and by an increasing number of Anglicans. The biretta is a square cap with three or four projections at the top, usually brought together with a round tassel. The English equivalent of the biretta is the square Canterbury cap, which is flat on the top. Canterbury cap or biretta may prove useful if the clergyman has to stand long in the open in bad weather. Otherwise they have little service to render today.

What about vestments for the choir? A choir seated in a rear gallery need not be vested, but one placed either in the chancel or in a transept must be, for the sake of uniformity and dignity. The cotta, a short surplice, will look better to most eyes than will a robe of any dark color, and it can be laundered and pressed with some frequency. Cassocks for choristers historically are either black or red, and may be purple in cathedral churches.

It is easily possible to spend too much for elaborate choir vestments of unhistoric and romantic design; but it is a false economy, whatever style may be chosen, to save money by using sleazy materials which offend the eye from the beginning and which rapidly become disreputable. If the church wishes to retain the tradition of the covered head, small skull caps for women and girls are more comfortable, less cumbersome, and less expensive than any other type of headdress. Mortarboards, per contra, are costly, awkward, and disturbing to the wearers, as well as being academic rather than churchly. Needless to say, all choir vestments, as well as those of the clergy, should be carefully hung up after every using, and should be checked often for any soiling or disrepair.

This may be the place to insert a word about the minister's wearing of the clerical collar when he is away from the church. The collar, like the vestments, is a token not of personal separation from the rest of humanity, but of a special responsibility to serve all men and women. Anyone who has worn the collar about town, or when traveling, knows how often it leads to important counseling of total strangers, who without seeing it never would have had the chance to seek the help they needed.

The respect accorded to the collar (and verily it is to the collar, not to its unknown wearer) by members of the more depressed groups in our society is a heartening tribute to the Church of Jesus Christ, whose ministers on the wrong side of town so evidently have approved themselves as friends and true servants of the underprivileged. One does not become less validly human when he has the collar on, though indeed he may be inclined to behave better than he might when hidden in the anonymity of a red tie or an aloha shirt. With the collar he does become a visible, living reminder that some men have given themselves wholly to God, and that they are not ashamed of their high calling in Christ Jesus.

"Honour and majesty are before him: strength and beauty are in his sanctuary." Rightly shall we give unto the Lord the glory and strength of a noble house meet for his service, and within it the beauty of tasteful and meaningful adornment. Every historic symbol speaks to us of our historic faith. Every worthy painting and every gleaming window unites us with all the heroes of the past, and with the artists and the craftsmen of all the generations. Every flaming candle reminds us of the Light of the World, and each change of color calls us to ponder yet another aspect of the Christian faith and life. Ministering to the people for Christ's sake, the minister wears not the garb of daily business, but the tokens of a sacred office which has been passed on through countless generations, and which has brought its own emblems with it.

We shall not worship the objects, and we need not worship any one particular way of selecting, arranging, and using them. Our sole concern is that we shall worship God. The objects have helped many toward this end; and they will help again and again, whenever they are chosen in thoughtfulness, and made with care, and used in reverence. For glory and for beauty in the house of the Lord, we shall find that always there will be more that we can bring as our gifts to him.

V

THE CHRISTIAN YEAR

TIME IS NOT real. It is only a category of our limited human experience. Plato and the author of the Fourth Gospel discerned this long ago, and modern physicists have added their supporting witness. But since we are human and limited, we have to deal with time, and we must learn to use it wisely as an instrument.

The truths of the Christian gospel are timeless, too. Every day is the day which the Lord hath made. The sacrifice of the Christ is eternal, and his Resurrection is a continuing reality. Within time, however, our own restricted capacities of thought and feeling preclude our giving full attention to every aspect of truth at once. Inevitably, therefore, we have associated certain particular emphases with certain points in time; and the recurring phenomena of the lunar month and the solar year have lent themselves readily to fixing regular seasons and days for such special observance.

This sort of thing has been done wherever man's sophistication has reached to the making of any sort of calendar, and in every aspect of life secular or religious. Ancient Egypt, whose calendar had twelve months of thirty days each, added five extra days at the year's end to make up the necessary 365, and assigned each of the five to the honoring of one major deity of the Egyptian pantheon: Osiris, Horus, Set, Isis, and Nephthys. In our America of today many a Protestant, who knows nothing of the feasts of the Conversion of St. Paul (25 January) and of the Presentation of Christ in the Temple (2 February), celebrates with scarcely less than religious zeal the birth dates of the secular saints Lincoln and Washington, to say nothing of the intervening feast of the patron of romantic love. Between ancient Egypt and modern America there have been calendars innumerable, each with its own series of special observances and celebrations belonging to its own cultural history.

THE JEWISH CALENDAR

Judaism derived its time measurements very largely from Babylonian sources. The year was solar, with twelve months originally of thirty days; but instead of the annual five-day addition of Egypt, the Babylonian priests inserted an extra month whenever they deemed it necessary. Modern Judaism follows the same procedure, with the extra month coming seven times in each nineteen years because some of the months now have only twenty-nine days. The seven-day week, on the other hand, was strictly lunar in origin, as one fourth of the moon's complete sequence of phases. The adjustment between the two always has been difficult, and accounts for some of the complexities which persist in our calendars of today.

The sabbath, whose name is from the root *shabath*, "to cease, desist," appears originally as a day of rest for man and beast. Not only field labor, but also trade, was forbidden on this day. From the Babylonian exile onward the keeping of the sabbath served to mark the Jewish people as distinct from their neighbors, and so became an important token of loyalty to the Jewish faith. Details of interpretation, as to just what was prohibited on this day and what was allowed, occasioned more and more discussion as time went on. Thus there were produced those scribal niceties, and perhaps cavils, which Jesus is said to have disapproved as contravening human value.

Within the Jewish year there developed, in the course of the centuries, a series of observances which survive in the well known festivals and high holy days of current Judaism. The seventh month, Tishri (September-October), very early was identified as a month of special holiness, and was marked with the Feast of Trumpets on its first day. The Masonic order, it may be noted, still recognizes a Feast of Tishri in its own traditional calendar. Each seventh year was a sabbatical year (a presage of modern academic custom?), with release from labor and from debt. Each fiftieth year, being seven sevens plus one, was idealized in the late priestly code as a time for the return of all property to its hereditary owners; but there is no proof that this ideal ever was fulfilled in fact.

The great solar festivals of Judaism were the Passover, Pentecost, and the Feast of Tabernacles. The Passover, celebrating the escape of Israel from Egypt, fell always on the fourteenth day of Nisan (March-April), and so on shifting days of the week from year to year. This was a nomadic feast, with the lamb as its primary physical object. After Israel's settlement into agricultural life in Palestine, there was associated with the Passover the seven-day Feast of Unleavened Bread (Matzoth), the beginning of the seven weeks' "joy of harvest."

Pentecost, fifty days later, marked the completion of the grain harvest. Its early name was the Feast of Weeks: that is, seven weeks from the beginning of the Feast of Unleavened Bread. The final agricultural festival of the year was the Feast of Tabernacles, or Booths, which corresponds approximately to the English "harvest home" and the American Thanksgiving. This came at the end of the harvests of fruit, oil, and wine, from the fifteenth to the twenty-second days of Tishri. It was observed by a token return to primitive conditions of life, for that one week, in temporary shelters which were erected in the orchards and vineyards. Today the booths commonly are set up inside the synagogue building, a sign that symbol has triumphed wholly over reproduction.

Purim, associated with the story of Esther, fell on 14 and 15 Adar (February-March). Probably it was at first a popular Babylonian festival, adapted by the Mesopotamian Jews as they adopted it from their neighbors, much as Christmas has come now to be observed by many Jewish families in America. It will be noted that there is an evident correlation between the names of the leading characters of the familiar story, Esther and Mordecai, and those of the Babylonian deities Ishtar and Marduk. Thus the Jews seem to have set the precedent which the Christians followed later, in their taking over existing festival dates from Greco-Roman paganism and transmuting the occasions for Christian use. Purim always has been a time of special gaiety, and in modern times is almost frivolous in its delight in the beauty of Esther and its unbridled glee over the fate of the villainous Haman.

The Feast of Dedication, or Lights (Chanukkah), originated in the rededication of the Temple by the Maccabees in 164 B.C., after their victory over the forces of the Syrian king Antiochus Epiphanes. Its date is 25 Kislev (November-December), and today it has become largely a Jewish surrogate for Christmas. Jewish children have the advantage, however, for they are supposed to receive gifts on each of the eight days of the total celebration.

The "high holy days" or "solemn festivals" of Judaism are the New Year (Rosh Hashanah) and the Day of Atonement (Yom Kippur). The beginning of the year was moved in medieval times from 1 Abib to 1 Tishri, and so falls in early autumn. Rosh Hashanah is largely a day of memorial, self-examination, and repentance, and it is almost wholly free from the nonsense elements of our secular-Christian New Year festivities. One recent concession to prevailing fashion has been the adoption of the practice of sending greeting cards at this time.

Yom Kippur, the Day of Atonement, is represented in the priestly writings as having been observed in the wilderness. There is no early evidence for this, and it seems more probable that this day of deepest solemnity originated during the dark days of subjection to alien rule. Its date is ten days after Rosh Hashanah, and the entire period between is a season of soul-searching comparable to the Christian Lent. Yom Kippur itself is a total fast for the devout Jew, and its services continue throughout the entire day practically without a break.

In Orthodox Judaism the great feasts and fasts are two-day observances, apparently because of early uncertainty about the precise dating of the new moon. This has been rationalized more recently, in terms of a spherical earth, by saying that the two days provide for a measure of simultaneous observance by the faithful round the world. Reform Judaism, taking into account modern astronomical and chronological precision, has reduced the time in each case from two days to one.

GROWTH OF THE CHRISTIAN CALENDAR

It is evident that Christianity borrowed much from the Jewish calendar, which its first adherents knew so well. The Sabbath was observed, though scarcely in a way that would have satisfied the scribes, as long as Christians remained in touch with Jewish circles. The Passover is inextricably bound up in the Christian story of the last days of Jesus' life. Pentecost has kept its ancient Greek-Jewish name, although few Christians know anything of its original connection with the grain harvest.

The first great change was the establishment of Sunday initially as an added day of worship for the Christians as a special unit, and then as a total replacement for the Jewish Sabbath. This was a celebration primarily of the Resurrection on the first day of the week, though its association with the sun was noted favorably by St. Justin Martyr as early as the middle of the second century. The attachment to the Christian Sunday of the Jewish regulations for the Sabbath was not thought of until the Protestant Reformation, when it was suggested by a Puritan clergyman named Nicholas Bownd (1606); and it never has been accepted by Rome, nor by most of the Christians of continental Europe.

With each Sunday regarded as a little Easter, it was natural that each Friday soon should be treated as a special memorial of our Lord's death on Calvary. Friday therefore became a day of fasting, and in the second century Wednesday was added to it, apparently in conscious rivalry with the established Monday and Thursday fasts of the Jews. "I fast twice in the week," says the Pharisee as quoted by Jesus. It would seem that the Christians had decided not to be outdone.

Easter Day was observed annually on a Sunday everywhere but in the province of Asia, where the Church held to the Passover date of 14 Nisan. Our present rule, setting Easter on the first Sunday after the first full moon after the spring equinox, dates from the Council of Nicea in 325. This was far from being a total solution, because of the difficulty of calculating the moon's phases, and soon both the Celtic Churches and the Eastern ones diverged from Rome as to its precise application. Orthodox Christianity still uses a different basis in computing the date, with the result that the Eastern and Western Easters sometimes are as much as five weeks apart.

Good Friday is mentioned in documents of the early second century, with its fast extending through Holy Saturday. Lent originally was an enlargement of the Good Friday fast. Its setting at forty days was first suggested, so far as we know, by St. Athanasius in about A.D. 340. In the seventh century four days were added to the six Lenten weeks, in order to provide a full forty fast days without counting the six (nonfasting) Sundays. Thus Ash Wednesday, named from the practice of marking the foreheads of the faithful with ashes, came to be the first day of Lent. The great feasts after Easter and depending upon it, Ascension Day and Whitsunday (Pentecost), first can be traced in the fourth century.

While these Christian festivals all had a Jewish and lunar calendar base, the dates of Christmas and the Epiphany (6 January) come from wholly different origins. Both are approximations of the winter solstice, become inaccurate with the passage of the centuries, and both have their roots outside the Hebrew-Christian tradition. In Egypt 6 January had been observed as a festival of the dying-rising Osiris as early as 2000 B.C.; and 25 December, a recalculated solstice dating, had belonged to the Roman Saturnalia from more than two centuries before the founding of the Christian Church. The Epiphany became a standard festival in the East before A.D. 300, and in Rome Christmas was assigned to 25 December in 336. It seems clear that in both cases the motivation was to provide Christian substitutes for familiar pagan holidays, without serious concern for historical accuracy; and indeed there was no existing evidence on which an accurate determination could have been based.

Not only the Lord, but also the great cloud of witnesses to him, came to be commemorated by the faithful in later years. Philocalus in Rome listed, in A.D. 354, the burial days of ten popes and twenty-five martyrs, and therein began the long story of the calendar of the saints. The earliest authorized celebration of a saints' day seems to have been a festival in honor of SS. Peter and Paul in the year 258, on the same 29 June which belongs still to both apostles in the Roman and Lutheran systems, though to St. Peter only in the Anglican. Other localities compiled their own lists of those regarded as worthy of special remembrance, and these in time were coalesced one with another and with that of Rome.

By the tenth century the Christian year had assumed the essential form in which we know it: a series of shifting dates and seasons depending on the date of Easter; some fixed festivals of the Christ and of the Blessed Virgin; and a growing list of saints' memorials also set on particular days of the solar year. Appropriate prayers and biblical readings came to be assigned to each Sunday and holy day from the fifth century on. The most important of these schematizations, called "sacramentaries," is ascribed to Pope Gregory I (590–604), but no doubt it underwent considerable revision before it assumed the ninth century form in which we have it. The Gelasian Sacramentary, attributed to Pope Gelasius I (492–496), exists today in a single eighth century manuscript.

The so-called Leonine Sacramentary, surviving in a seventh century copy, is a fragmentary work conjectured, without compelling evidence, to have been the work of Pope Leo I (440–461). Alcuin, the religious adviser of the Emperor Charlemagne, edited the Gregorian compilation and made a number of additions to it, notably including the Communion Collect, "Almighty God, unto whom all hearts are open." To a very large extent the collects, epistles, and gospels in Roman, Lutheran, and Anglican use today are taken from these early collections; and the high degree of persisting identity will be apparent to anyone who will compare the Roman Missal with a Lutheran *Common Service Book* and with the several Anglican Prayer Books.

THROUGH THE CHRISTIAN YEAR

The Christian year, which in the fourth century began with the celebration of the Nativity of Christ as settled on 25 December, has opened since the eighth century with the preparatory season known as Advent. Advent Sunday, the New Year's Day of the Christian cycle, is the Sunday nearest to St. Andrew's Day, 30 November. There always are four Sundays in Advent, to which in time there were assigned the themes respectively of the Lord's second coming, the Holy Scriptures, the ordained ministry of the Church, and the work of St. John Baptist as the Christ's precursor and herald. The third Sunday is also the Roman Gaudete, a day of joy symbolized by the use of rose as the liturgical color.

Confusion between 25 December and 6 January as feasts of the Nativity was resolved in the West by assigning the birth to the earlier date, and the coming of the Magi to the later. The Feast of the Holy Innocents (28 December) thus comes, rather curiously, before the visit of the wise men to Herod. Only in Spain was it removed to a more logical position after the Epiphany.

"The manifestation of Christ to the Gentiles" was seen not only in his discovery by the travelers from afar, but also in his boyhood visit to the Temple in Jerusalem, in his baptism by John, and in his first miracle at Cana of Galilee. These accordingly became the standard subjects of the first three Sundays of Epiphanytide. The variable date of Easter means that there may be from one to six Sundays between the Epiphany and Septuagesima. Materials omitted in this earlier part of the year are transferred to the end of the Trinity season, which necessarily is longer when Easter is early.

The forty days of Lent were further amplified at Rome in the seventh century, by the institution of three explicitly pre-Lenten Sundays, and the assignment to them of special liturgical materials. Quinquagesima is fifty calendar days before Easter. Sexagesima (sixty) and Septuagesima (seventy), one and two weeks earlier still, seem to have been named by analogy, and without reference to exact counting. The liturgical purple appears first on Septuagesima, and it is retained, except for a few festivals and saints' days, to the end of Lent.

The word "Lent" is akin, etymologically, to "long" and "lengthen," and it referred originally to the lengthening of the hours of sunlight in the springtime. The forty-day fast early was associated with Jesus' forty days of fasting in the wilderness after his baptism, and so with his temptation by the devil. This experience of course came at the very beginning of his earthly ministry, while the first Good Friday marked its close. Thus our observance seems to involve an anachronism, in which early and late events are crowded together and the intervening years left out.

Something of this sort is inevitable, however, when the occurrences of several years are to be remembered within one; and we have to allow for a total of some thirty years of Jesus' life, and for two-plus years of his active work between the baptism and the crucifixion. It is clear, too, that the association of the initial tempting with the final sacrifice is closer in meaning than it is in chronology. The choices which Jesus made in the desert led him straight to the cross: the choice of spiritual rather than material goals, of quiet rather than spectacular means, of service to God rather than to Satan. Nor did the temptation come to an end in the wilds beyond the Jordan. It continued when the crowds would have made him a king, when he heard of the threatenings of Herod, when he looked in despair at a willful and unrepentant Jerusalem; and it reached its climax in Gethsemane on the night before Good Friday.

Thus when the Christian sets himself to sober reflection and solemn consecration, throughout the days of Lent, he shares personally in the intense moral struggle which Jesus underwent from the beginning to the end. He lives in the conflict of goals and means as he must all through his life, and he looks ahead to that final choice of his Lord in which life everlasting was attained by the choosing of the way of death. Lent is preparation for Easter indeed; but first it is preparation for that total giving of one's self without which there can be no Resurrection unto eternal life.

Reference already has been made to Laetare Sunday, the fourth in Lent, which in the Roman use is one of festival spirit and relaxation of the Lenten rules. In England this was called "Refreshment Sunday," perhaps because of the assignment of the miracle of the loaves and fishes as the Gospel for the day; and also "Mothering Sunday," which at first may have been a corruption of "Midlenten Sunday," but which became an occasion for visiting one's mother and taking her a gift of cakes.

The deepest intensification of Lenten seriousness begins the following week with Passion Sunday, the fifth in Lent; and recent Anglican usage has described the succeeding period as Passiontide. Palm Sunday began to be observed in Jerusalem from the fourth century on, with a festival procession from the Mount of Olives into the city, and with the bishop riding on the traditional ass. It should be noticed that the liturgical materials specified for this day are not triumphal, save in the Roman service of "The Blessing of the Palms." They belong rather to the continuation of solemn thought about the passion of our Lord, and include St. Matthew's account of his trial and crucifixion.

Holy Week (not Passion Week, which is the one before) is the oldest "octave" in the Christian tradition. Special collects, epistles, and gospels are assigned day by day, and the selections in general are much longer than at any other time of the year. The term "Spy Wednesday" was a popular allusion to the traitorous activities of Judas, and is unknown in the Prayer Books. "Maundy Thursday" is from *mandatum novum*, "a new commandment give I unto you." The evening celebration of the Lord's Supper on this day, in special remembrance of the last meal together in the upper room, goes back at least to the Gelasian Sacramentary; and the ceremonial washing of the feet of the poor by high dignitaries, ecclesiastical and civil, has a history extending from the earliest days to the present time.

Good Friday, as the day of the one oblation once offered, is the single day in the Christian year on which the Eucharist never should be celebrated. Rome developed the "Mass of the Presanctified," for which the consecration of the elements was made in advance. Black is the liturgical color, pictures and statues are somberly draped, and in Anglican practice the altar is completely bare.

Custom has sanctioned the three-hour service as the chief memorial on Good Friday, though this is a comparatively recent development, and there are no clear regulations as to what should be its specific content. If it is to include meditations on the "seven words from the cross," these are better assigned to one minister than to seven, to guard against the confusion of teaching, and the obvious competition for effect, so often apparent in "union" Good Friday services. Whatever the Good Friday service or services may be, the whole day ought by all means to be set apart for single-hearted devotion, uncumbered by business or amusement in any part. The closing of offices and shops from twelve o'clock to three is a step in the right direction, but it is not recognition enough of the tragic significance of this day of sacred memory; nor is any teacher or employer likely to be strongly antagonistic if for reasons of conscience the student or worker claims the entire day for devotional purposes.

Easter Even, or Holy Saturday, is more prominent in Eastern than in Western observance. The Orthodox lighting of candles is the most dramatic example, and an unforgettable one to those who have witnessed it. *Christos aneste, Kyrios aneste*, "Christ is risen, the Lord is risen," chants the whole Greek congregation for what seem to be hours on end; and the risen Christ evidently is a reality and an abounding joy to all who join in the chanting. There actually is much more point in holding a midnight service on this date than on the fashionable Christmas Eve; and the increasing multiplication of lights is a wholly fitting symbol of the brightening splendor of the Resurrection.

Easter, far more than Christmas, is the crowning glory of the Christian year. It is debased rather than glorified by the wholly secular custom of putting in an appearance at church on this one morning and on no other. Nevertheless the service ought to be so compelling in its note of triumph, and the sermon so clear a declaration of the eternal life that is in Christ Jesus, that they who have come to parade will be challenged to come again to pray. The Easter services properly belong in the church, and first of all to the church's people. Sunrise services on chilly hilltops, especially with the secular promotions that usually accompany them, are of dubious religious value.

The first Sunday after Easter popularly is called "Low Sunday."

This may have been a corruption of *Laudes,* from the opening word
of its sequence hymn, but it seems sadly appropriate as reflecting the
very obvious slump that affects so many congregations after the
Easter mood of victory. Rogation Sunday, the fifth after Easter, leads
into the three Rogation Days, or "days of solemn supplication." These
originally had an agricultural significance, and were observed by the
processional singing of the Litany around the boundaries of the
parish, as a plea for the granting of a fruitful season.

Forty days after Easter is the Feast of the Ascension, and ten days
after that Pentecost, in English parlance "Whitsunday." (This is
"white Sunday," with reference not to the liturgical color, which is
red, but to the white robes worn by candidates for baptism.) These
two post-Easter festivals, the one hailing the Lord's final exaltation,
and the other assuring us of the abiding presence of his Spirit, bring
to a fitting close the story which began some four or five months
earlier with the celebration of his birth. Unfortunately the American
custom of going to church on Sundays only has led to a very general
neglect of the Ascension, which inevitably is commemorated on a
Thursday; and not always is the coming of the Holy Ghost remembered, and sought, as it ought to be by those who so much need his
inner strengthening.

The next Sunday after Pentecost, anciently in Rome that on which
repentant heretics were readmitted to the orthodox Christian community, came therefore to be known as Trinity Sunday. Roman usage
dates the subsequent Sundays, up to the beginning of Advent, from
Pentecost. The Anglican calendar, following the Sarum (Salisbury)
Missal of the eleventh century, uses Trinity as the point of reference.
Thus what is the fourth Sunday after Pentecost in Rome is the third
after Trinity in England.

The Sundays after Trinity, from twenty-two to twenty-seven in
number, constitute what some have felt to be a long, depressing valley
after the almost unbroken series of high points between Advent and
Whitsuntide. The sacramentaries and lectionaries have used this time
to stress various aspects of Christian faith and life which have received
less of direct mention in the special penitential and festival periods.
Functionally it may be well that so much of this Trinity season coincides with the long summer vacations of our time, when church activity everywhere lags and in some places reaches almost the vanish-
ing point. There is no excuse, however, for allowing indifference thus

ST. ANN'S CHAPEL OF THE NEWMAN CLUB, STANFORD UNIVERSITY, CALIFORNIA (1951)

Vincent G. Raney, architect   Father John P. Tierney, chaplain

ST. ANN'S CHAPEL OF THE NEWMAN CLUB, STANFORD
UNIVERSITY, CALIFORNIA (1951)

Vincent G. Raney, architect   Father John P. Tierney, chaplain

UNIVERSITY CHRISTIAN CHURCH, BERKELEY, CALIFORNIA
(1931)

W. H. Ratcliff, architect   Jack Finegan, minister

to supervene after high enthusiasm; and the long season in which green dominates the sanctuary well may be one of genuine if quiet growth in Christian understanding and devotion.

Scattered throughout the year are many festivals fixed by the solar calendar, relating both to our Lord and to the early heroes of the faith. A special case, with mixed points of reference, is that of the Ember Days "at the four seasons." These are the Wednesdays, Fridays, and Saturdays following respectively the first Sunday in Lent, Whitsunday, 14 September, and 13 December. The name derives either from the Old English *ymb*, "about," and *ryne*, "course," or from the Latin *quatuor tempora*. In either case "Ember" has here no reference to glowing coals, but points to the regular occurrence of these periods. Embertide is the traditional season for ordinations, and the liturgical materials assigned to its stress "the ministry of reconciliation."

The chief variable dates and seasons of the Christian year, and the principal fixed holy days, with indication of their recognition in the several Western traditions, will be found listed in Appendices B and C. The extreme multiplication of saints' days in the Middle Ages became a decided encumbrance upon normal activity. In 1532 the House of Commons petitioned for a reduction in the number of holy days, especially in harvest time. In general the English Church did away with all festivals of saints other than biblical, though there were slight variations in the successive Prayer Books, as there are today among the several autonomous Anglican communions. It is interesting to note that the feast of St. Thomas of Canterbury, loyal defender of the papacy against an English King, was the first to be eliminated; and that the services relating to Charles I, "King and Martyr," were removed from the Prayer Book by order of the Hanoverian Queen Victoria.

USES OF THE CALENDAR

The extreme of distaste for the historic calendar was manifested by the early Quakers, who objected not only to the multiplicity of elaborate ceremonials that Rome had developed, but also to the surviving pagan names of the months and days. Both days of the week and months of the year were by the Friends referred to by their numbers only, a practice which created some little confusion in dating.

Calvinism was quite as negative about the Christian festivals, if not about the Latin and Norse words, and on principle rejected all the traditional observances.

Human nature nevertheless demanded special notice of special times and seasons. The Scottish delight in New Year's Day thus was a direct product of the Puritan denial of Christmas. In just the same way American Christianity adopted secular holidays into quasi-religious recognition, even while it continued to look askance at the holy days of ancient Christian faith. Independence Day and Thanksgiving Day are provided with special liturgical materials in the American *Book of Common Prayer*, and in many churches Mothers' Day and Memorial Day are treated as if they were holy days of obligation.

Gradually Easter and Christmas, as the greatest of the Christian feasts, made their way back into observance in almost all the Protestant groups; though both of them now with secular and commercial involvements wholly alien to the Christian way. Palm Sunday and Pentecost next gained a measure of recognition, and in our time Lent has commended itself widely as a necessary reminder of the serious responsibilities imposed in one's bearing allegiance to the Christ. As yet there is little else of the Christian calendar that is noticed by, or known to, the average American Christian; but the trend seems to suggest that soon there will be more.

Surely there should be. To observe the days of national and nationalistic pride, and not those of Christian joy and solemnity, is patently absurd for the universal Church of Jesus Christ. Memorial Day no doubt is akin in mood and content to the feasts of All Saints and All Souls, but it is a narrowed and ethnocentric expression of our desire to honor those whose work on earth is ended. Mothers' Day, in its inception a lodge festival and now sentimentalized and commercialized to the worst degree, is a poor surrogate for those tributes to ideal motherhood which are the feasts of the Blessed Virgin. To glorify American Presidents while ignoring Christian apostles and martyrs is a curious and indefensible reversal of values. It is high time that Christianity became again explicitly Christian; and the calendar of the Church is a useful means to the expression of an authentically Christian Christianity.

The teaching value of the calendar is evident to all who will consider it. The orderly progression from the expectant days of Advent, through the birth and ministry and passion of Jesus, to the mighty

Resurrection and glorious Ascension of the triumphant Christ, provides annual opportunity to review our Lord's life among men, and to meditate with joy upon those mighty acts whereby he has given unto us life and immortality, as well in the twentieth century as in the first. He comes anew to us each Christmas, in great humility. He strives with us in our temptations, and by his grace aids us to conquest over them. He dies for our sins each Good Friday, and he rises as the Lord of Salvation each Easter morning. He ascends where Christian faith must place him, at the right hand of God; and withal, at every Pentecost, he sends us his Holy Spirit to give us strength.

The following of the calendar as an outline for reminder and instruction is an important safeguard against the monotonous repetitions and the distorted emphases which have marked so many sects that lack this kind of teaching plan. The sacrifice on Calvary is critical indeed, but it is not the only item of Christian faith that needs to be considered. Lent and Passiontide and Good Friday, along with the regular celebrations of the Holy Communion, present and interpret the cross more effectively than does continuous revivalist preaching on this single theme. The doctrine of the second advent is an important one for all Christians to understand, but it has title to no such central place as some of the sects have given it. Advent Sunday provides for it quite enough of attention, and in a context that has meaning in its relation to the Lord's historic ministry of so many years ago.

As to the liberals, who have had little to say about either the second coming or the cross, they well may be reminded too that the theme of Christian teaching should be the whole Christian gospel, which includes theology as well as sociology, and everlasting truth as well as contemporary affairs. It is all too easy, without the guidance of the calendar, to allow the faith to be subordinated to current fashion, and its great affirmations to be crowded out by the incidental questionings and the popular books of today. This is not at all to say that our present life is to be ignored. It is to contend that our life has meaning only in the light of eternity, and that our Christian values will be maintained only if they are continuingly related to their authentic sources.

More specifically, the old and wearisome question of "what to preach about" frequently will find a ready and creative answer in the calendar, and in the materials which the Church has provided for use on each Sunday and each great festival. The first Sunday in August, for example, is likely to be a very dull one, in the middle of summer vacations and summer heat. What can one use as the theme of such a Sunday's service? Immediately the tradition calls to mind the Transfiguration of Christ, celebrated from the ninth century on the sixth day of August, and offering as its theme the fulfillment of Law and Prophets in the newly visioned Man of Galilee. Similarly the occurrence of a saint's day in a given week may suggest consideration of a major Christian hero such as St. Peter or St. Paul, or a neglected one such as St. Andrew or St. Barnabas.

The Sunday materials too, and especially in the long stretch of the Sundays after Trinity, frequently will stir the imagination of the preacher to the discussing of some long-unmentioned aspect of the Christian life, and so by God's grace may inspire the congregation toward its more complete and better living. The first draft of this chapter is being written between the seventh and eighth Sundays after Trinity, surely a time when sermon subjects and service themes may be hard to hit upon. Is there not challenge in the seventh Sunday's Epistle, "The wages of sin is death; but the gift of God is eternal life through Jesus Christ our Lord"; and also in the eighth Sunday's Gospel, "By their fruits ye shall know them"?

So much of variety is available, in all the wealth of Sundays and festivals, of fixed and variable holy days, that there need be no monotony from year to year. Obviously one ought always to recognize the major festivals of the Christ, but one need not preach annually about St. Matthew and St. Luke. Perhaps a fair rule of thumb would be to preach about any given saint in a year when his feast falls on the Sunday itself. This would guarantee no repetition within five or six years, unless there seemed sufficient reason to remember one or another of these saints more often.

Nor is there any requirement that we should be forever bound by Archbishop Cranmer's dropping of the postbiblical saints from the Prayer Book. St. Augustine of Hippo, St. John Chrysostom of Constantinople, and St. Francis of Assisi belong to the common heritage of all Christians, and well may be honored on or near their feasts, respectively 28 August, 29 January, and 4 October. St. Augustine of Canterbury and St. Columba are heroes of early Anglo-Saxon Christianity of whom our people ought now and then to be reminded, or (let's be real about it) for the first time to be informed; and their stated days of 26 May and 9 June provide fitting opportunity for their occasional commemoration.

Sunday is the holy day of the Christian week, when all Christians are called to join together in worship. It is unfortunate if Sunday is regarded, as in the Puritan Sabbatarian tradition it commonly has been, as the only day on which it is proper to go to church. One tragic consequence of the Sunday-only habit is seen in the fact that so many Christians pass immediately from Palm Sunday to Easter Day without having given any thought to the events of Holy Week, and so that they claim two triumphs without having admitted any tragedy. It is scarcely too much to say that the lack of a sense of serious moral responsibility on the part of so many modern Christians may be related to their habit of leaping thus from one Sunday to the other, without remembering Good Friday at all. The way to the Resurrection is but by the cross and the grave; and the Church never may be excused from the obligation to insist upon this basic truth.

Even in our busy and overscheduled world it should be possible to initiate and develop a number of weekday services which would have sufficient appeal, because they would have sufficient meaning, to bring Christians to Christian devotion, and to the consideration of Christian teaching and Christian history, even in the middle of a crowded week. The Wednesday-evening prayer meeting used to serve something of this purpose, but it is dead: I suggest not of religious indifference as such, but simply of utter boredom. The use of the calendar, with its changing themes and its vivid points of reference, would do much to prevent any mere repetition from week to week; and the increase of the opportunities for worship is likely to mean a larger, rather than a smaller, average attendance at those services which previously have been held. Such at least has been our experience at Mills College, where the average number present at early morning Communions has grown steadily as the number of celebrations has been increased.

From the beginning the Christian calendar has been at once a record of pride and a device of teaching. We who are proud of the Christian story ought continually to retell it, and we who believe in Christian teaching ought to present it in a coherent and meaningful sequence. The calendar is far from being a strait jacket, forbidding freedom of intellectual and spiritual activity. It is a useful guide to those who will use it discerningly: a guide by whose following the total Christian faith will be assured of recognition within each passing year, and the entire Christian heritage set forth in orderly and constructive fashion.

Truth remains eternal and indivisible. But our apprehension of truth must occur in time, and our understanding of truth is in part and part.

> Our little systems have their day:
> They have their day, and cease to be.
> They are but broken lights of thee,
> And thou, O Lord, art more than they.

Hour by hour, day by day, we catch our glimpses of the light of everlasting truth; and the calendar is a convenient lamp by which we may be helped to see. We live in time, and it is in time that we must carry on our work. The thoughtful measuring of time, as we find it in the calendar of the Church, offers itself as a vital means toward our apprehending of the verities that transcend all time. By its using we may redeem the time, and thus bring time itself into the service of the life which is eternal.

VI

FITLY FRAMED TOGETHER

THE CONTINUITY OF the Christian year binds all the variety of its content into an effective unity of meaning. By its ordered sequences, too, the calendar ensures that variety as well as unity shall be preserved. The same objectives are to be sought, and the same principles are relevant, on the much smaller scale of the single service of worship. There needs to be variation from one service to the next, and variation also within each service in itself. There needs no less to be unity of impact, unity of thought, and unity of tone. The way to present variety while maintaining unity is the same for the one hour as it is for the year: the way of considered continuity.

This means that the service must be carefully organized in advance, with none of its elements left to guesswork or to momentary whim. It means also that the services from day to day, and from week to week, must be planned in terms of a coherent relationship throughout a considerable period. No two services ever will be quite identical, but all should be enough alike to enable the worshiper to feel at home. Each service ought to mean most to those who attend all, but every service must offer meaning as well to him who is present for a single occasion. Sixty minutes on Sunday, multiplied by the number of members of the congregation, count up to a phenomenal amount of time. It is the sober duty of each church, each minister, each musician, to be sure that none of this time shall be wasted by allowing ragged individualism to take the place of informed and ordered planning.

FRAMEWORK OF THE SERVICE

The Roman, Anglican, and Lutheran forms of worship are relatively fixed, and permit of a minimum of local departure from them. Recently the other great Churches of America, as was noted in Chapter II, have one by one been issuing detailed worship materials, and at least commending them to the use of their local congregations. The motive clearly has been to assure, by continuity, at once the variety and the unity both of which have been so largely lacking in American Protestant worship. The means, quite as patently, has been that of returning more and more nearly to the historic usages of worship that have come to us from the former days.

The structure of the service of the Holy Communion will come before us for special attention when we examine that supreme Christian service in Chapter XI. For the moment we may use, for illustration of the principles of order and sequence, the type of service most common and best known among us: that "morning worship" which stems from the synagogue service of instruction, by way of the medieval choir offices of the monks, and of Cranmer's compilation called Morning Prayer. Anglicans and Lutherans specify its precise procedure, and allow little of variation by individual preference. Methodists and Presbyterians have the same service in its essential form in their official books, though less often in their actual practice. The other Churches diverge from it more largely, though in varying degrees.

Morning Prayer is still in the Anglican Prayer Books entitled "Daily Morning Prayer," though there are few churches in which it is used as a daily observance. Anyone who will follow its course in the early morning, without the addition of hymns and sermon, will realize how effectively it is designed as a daily office of devotion. With some supplementation, however, it lends itself admirably to the chief function which it serves today, as the outline of Sunday-morning worship for the general congregation.

There is a strong case to be made for the greater fitness of the Ante-Communion as the standard Sunday service: that is, the Communion Office through the Prayer for the Church (Anglican) or the General Prayer (Lutheran). The Lutherans indeed follow this practice consistently, treating Matins as a secondary order. Prevailing custom elsewhere, however, holds to the service of instruction rather than that of thanksgiving for most Sundays at eleven o'clock. Without attempting at the moment to determine the relative merits, let us examine the service as, *mutatis mutandis*, we most commonly use it.

In practically every church the service begins with an organ prelude, followed by a hymn and something approximating a call to worship. If the hymn be a processional, the first spoken sentences inevitably must follow it; and this may be preferable in any case, as assigning to the whole congregation rather than to one minister the day's first vocal expression of praise. There was one large church whose service for years opened with the choir's singing "The Lord is in his holy temple" just as the pastor made his first (and very dramatic) appearance; and the congregation did not miss the point. It is better on the whole to take no such risk.

There is indeed no reason why the minister should be particularly visible (though he ought always to be fully audible in his "solo" parts) during most of the service. He worships not for the congregation, nor at it, but with it and as one member of it. Accordingly he should face the people from the lectern, or the pulpit, only when his duty is clearly distinguished from theirs, that is, for the instructional items which are the lessons and the sermon. Otherwise his place is in the chancel or at the altar. There is no reason for his leading the hymns, or for his appearing to do so while he counts the house. For hymns and chants he should stand before his chair, facing across the chancel. For the prayers, in which humbly he and the people together present themselves before God, he turns with them toward the altar; and in the prayer or prayers after the sermon he should kneel immediately before it. It is traditional practice, and fitting as recognition of special high points in the worship, to face directly toward the altar for the *Gloria Patri* each time it is said or sung, and for the saying of the Creed.

The opening sentences of the service are uniform in the Lutheran ritual, and specified, but with some options, in the Anglican, Methodist, and Presbyterian. Always they should be ascriptions of praise, but they well may be chosen in terms of the season, the day, and the service's particular theme. Frequently it will be found that other passages than those printed in the service books will be more fitting under a given day's circumstances; and where there is no legislation to the contrary some personal initiative and ingenuity surely are permissible. Two sentences normally are quite enough at this point. Any more are likely to seem to be an additional and misplaced lesson from the Scriptures.

Lutheranism omits any general confession from Matins, though it provides for one at the very beginning of "The Service," that is, the Communion. The Anglican use, followed by the Methodists and the Presbyterians, places a humble confession of sins at this very early point. Immediately upon the Confession there follows a "declaration of absolution" (Anglican), "assurance of pardon" (Presbyterian), or "prayer of pardon" (Methodist). This is said by the minister, as a word of promise to the people. Whether the form used employs "you" or "us" is a matter of theological preference, including the particular view taken of the nature of holy orders. In either case some form of reassurance is required here to balance and complete the people's united act of contrition.

Then comes the Lord's Prayer, in which all present seek to pray as Jesus taught his disciples. Because of the familiarity of the words, and the extreme tendency to gabble them without thought of their content, it may be desirable to sing this prayer rather than say it. The singing should be done by all the congregation, however, not by the choir only, and definitely in the spirit and attitude of prayer. It follows that a simple chant setting, and not a florid concert one, is to be used.

With confession and prayer completed, and the word of comfort spoken, the tone of the service changes now to one of exultant praise. Introduced by the Preces, "O Lord, open thou our lips . . . Praise ye the Lord," the *Venite, Exultemus Domino* (from Psalms 95f) long has been the one traditional chant at this point; so much so, indeed, that the Congregational book of 1931 referred to each of its varying initial praise selections as a *Venite*. After the regular *Venite* comes the variable Psalm of the day, perhaps better read responsively than sung, at least until a congregation has learned (in the regular canticles) to chant with ease and comfort. The Psalm, a Hebrew writing, concludes with the singing of the Christian *Gloria Patri*, most conveniently to the same setting as has been used for the *Venite* just before, and serving thus to bind the two together.

Now the service turns specifically to the instruction of the people, in the lessons from the Old Testament and the New. The two lessons are separated by a chant, commonly the early Christian *Te Deum*

Laudamus, though in some cases it may seem wise to substitute an appropriate anthem at this point. Another chant, most often the *Jubilate Deo* (Psalm 100), resumes the mood of praise after the second lesson, and leads to the united affirmation of the faith in the reciting of the Creed.

Then, with the graceful transition provided by the ancient Salutation and Suffrages, "The Lord be with you," the whole company of the faithful joins in prayer. Twice already the people have prayed aloud together, in the Confession and the Lord's Prayer. The General Thanksgiving provides a third opportunity for explicit congregational participation, and on a third level of feeling tone. The other prayers used here are both general (the fixed Collects, prayer for all conditions of men, and so forth) and specific (Collect for the day, and any special petitions).

Morning Prayer proper ends at this point, with the saying of the apostolic Grace (II Corinthians 13:14). Within its approximately thirty minutes there have been encompassed confession, praise, instruction, and prayer. Custom provides now for a hymn leading into the sermon; and after the sermon another brief prayer or prayers, a closing hymn, and a final Blessing. With a twenty-minute sermon the entire period of worship will last almost exactly one hour; and organized in this way it will have given opportunity, and continuously related opportunity, for every phase of Christian worship save the strictly sacramental.

The taking of an offering no doubt is unavoidable in most churches. It may come before or after the sermon, but in no case should it break the continuity of the Morning Prayer sequence which has been described. It can be handled with decency, and made a genuine act of worship, if church and minister will think of it thus. Certainly the practice of the ushers' taking the plates out immediately to count the take is inexcusable. The offerings need not be left on the altar; but they should be reverently offered before it, and then may be placed quietly on a side table in the chancel.

JERRY-BUILT SERVICES

Consider now what happens to the totality of worship if we discard any of the parts of the service as we have been following it through. The Creed is the element most usually omitted. To leave it out is to imply either that the church lacks a common faith, or that for some reason it is afraid to assert it. Without the Creed there is no clear opportunity for the people with one voice to declare their Christian position, and the whole service suffers from a consequent vagueness and lack of specific anchorage. Admittedly the ancient phrases of our Creeds require some interpretation to the naïvely literal minds of today. Once their nature as Symbols (their original name) is understood, however, their symbolic value as declarations of united Christian conviction is immediately available.

The Confession also has become unpopular in the smugness of our time. Yet to think to begin the worship of God without an admission of our unworthiness is to approach him quite unprepared to face his majesty. The sinner's earnest repentance of his sins is his first step toward the salvation that is in Christ Jesus; and the Christian needs ever and again to remind himself of this, as ever and again he falls short of the glory of God. "I am not a miserable offender," said a well born and charming visitor from New England. The only possible answer to that was, "The fact that you say you're not is the absolute proof that you are."

Very strangely in a culture that commonly has held the Bible to be more important than the Church, it has become widely customary to use only one lesson from Holy Scripture, and in some churches none at all. Thus to eviscerate the service is to rob our people of the heritage that is theirs by right in the Hebrew-Christian tradition. Whatever the theme of the day, it gains in depth of perspective when it is seen in the dual light of Hebrew backgrounds and of Christian valuation. The lessons need not be long; indeed, they should not be. But both of them should be provided always, and thoughtfully chosen and read in view of the meaning of the day's entire service.

To omit the responsive Psalm is likewise to cheat the people of a chance to use for themselves the majestic phrasing of the world's supreme collection of religious poetry, and so of their own full sharing in the faith and aspiration of the poets of the ancient days. Of course if the responsive material is perfunctorily selected and carelessly read it will fail of its purpose, and in that case it might as well be skipped. But its skipping inevitably will leave the service without one of the important supporting beams of its total structure.

The chants are musical expressions of the Psalms, or of cognate poems from the early Christian tradition. It is absurd to say that the average choir or congregation can't learn to chant. With all due respect to Lutherans and Anglicans, they average no higher in general intelligence and in musical ability than do other Christians. They do have the advantage of tradition and training; but a modicum of training soon will rebuild the tradition elsewhere. The recurring canticles, with their noble language and their clear, compelling melodic lines, rapidly become high points in congregational praise; and a church once accustomed to their singing will not lightly let them go.

Strange as it seems, even a time for prayer currently is omitted from some orders of service, and in some churches of no little size. What was said above about the Confession applies a fortiori here. If a congregation doesn't feel the need of prayer, it stands very deeply in that need. The effectual fervent praying of a sincere congregation, in the words which it says itself and in those which it hears, availeth much toward uplift of spirit and consecration of life. True worship without prayer is unthinkable, and a service without prayer falls of its own weight of self-satisfaction.

There should be at least three hymns in a full-scale Sunday service, and for a number of reasons. One is that the people shall have at least that many chances to join unitedly in praise. Another is that added opportunity is afforded for acquaintance with our treasures of religious poetry and music. A minor one is that changes of activity are psychologically and physiologically essential to a real continuity of interest and attention. The bad habit of leaving out the final hymn, and pronouncing the benediction immediately at the close of the sermon, is bad because it says flatly that the preacher thinks his own words are the most important thing for the people to have in mind as they leave. If he really believes this, let him hire a hall and deliver a lecture.

The point about hymns as a change of activity applies to the service as a whole. In one service at which recently I was the guest preacher the congregation sat continuously from the end of the opening hymn, while all the rest of the vocal music was supplied by a tenor with a poor voice and worse taste. The seats in that church were uncomfortable, and so the people suffered. Had they been comfortable, the congregation inevitably would have gone to sleep on that August morning. There is no reason for such monotony, whether in the event it is painful or only soporific.

The twenty-minute sermon time is the longest during which the worshipers should be required to remain in a single position. The Anglican rule of "Kneel to pray, stand to speak or praise, sit to listen," is a useful one; and in the Anglican service it provides a healthy and meaningful variety of movement from beginning to end. Even where willful pride and/or unduly economical spacing of pews forbid the historic posture of prayer, alternation between sitting and standing will do much toward keeping the congregation mentally alert and spiritually aware.

They should not be standing, however, at the very end of the service, as if poised for immediate escape. After the last hymn, whether or not it is a formal recessional, the people should kneel (or sit, if that is as far down as they have learned to go) for the final Blessing. The ceremonial extinguishing of the sanctuary candles is the concluding act of worship, and the organist should not begin a vigorous postlude until this has been completed, and without haste. Only after these final moments of peaceful devotion should there be any movement from the pews; and then it should be quiet, orderly, and unhurried.

A well built service requires all of the structural elements we have considered. To omit any one of them is to weaken the whole. The pillars of public worship are praise, confession, enlightenment, and prayer, and all of them strengthened and secured in a communal and unbroken attitude of reverence. If our framework thus is constructed, with none of the factors left out or impaired, each service may become for each worshiper a valid and vital experience of fellowship with God. If we think to get along without any of them, the balance is destroyed and the entire structure distorted. The total plan is a very old one; and all the experience of all the years identifies it as an architecturally sound one.

CONTINUITY AND UNITY

Within the structure of the service there is a continuous pattern of significant movement from each phase into the next. Rightly seen, the service has no separated parts but is a single flowing whole. This means that it should be interrupted as little as possible by announcement of what is coming next. The Preces before the *Venite*, and the Suffrages after the Creed, technically serve the purpose of getting the congregation up and down without explicitly telling them to rise or kneel; but they are themselves acts of devotion, swelling rather than blocking the stream of worshipful experience.

Even with an unpractised congregation it is not at all difficult, by the use of an adequate service leaflet, to secure united sharing in hymns, chants, and prayers without a single word of oral direction. Indeed a congregation normally will find challenge and stimulus in being thus expected to use its intelligence in following the progress of the service, and will take pride in the effect that it discovers itself achieving. The total product will be an unbroken expression and realization of the worship of God, blessedly set free from repeated interruptions and mood-shattering chatter.

Manifestly this command of silence applies also to the advertising of coming events in the parish. These can and should be planned long enough in advance to be published in the leaflet, and it is an insult to a literate congregation to tell them again what already they have read. The datum that the Golden Girls (*aetat. 75*) will meet on Tuesday afternoon at Miss Agatha Twombley's will be more useful to them in print than in a quick oral statement half heard amid the familiar relaxed buzz of "announcement time." Absolutely necessary emergency announcements, and important personal news such as baptisms, marriages, and deaths, conveniently may be placed at the close of the service proper and before the sermon hymn.

The continuity of each service is not alone that of the regular structure from week to week, but also that of the variable materials within each week's own order. These should be selected always with the greatest care, and in direct reference to the particular season and to the theme of the day. The "common" or "ordinary" parts of the service, never or seldom altered, bind the whole together and keep the congregation at ease in the familiar. The "proper" or changing parts belong to that day only, and all of them should help specifically to carry that day's own message. From service to service these last correspond severally in type and place, but they are and should be quite different in detail.

In general the Confession, the chants, the Creed, and a few congregational prayers, are best maintained practically without variation. There remains for each service the duty of selecting hymns, responsive reading, the lessons, and the variable prayers. All this is most satisfactorily done by the minister, for only he can have a clear idea of how the several parts will fit together in the total pattern he is hoping to develop.

A possible exception is in the matter of hymns. If (as is to be expected) the choir director has more musical knowledge than the minister, he ought at least to be consulted. Only, however, if he adds to musical knowledge a true spiritual apprehension, and also a willingness to take the task with complete seriousness, can he be trusted to choose the hymns altogether on his own responsibility; and even so it is important for the minister to retain veto power.

The selection of hymns without reference to the service theme results at best in irrelevance, and sometimes in absurd incongruity. Once, as guest preacher, I was told that the organist would make the selections. I was not greatly troubled, for I knew the pastor to be a man of scholarly discernment and conscience, and the services of his church to be thoughtfully planned. He was away, however, and apparently the organist had decided to seize this one chance to give free rein to his own quite different tastes. That morning I preached a sermon insisting on the duty of all Christians to take a vigorous part in all of the community's life. Fittingly then we might have sung "A Charge to Keep I Have," or "Fight the Good Fight." What we did sing was "Safe in the Arms of Jesus."

The first hymn of the service well may be one of general praise, but the sermon hymn and the one after the sermon respectively should lead up to and reenforce that aspect of truth which the sermon discusses. The responsive reading holds a middle ground, but its general aspects often may be related to specific ones; and it should be always in the prevailing mood, penitential if the general theme is somber, triumphant if the day is one primarily of Christian joy.

The lessons most decisively, as direct instruction, should illustrate and support the particular message of the sermon. Churches which use the calendar regularly have the advantage here, in lectionaries worked out with immediate reference to seasonal and festival themes. Any adequately trained minister, however, should be able to recall (or to use a concordance to look up) fully appropriate passages in both the Old Testament and the New.

Prayers are, and ought to be, both general and specific. The very act of planning the day's prayers in advance is itself the best guarantee that the praying will be real and relevant, and that no important and immediate concern of the congregation, and of its individual members, will be left unmentioned before the throne of God. The comparative merits of traditional and new prayers, and of written and unwritten ones, will be considered at some length in Chapter IX. Whether old or new, prepared or apparently extempore, the prayers of the service ought never to be left to the chance inspiration, or (as more commonly) to the chance amnesia, of the moment of their utterance.

A service thus built on a framework which has proved its survival value through the ages, and worked out in detail as a coherent and significant unity for the day, will provide for all its participants at once a restatement of the essentials of Christian faith and experience, and a new apprehension of the particular values which have been integrated into this particular structure. This undeniably means hard work: probably many hours of work in looking up materials, in comparing possible choices, in selecting some and discarding others. It means also doing the work well ahead of time, especially if the service is to be helped and smoothed in its course by the use of a leaflet, instead of being jarred to a halt every so often by a distracting announcement. The product of the work, however, can not be other than the provision of a more significant hour of worship for all who attend. If worship is worth while, the job of preparing adequately for it is worth doing at whatever cost in labor.

UNITY IN VARIETY

One immediate consequence of planning each service with a maximum of thought and care is that new ideas and long unthought-of materials will crowd to mind, and will replace the frequent needless repetitions that have marred so many services and bored so many congregations. Here again the Lutheran and Anglican procedures are relatively fixed, so that even the variety of the service is itself largely uniform from year to year. Oddly, however (or is it odd?), the lack of such specifications has led many other Churches into much more frequent, because quite unconsidered, repeating of a few favorite materials. Nevertheless the denominations without fixed rules offer the greater room for creative flexibility, if their people will but enter upon it and use it aright.

Any given hymnal does set certain practical limits on the local church which has bought it, but certainly no such cramping restrictions as the average church has placed on itself by its unimaginative and repetitious selections. With a hymnal of five hundred hymns it is theoretically possible to go through almost three years of Sunday-morning services without repeating once. No church is going to do this, indeed. But no church needs to confine itself, as so many do, to a total of some fifty hymns out of the five hundred, year in and year out. Again attention to seasons and meanings will lead perforce to greater variety in use, and so to heightened richness of experience.

The Bible too has many treasures in it other than Psalm 23, St. John 14, and I Corinthians 13. These ought we to read, but not to leave the others unread. A lectionary is useful to provide suggestions, even when it is not accepted as a control. There is no real substitute, however, for the minister's own acquaintance with the Scriptures, and his persistent re-searching of them. The regular practice of personal Bible reading, which too many of us advise more than we pursue, will bring to light many passages that ought to be shared with the congregation, and that will both support the preaching ministry and suggest new and refreshing themes for treatment in the sermon.

In addition to the prayers set forth in any given denominational book—and these increase in number and variety with each new edition of each—it is permitted to clergy of the "free" churches to seek further afield for forms of prayer that are universal in spirit and vital in impact. Every minister should have on his shelves a number of prayer books of Churches other than his own (including by all means the Jewish, both Orthodox and Reform), and he should search them regularly for materials that will vary, enrich, and strengthen the praying of his people. There also are numerous unofficial compilations of prayers and other devotional materials, which indeed must be used with extreme care and discrimination, but which contain many usable and worthy expressions of the Christian's rightful supplication to his God.

In music, Scripture, and prayer alike, there is open to us the entire treasury of all the ages of Hebrew-Christian religious life. To fail to use its wealth fully and freely is to impoverish our worship, and so to impair the religious life of every worshiper. Without ever departing from the central Christian faith, without allowing the intrusion of any sub-Christian sentimentality, without abandoning for a moment the unity of Christian conviction and the continuity of Christian living, we can make of each service an art work harmoniously decked with ever changing, but all authentic, jewels of Christian devotion. The one requirement is that we shall seek diligently for our pearls where they are to be found.

Not the least important aspect of unity in worship is that of full community in the active part taken by the members of the congregation. A church is not a theater, and a service is not a performance to be observed. Passively to sit back and listen to choir and cleric is not to worship in spirit and in truth. Everyone present should be given a chance, and positively should be challenged, to sing, to pray with his voice as well as in his heart, to speak at least in the Psalmist's words of praise. An unplanned service will not permit of this. A well planned one will increase the people's opportunity to the maximum, and will encourage the people actively and eagerly to seize upon it.

Our continuity thus moves within our historic tradition as a whole, and each week in the orderly sequence of the service's constituent parts. Our available variety is great, though it needs testing always by the unities of teaching, of manner, and of feeling tone. The first and final unities are those of Christian doctrine as a coherent scheme of thought, of Christian experience as a balanced way of life, and of Christian people as the one body of Christ on earth.

The framework of the service has several pillars, the doctrine has many aspects, and the body has innumerable members. No part of the framework of worship may be neglected, lest the structure be warped and ultimately collapse. No phase of Christian faith may be ignored, or our Christianity is incomplete. No person may be excused from active participation, or our fellowship is broken.

A year's services organized within the sequence of the Christian calendar will guard us from incompleteness of thought. Each single service of the year, planned as an organic unit in itself, will express the full essence of Christian devotion. Each chance for the worshiper personally to take active part will enable him the more readily and the more really, in his own right, to enter into the very presence of God. The whole service fitly framed together, and compacted by that which every joint supplieth, indeed will make increase of the body unto the edifying of itself in love.

VII

SING UNTO THE LORD

IT IS A commonplace that religion is the mother of all the arts of man. Architecture and decoration, drama and the dance, literature and music, each sought first and foremost to express religious feeling and meaning. The story of music is the story of worship, entirely in its origins and importantly at every point in its history.

With the increasing complexity of human life, and the separation of its multiple strands, the distinction between sacred and secular came to be discerned in music as in every other field. Always there has been interplay, and a measure of reciprocal borrowing. But as there are distinct interests and purposes, so there have developed quite distinct means of expression.

Our problem in church music today is that of finding a satisfactory balance between so stern a maintenance of a separate religious music as will divorce it from ordinary human appreciation, and so ready an acceptance of popular musical fashion as will make religious music quite indistinguishable from the secular. If Rome at the moment may be thought to err on the former side, Protestant habits surely have gone much too far toward the latter. Before we can decide wisely what now we ought to do in our singing of the Lord's praises in his house, we shall need to review briefly the several musical legacies that are ours within the Hebrew-Christian tradition.

HYMNS OF THE SECOND TEMPLE

That, very early in history, music played a large part in the life of the people of Israel is evident from their records. Probably some

102

of the oldest passages in the Scriptures are such fragments of folk song as the obscure "song of Lamech" in Genesis 4, the battle ballad quoted in Joshua 10, the "song of Deborah" (another battle ballad) in Judges 5, and David's lament for his friend Jonathan in II Samuel 1. The first certain mention of the use of music for religious purposes is in the account of David's joyous processional with the ark from Gibeah. Here no less than five different musical instruments are specified, though their identification remains in every case most uncertain.

The greater development of ceremonial religious music no doubt took place after the settlement in Palestine. Amos, ever the recalcitrant nomad, is characteristically negative about this aspect of civilization as he is about others:

> Take thou away from me the noise of thy songs;
> For I will not hear the melody of thy viols.

He is bitter about those

> That chant to the sound of the viol,
> And invent to themselves instruments of musick, like **David**;

and he threatens that

> The songs of the temple shall be howlings in that day . . .
> I will turn your feasts into mourning,
> And all your songs into lamentation.

Amos, however, was little heeded in his own time; and the religious music of Israel continued to grow despite his protests. The book of Psalms as we have it is the hymnal of the second Jerusalem Temple, not finally edited until perhaps the second century B.C., but including materials of much earlier origin. It may be doubted whether King David wrote many, or any, of the seventy-three Psalms ascribed to him in the titles; and it is possible that such Psalms as 44, 74, and 79 belong to the period of the Maccabees, about 160 B.C. (John Calvin, among others, held this latter judgment.) There are in the present arrangement five "books," of which Book I (1–41) probably is the most recent, as a sort of introduction prefixed to the whole collection, II and III (42–89) contain a majority of quite early materials, and IV and V (90–150) are relatively late products of Temple worship.

As in our modern hymnals, there are accompanying notations which are designed to inform the reader and to instruct the singers.

Among these the ascriptions of authorship, being evidently of late date themselves, are the least revealing. In many cases the internal evidence of language or of specific historical reference disproves the tradition as it is recorded. Much more significant are the headings which point to the specific use of a given Psalm in the Temple service, or which indicate the tune to which it was intended to be sung.

Notable among such captions is "A Song of degrees" (thus the version of 1611), better rendered as in the Revised Version, "A song of ascents." The Psalms thus marked (120, 122–134) appear to have been processionals, used either by pilgrims on their way up to Jerusalem for the feasts, or by the Levites as they ascended the temple steps. *Alamoth* (Psalm 46) and *Sheminith* (6, 12) are understood to refer respectively to soprano and bass ranges, vocal or instrumental, and *Neginoth* (4, 6, 54, 55, 67) and *Nehiloth* (5) to stringed and wind instruments. *Gittith* (8, 81, 84), *Muth-labben* (9), and *Shoshannim* (45, 69) appear to be the names of familiar tunes: "A vintage song," "Die for the son," and "Lilies." Dr. James Moffatt's ingenious renderings in *The Holy Bible: A New Translation* will do much to clarify the Psalm headings for the general reader.

Selah, a word which occurs seventy-one times in the Psalter, never is part of the Psalm text, and no more should be read aloud in the service than a soloist should vocalize the term *pianissimo* from his expression marks. Probably, though not certainly, the root is *salal*, "to lift up." Since *Selah* appears invariably at a break in thought, corresponding to what we would consider the end of a stanza or paragraph, it seems to indicate the "lifting up" or heightening of the instrumental accompaniment, while the singers pause before making a start on a new section.

The chief structural element in Hebrew poetry is parallelism, the repetition or completion of the thought in the second line of each couplet. This strongly suggests antiphonal or responsive use from the earliest days. It will be noticed, for example, that this form appears decisively in both Deborah's song and David's lament:

Awake, awake, Deborah:
Awake, awake, utter a song . . .

Then he made him that remaineth have dominion over the
   nobles among the people:
The Lord made me have dominion over the mighty . . .

Out of Machir came down governors,
And out of Zebulun they that handle the pen of the writer.

and,

Tell it not in Gath,
Publish it not in the streets of Askelon;
Lest the daughters of the Philistines rejoice,
Lest the daughters of the uncircumcised triumph . . .

How are the mighty fallen,
And the weapons of war perished!

Metrically, the Hebrew poem was comparable to modern free verse as Yvor Winters of Stanford University has sought to define it: a pattern fixed as to major stresses only, with the unaccented syllables left uncounted and falling where they might. Common forms of the Hebrew couplet exhibit four and four principal accents, three and three, and three and two. This type of verse lends itself well to translation, since there need be no slavish counting of syllables to the line, and since the principal vocal emphases are likely to be about as many in one language as in another. Especially in English, which like the Hebrew depends for its metrical effects upon accent rather than upon vowel quantity, the reproduction of the original form and the original effect can be very close indeed.

Miles Coverdale's rendering of the Psalms in the "Great Bible" of 1539, and the King James version of 1611, both were highly successful in achieving the transfer from Hebrew to English without serious loss either of meaning or of poetic quality. These are the texts on which almost universally we depend today for our responsive readings, and they are good ones. Alike the rhythm and the parallel structure have been retained, and both offer themselves for our ready use.

It is therefore illiterate, and quite destructive to appreciation either of the Psalmists' design or of their achievement, to follow the common practice of allowing the minister to read one whole verse, and the congregation the next. This way each voice answers only itself, instead of responding quickly to the other. Many of the readings as printed in the current Methodist and Presbyterian books are quite unusable, if there is to be any interest at all in reproducing the intended antiphonal effect.

The English *Book of Common Prayer* uses an arbitrary colon between the two lines of each distich. The star printed in the American book, being distinct from the punctuation proper, is more helpful. Either, however, will provide guidance for the correct responsive using of the Psalms; and every Anglican church thus has the chance to use them aright if it will. Most of the churches of other denominations, if they hope to realize the genuine responsive force that is integral to the structure, will have to supply the readings rightly rearranged in their own Sunday leaflets, pending a sounder editing of their official service books.

Some biblical materials outside the book of Psalms are appropriate also for responsive use. The test is simply whether they employ the standard parallel-antiphonal device of Hebrew poetry. On this basis Habakkuk 3 and Job 28 are permissible choices, and so are the New Testament canticles *Magnificat, Benedictus,* and *Nunc Dimittis.* The Beatitudes also may be, if the congregation comments on each blessing from the dividing word "for"; but neither St. John 14 nor I Corinthians 13 is responsive material, and both of these are much better read by one voice from the lectern.

GREGORIAN CHANTS

The early Christians followed the Jewish pattern in music, as they did in other areas. The Psalms long had been used in the synagogues, as a natural borrowing from the practice of the Temple. St. Paul in his letter to Colossae seems to differentiate among "psalms and hymns and spiritual songs," but to approve them all. The "psalms" presumably were those of the Old Testament, the "hymns" such Christian compositions as the canticles of St. Luke's Gospel, and the "spiritual songs" freer and less formal compositions which had sprung up in the primitive Christian community. Particularly in the book of the Revelation it would appear that we have a number of fragments of early church hymnody, such as

> The kingdoms of this world are become
> The kingdoms of our Lord, and of his Christ;
> And he shall reign for ever and ever;

and the triumphant "Worthy is the Lamb" which was quoted at the inception of the present enquiry into the nature and meaning of Christian worship.

While the texts first used for Christian singing were Jewish, or were based very largely on Jewish models, the musical settings became dominantly Greek as soon as Christianity moved out into the Mediterranean world. With the Church's gaining of official status in the empire, its music, along with much else of its practice, required to be regularized. St. Ambrose of Milan (A.D. 340–397) is credited with adopting four of the existing Greek modes and specifying their Christian use. To these four, each of which ranged upward from the "final" (corresponding to our keynote), Pope Gregory I is said to have added four associated ones each ranging from the fourth note below the final to the fifth above. The first four are called "authentic," the second group "plagal," which is to say "oblique" or "borrowed." Yet two more pairs were added in later years, making twelve ecclesiastical "tones" in all. The Greek names (Dorian, Phrygian, Lydian, Aeolian) were subsequently restored, but by accident or design they now were attached to other modes than those to which first they had belonged. It is simpler therefore to follow the practice enjoined by Ambrose himself, referring to the tones simply by their numbers.

The Gregorian chant, generically known as "plainsong," was in one voice only, was unaccompanied, and normally did not exceed one octave in range. Roughly speaking, the notes may be thought of as corresponding to the white notes on the modern piano (with a fairly early addition of B flat), though the mode as such carried no absolute determination of pitch. There are no regular bars, though the ends of sense phrases came to be marked off for convenience. Notation in our sense (though not identical with ours) dates from after A.D. 900, and so it is not available to give us specific information about earlier usages.

Gradually the entire body of ritual texts, both in the Mass and in the monastic Offices (respectively Missal and Breviary) came to be attached to specific settings. These were formally codified after the sixteenth century Council of Trent, which at many points solidified Roman positions and practices in reply to Protestant challenge. More recently historical criticism, led by the Benedictine monks of the Abbey of St. Pierre de Solesmes in France, has led to a reestimate of the usages that had become traditional; and from 1904 on the Roman Church has been reissuing its authoritative musical texts in what is believed to be closer conformity with the practice of the earliest days.

Nineteenth century romanticism ran riot in producing hyperdramatic settings for masses, canticles, and motets, turning the service into a concert performance rather than an act of worship. The reaction came sharply in 1904, with the *Motu proprio* of Pope Pius X. This edict established plainsong as the standard music of the Church, though it permitted the continued use of some of the stricter forms of polyphony which had come down from Palestrina (1526–1594) and his associates; and it flatly ruled out all the concert materials as being improper for use in the services.

Plainsong as a specialized art manifestly required specialists for its performance. The insistence that the chants should be rightly sung meant that the ignorant and untrained might not be allowed to tamper at all with their effect. Church music thus became a monopoly of clergy and choir (itself largely clerical), and the congregation was effectually debarred from taking any active part in the music of worship. The continued use of Latin, too, while each nation was developing its own vernacular, and in practice confining itself to it, created another barrier to the people's sharing vocally in the musical parts of the service. The consequence was that almost total silence of the congregation which is so evident in Roman worship today. The development of polyphony in the Renaissance but intensified the situation, as it made any active participation quite impossible except for the meticulously trained.

A year after the first appearance of the liturgy in English, in Cranmer's prayer book of 1549, there followed a harmonized adaptation of Gregorian melodies to be used with it, and entitled *The Booke of Common Praier Noted*. This was the work of John Merbecke, organist at St. George's Chapel in Windsor. It was to all intents and purposes suppressed with the appearance of the much more stringently Protestant book of 1552. In recent years, however, Merbecke's work has been restored to notice and to use, and it is represented not only in Anglican books but also (though a shade tentatively) in the current Methodist and Presbyterian hymnals. *The Hymnal 1940* of the Protestant Episcopal Church includes Merbecke's full Communion Service, no part of which had appeared in the preceding book of 1916. The 1940 book, however, supplies also a service, and canticle settings, much more nearly approximating the authentic plainsong forms of pre-Reformation days.

Plainsong as yet sounds strange to most people who do not attend

Roman services regularly, and so it is generally supposed to be extremely difficult. It is of course difficult to sing music of any kind really well, and concessions always must be made to human weakness. With the general literacy of today, however, musical as well as verbal, there need be no such barrier maintained between professionals and laymen as existed during the Middle Ages.

Plainsong lends itself admirably to use with nonmetrical texts, and notably better than does the more recent Anglican chant, with its rigid three-note and five-note cadences in unbroken alternation. The effect of plainsong is strong, straightforward, and above all, because of its complete dissociation from all secular forms, churchly. Only a little habituation to a few plainsong settings will enable a perfectly average congregation to sing this music, and to sing it with enjoyment; and added chants may be brought successively into use, with greater ease in each new case because the general treatment has become more and more familiar.

LUTHERAN CHORALES

Martin Luther hit upon a quite different means, and for his time a more immediately practical means, toward the restoration of congregational singing. He seized upon the popular secular melodies of his day, wrote new religious texts to fit the tunes, and made the singing of these "chorales" an essential part of the Lutheran service. How many tunes Luther himself composed is a matter of dispute. Probably *Ein' feste Burg*, "A Mighty Fortress Is Our God," is an adaptation which he made from the Roman Gradual. Certainly the beloved "Cradle Hymn" is not his, for it was nowhere known until the early part of the nineteenth century. Of verbal hymn texts some thirty-five may be assigned to Luther with a fair degree of assurance.

Many Lutheran musicians, and among them not a few clergymen, soon made their contributions to the chorale literature. Among those who are generally known today, because of the inclusion of some of their work in a number of standard hymnals, are Philipp Nicolai (1556–1608), pastor at Hamburg; Johann Crüger (1596–1662), cantor of St. Nicholas' Church in Berlin; and Johann Rudolph Ahle (1625–1675), organist at Mühlhausen. To Nicolai we owe the tune generally known as "Frankfort," *Wie schön leuchtet der Morgenstern*, "O Morning Star"; to Crüger *Nun danket*, "Now Thank We All Our

God"; and to Ahle *Liebster Jesu*, "Blessed Jesus, at Thy Word." The Lutheran hymnals of our time, and especially that of the Missouri Synod, will be found to contain the most generous representation of the historic German chorales; but increasingly the books of other communions are drawing upon this rich and fertile source of stately congregational song.

The chorale at first was sung in unison, and then was harmonized with the melody in the tenor. By the end of the sixteenth century the soprano part had captured the melody for itself, thus setting the pattern which we take for granted in almost all our choral music. The classic chorale harmonizations are those of Johann Sebastian Bach (1685–1750), whose thirty-seven years as cantor at Leipzig produced the amazing wealth of some two hundred church cantatas. In each of these one or more chorales provided opportunity for the whole congregation to take part.

Luther's ready borrowing of music from secular sources was continued by his successors. Even the famous "Passion Chorale," with all the poignancy that now we find in its "O Sacred Head, Now Wounded," originally was Hans Leo Hassler's entirely secular love song, *Mein G'muth ist mir verwirret*, "My Feelings Are Bewildered." The mournful *O Welt, ich muss dich lassen*, "O World, I Now Must Leave Thee," was first a soldier's protest at giving up the social amenities of his beloved Innsbruck. On the other hand, many of the chorales were taken directly from the familiar plainsong of the Roman Church. Well known examples are *Kyrie, Gott Vater*, from a ninth century *Kyrie Eleison; Allein Gott in der Höh'*, from an Easter *Gloria in Excelsis; Christ lag in Todesbanden*, from a twelfth century Latin hymn; and *Gelobet seist du*, from a fifteenth century *Grates nunc reddamus*.

CALVINIST PSALM PARAPHRASES

A much sterner view than Luther's, as to what was permissible in church music, was held by John Calvin. To him only the inspired words of Holy Writ were worthy to be used in Christian worship. This limitation did not extend, however, to forbidding the use of vernacular metrical versions of the Psalms, in the poetical and musical fashion of the time, to facilitate popular use. The consequence was the immediate burgeoning of another great aspect of Christian hymnody, that of the Psalm paraphrases. Calvin himself made five such paraphrases, in French, before 1539.

French Psalters were issued in Geneva in 1551 and 1552, and the famous "Anglo-Genevan Psalter," in English, in 1556. The Psalter of John Day, a complete revision with tunes supplied, was published in London in 1562. The "Bay Psalm Book" (*The Whole Book of Psalms*), an independent and singularly graceless set of paraphrases, appeared in Cambridge, Massachusetts, in 1640, and holds the distinction of being the first book of any kind to be published in British North America.

The Scottish Psalter of 1650, issued under the authority of the General Assembly of the Church of Scotland, remains generally in use in that country to the present day. Its style is fairly well represented in Psalm 23:

> The Lord's my Shepherd, I'll not want;
> He makes me down to lie
> In pastures green; He leadeth me
> The quiet waters by.

The Psalter in Metre, published in 1900 jointly by the Church of Scotland, the Free Church of Scotland, the United Presbyterian Church, and the Presbyterian Church in Ireland, presents first the 1650 rendering of the Psalms without change, then metrical paraphrases of 67 other passages of Scripture, and finally 626 hymns, 13 "doxologies," and 11 chants, most of these last to settings by the nineteenth century Anglican Sir John Stainer.

"All people that on earth do dwell," from Psalm 100 (the *Jubilate Deo* of Morning Prayer), belongs to the first age of Calvinist psalmody, and is attributed to William Kethe, a Scottish refugee in Geneva. The name of the tune, "Old Hundredth," derives from Day's English Psalter; in Geneva this melody was set rather to Psalm 134. In his boyhood John Milton made a number of Psalm versions, including the still widely known "Let us with a gladsome mind," from Psalm 136. In 1696 the *New Version of the Psalms of David*, made by the poet laureate Nahum Tate (John Dryden's Protestant successor), in collaboration with Nicholas Brady, came quickly into popularity and remained generally in use in England for a century and a half. "As pants the hart for cooling streams" (Psalm 42) is today perhaps the best known of the Tate and Brady paraphrases.

Even more familiar are many selections from *The Psalms of David Imitated in the Language of the New Testament, and Apply'd to the Christian State and Worship*, a 1719 publication of Isaac Watts, then minister of the Independent Chapel in Mark Lane, London. Among them are "Sweet Is the Work" (Psalm 92), "Before Jehovah's Awful Throne" (Psalm 100), "Our God, Our Help in Ages Past" (Psalm 90), and the decisively Christian adaptation of Psalm 72, "Jesus Shall Reign Where'er the Sun." A better known literary figure, though no doubt an inferior writer of hymns, was Joseph Addison, whose "The Spacious Firmament on High," a rather labored version of Psalm 19 in eighteenth century couplets, concluded an article on "Faith and Devotion" in *The Spectator* of 23 August 1712.

The practice of writing new verse renderings of the Psalms was carried on well into the nineteenth century. Henry F. Lyte (1793–1847), curate in a little fishing village in Devonshire, and best known as the author of "Abide with Me," is responsible also for "Praise, My Soul, the King of Heaven," from Psalm 103, and "God of Mercy, God of Grace," from Psalm 67. James Montgomery (1771–1854), Moravian editor of the Sheffield *Iris*, wrote not only "In the Hour of Trial" and "Prayer Is the Soul's Sincere Desire," but also the magnificent rendering of Psalm 72 which is "Hail to the Lord's Anointed." "The King of Love My Shepherd Is," which conflates Psalm 23 with the parable of the Good Shepherd, is a revision of a George Herbert paraphrase made by Sir Henry Williams Baker, editor of *Hymns Ancient and Modern*, for its supplement of 1868.

Many of the early Psalm tunes, as well as the texts, have passed into general and continuing use. These are firmly syllabic, with one note for each syllable of the text, and they march forward with unbroken stride and scarcely varying rhythm. Among them, in addition to "Old Hundredth," are "Old 134th" from the Genevan Psalter of 1551, "Old 124th" from that of 1552, "Old 22nd," from the Anglo-Genevan of 1556, "St. Flavian," from Day's Psalter of 1563, "Dundee" from the Scottish Psalter of 1615, and "Old 107th" from that of 1635. The familiar canon of Thomas Tallis ("All Praise to Thee, My God, This Night") originally was a setting for Psalm 67 in Archbishop Parker's Psalter of 1567.

Today the Presbyterian hymnbooks are the most readily available source for Psalm paraphrases. I count no less than forty-three such (not all of them so marked) among the 512 hymns contained in *The*

Hymnal of 1944. *The Methodist Hymnal* of 1935, stemming from a tradition quite different, and even more casual about identifying metrical Psalms as such, includes at least twenty-one among its 564 hymns: less than one-half as many, by the way, as the hymn poems (56 of them) which it attributes to Charles Wesley. *The Hymnal 1940* of the Protestant Episcopal Church has eighteen Psalm paraphrases among 600 hymns, despite the Anglican custom of using the Psalms much more regularly in other parts of the service than is usual in most other Protestant groups. Charles Wesley, who after all was an Anglican, exactly matches this quota with eighteen appearances in the same book.

ENGLISH HYMNS

The Methodists were by no means the first in England to write what the Calvinists long continued to call "profane hymns." Nicholas Tate produced not only Psalm paraphrases, but also the beloved "While Shepherds Watched Their Flocks by Night," a very close transcription of St. Luke 2. To Isaac Watts we owe, in addition to his "imitated" Psalms, such independent hymns as "When I Survey the Wondrous Cross," "Joy to the World," and "Am I a Soldier of the Cross?" John Dryden gets into modern hymnals with his version of the *Veni, creator spiritus,* "Creator Spirit, by Whose Aid." Whether the Romanist Alexander Pope had any intention of being a hymn writer may be doubted, but his very free rendering of Vergil's fourth Eclogue, which he captioned "The Messiah," gave to our use the glorious "Rise, Crowned with Light, Imperial Salem, Rise."

Isaac Watts published his first collection, *Horae Lyricae,* in 1706, and his *Hymns and Spiritual Songs* in 1707. This latter contained two hundred hymns, classified in groups as "Paraphrases," "Hymns on Divine Subjects," and "Hymns for the Lord's Supper." All told, Watts was the author of some six hundred hymns, and more than any other one man created the English hymn as a genre different from that of the metrical Psalm.

The Wesleys, personally more vigorous and active than Watts's feeble constitution permitted him to be, popularized the use of hymns wherever they went. Their first collection appeared not in England, but in Charleston (then Charles-Town), South Carolina. Issued in 1737, this was the earliest of American hymnals as distinct from metrical psalters. It included, beside a number of texts by Charles and John Wesley, seven selections from *The Temple* of George Herbert. In 1740 the Wesleys published *Hymns and Sacred Poems* in London, and two years later *A Collection of Tunes, set to Music, as they are commonly sung at the Foundery*. (The "Foundery" was a building bought by Wesley in 1739 for the holding of services; its name is derived from the fact that till 1716 it had been used as a plant for the casting of cannon.)

The definitive Wesleyan book, *A Collection of Hymns for the use of the People called Methodists*, appeared in 1780. It contained 539 hymns, organized in sections dealing with phases of the Christian life, from "Exhorting Sinners to Return to God" through "For Backsliders Recovered" to "For Believers Interceding for the World," and concluding with groups of hymns "For the Society Meeting," ". . . Giving Thanks," ". . . Praying," and ". . . Parting." Between them the two brothers had written 504 of the hymns in the book, and John had translated twenty-one more, nineteen of these from the German and one each from the French and Spanish. Isaac Watts, with nine of his hymns and Psalm paraphrases, was the only other author represented more than once. When in 1874 the Wesleyan Church in England published a supplement, its editors were able to add no less than 195 more hymn poems from the inexhaustible pens of the Wesleys.

What John Wesley claimed for his book of 1780 well may stand as an ideal for the hymn writer of this and all days:

1. In these hymns there is no doggerel; no botches; nothing put in to patch up the rhyme; no feeble expletives.
2. Here is nothing turgid or bombast, on the one hand, or low and creeping, on the other.
3. Here are no *cant* expressions; no words without meaning. . . . We talk common sense, both in prose and verse, and use no word but in a fixed and determinate sense.
4. Here are, allow me to say, both the purity, the strength, and the elegance of the English language; and, at the same time, the utmost simplicity and plainness, suited to every capacity.

The confident editor gave free permission to others to reprint, but under the condition that "they print them just as they are. But I desire they would not attempt to mend them; for they really are not able."

Gavien F. McCullagh

THE CHAPEL OF TRINITY METHODIST CHURCH,
BERKELEY, CALIFORNIA (1952)

Carlton A. Steiner, architect   F. Marion Smith, minister

A. J. Edwards

LAUREL METHODIST CHURCH, OAKLAND, CALIFORNIA
(1941)

George P. Simonds, architect   Donald G. Smiley, minister

Herrington-Olson

HIGH STREET PRESBYTERIAN CHURCH, OAKLAND,
CALIFORNIA (1950)

Irwin M. Johnson, architect   Fred B. Trevitt, minister

In 1779, a year before the appearance of Wesley's *Collection,* the poet William Cowper and his friend John Newton issued the first edition of their *Olney Hymns.* Newton, a converted slave-ship captain turned curate, wrote 280 of the 348 hymns in this book, including "Glorious Things of Thee Are Spoken" and "How Sweet the Name of Jesus Sounds." Among Cowper's sixty-eight contributions were "God Moves in a Mysterious Way," "O for a Closer Walk with God," and "Sometimes a Light Surprises." The Moravian James Montgomery published his *Songs of Zion, Being Imitations of Psalms,* in 1822, and his *Christian Psalmist* in 1825. "Angels, from the Realms of Glory" and "Go to Dark Gethsemane" will serve to suggest the wide range of religious feeling expressed in this lonely man's work.

The year 1827 saw the publication of two volumes which definitely assimilated hymnody to the liturgical tradition of the English Church. One was John Keble's *The Christian Year,* a single-handed production including a hymn for each Sunday and holy day, and also for the special services of the prayer book. The third edition, 1828, added poems even for "Gunpowder Treason" (Guy Fawkes) and "King Charles the Martyr." The only parts of this collection generally used today are "New Every Morning Is the Love" and "Sun of My Soul," each of which in its present form consists of a few stanzas taken from the much longer morning and evening hymns (respectively sixteen and fourteen quatrains) with which the book begins.

The other 1827 landmark, and a more enduring one, was Reginald Heber's *Hymns, written and adapted to the Weekly Church Service of the Year.* This was a compilation in which Heber included only nine of his own works, but all the nine survive in the Protestant Episcopal hymnal of today. Among them are "Brightest and Best of the Sons of the Morning," for the Epiphany; "From Greenland's Icy Mountains," noted as "before a collection made for the Society for the Propagation of the Gospel"; "The Son of God Goes Forth to War," for St. Stephen's Day; and the immortal "Holy, Holy, Holy," for Trinity Sunday. Heber did his literary work while he was rector at Hodnet, in Shropshire. In 1823 he became Bishop of Calcutta, and died at Trichinopoly the year before his volume of hymns was published.

The chorales of Germany, of which a sampling had become known in Britain through the work of the Wesleys, were made available in quantity by the activity of a young woman in London.

Catherine Winkworth's *Lyra Germanica*, a selection of 103 texts translated from a Lutheran collection of about nine hundred, appeared in 1855, when the maker was only twenty-eight years old. A second series, including some hymns "of a more personal and individual character than in the former," followed in 1858. There were 121 new renderings in this volume. Almost a hundred years later Miss Winkworth is represented nine times in the American Episcopal hymnal, seven in the Methodist, and ten in the Presbyterian. Typical are her versions of Paulus Gerhardt's *Fröhlich soll mein Herze springen*, "All My Heart This Night Rejoices" (1651), and Martin Rinkart's *Nun danket alle Gott*, "Now Thank We All Our God" (1636).

The Oxford Movement, concerning itself with the early liturgical traditions of the Church, brought to light a mass of hymn material from Latin and Greek sources. The great name here is that of John Mason Neale, who combined his researches with the wardenship of Sackville College and the operation of a women's hospital, St. Margaret's, which he established in East Grinstead. His *Mediaeval Hymns and Sequences* appeared in 1851, and his *Hymns of the Eastern Church* in 1862. Notable among his renderings from the Latin are "All Glory, Laud, and Honor" and "Jerusalem the Golden"; and of Greek hymns we owe to him our knowledge of "Christian, Dost Thou See Them?," "Come, Ye Faithful, Raise the Strain," and "The Day of Resurrection."

Hymns Ancient and Modern was the fully appropriate title of the first hymnal generally accepted as standard in the Church of England. Issued in 1860, it included 131 English hymns, 132 translations from the Latin, and ten from the German. Bishop Heber, Miss Winkworth, and Dr. Neale all were well represented. An appendix in 1868 added 114 hymn texts, including a few from the Greek.

Two epoch-marking if not epoch-making hymnals appeared in England at the turn of the century. *The Yattendon Hymnal* (1899) of Robert Bridges (1844–1930), a physically exquisite collection of just one hundred hymns, united the poetic taste of the future laureate with the musical erudition of H. Ellis Wooldridge (1845–1917), Slade Professor of Fine Arts at Oxford. Bridges wrote seven of the hymns, translated twenty-three, and "adapted" ten others. The music ranged from plainsong to several new compositions by Professor Wooldridge. Among Bridges' renderings, first published in this work, were "O Splendor of God's Glory Bright," from St. Ambrose's

Splendor paternae gloriae, and "Ah, Holy Jesus," from the medieval Latin by way of Johann Heermann's *Herzliebster Jesu* (1630).

The *English Hymnal* of 1906 was a much more comprehensive work, containing 656 hymns, which its sponsors "offered as a humble companion to the Book of Common Prayer for use in the Church." Included among the compilers were Percy Dearmer (1867–1936), later Canon of Westminster, and Athelstan Riley (1858–1945), a lay liturgiologist. The musical editor was Ralph Vaughan Williams (1872–   ), dean of contemporary British composers. It was for this book that Williams composed *Sine Nomine*, "For All the Saints," and arranged the plainsong *Christe sanctorum* as a setting for Dearmer's new rendering of St. Ambrose's *Nocte surgentes*, "Father, We Praise Thee, Now the Night Is Over." Dearmer contributed also "Jesus, Good Above All Other," and Riley was represented by "Ye Watchers and Ye Holy Ones." This book and that of Bridges did much at once to stimulate renewed interest in hymnody, and to establish stricter canons of scholarship and taste than had prevailed in Victorian days.

HYMN TUNES

Tune composition during the two centuries gradually moved abreast of the writing and translating of hymn texts. The first break from the strictly syllabic psalm-tune manner came with the anonymous *Lyra Davidica* of 1708, whose compiler recorded his intention to provide "a little freer air than the grave movement of the psalm tunes, as being both seasonable and acceptable." This book contained thirty-one hymns, largely translations from the German and the Latin, and twenty-five tunes. Typical of the change in musical style is the familiar "Easter Hymn" ("Jesus Christ Is Risen Today"), with its florid "Alleluias." Also in 1708 William Croft, organist at the Chapel Royal, published his *Supplement to the New Version of Psalms* (that is, Tate and Brady), in which first there appeared "St. Anne" ("Our God, Our Help in Ages Past") and "Hanover" ("O Worship the King").

The Wesleys made use of tunes new and old, including both chorales and psalm settings on the one hand, and eighteenth century compositions on the other. In the "Foundery Collection" of 1742 were Georg Wittwe's *Wer nur den lieben Gott* (1690), now known as "Winchester New"; the "Easter Hymn" from *Lyra Davidica;* and "Herrnhut" (also called "Savannah") and "Amsterdam" ("Rise, My Soul"), from the *Geistreiches Gesangbuch* (1704, 1714) of the Pietist minister and poet Johann Anastasius Freylinghausen. Thomas Olivers, a protégé and editorial employee of Wesley, contributed "Helmsley" ("Lo, He Comes with Clouds Descending") to the *Select Hymns* of 1765, and was responsible for the introduction of "Leoni," derived from the Jewish *Yigdal,* into *The Pocket Hymn Book* of 1785.

Aaron Williams, clerk of the Scottish Church in London, published *The Universal Psalmodist* in 1763, and saw its fifth edition as early as 1770. The best known of its tune innovations probably is "St. Thomas" ("I Love Thy Kingdom, Lord"). *An Essay on the Church Plain Chant,* published in London in 1782, provided tunes for well known Latin hymns. This Roman Catholic work marked the first publication of *Adeste fideles,* previously included in at least six manuscript copy books made by John Francis Wade at Douay in France. "Corinth" or *Dulce carmen* ("Alleluia, Song of Gladness") and Samuel Webbe's "Melcombe" ("Spirit of Mercy, Truth, and Love") are other standard tunes which made their first appearance in this collection.

The musical equivalents to John Mason Neale were John Bacchus Dykes (1823–1876), precentor of Durham Cathedral, and Sir Joseph Barnby (1838–1896), organist at St. Anne's, Soho, and precentor at Eton College. Dykes is represented today by twenty-two different tunes in the Protestant Episcopal hymnal, twenty-one in the Presbyterian, and eighteen in the Methodist. From Barnby's work the Episcopal book derives nine hymn tunes and three chants, the Presbyterian nine tunes and two chants, and the Methodist ten tunes and three chants.

In contrast to the early interchangeability of a few Psalm melodies, the tunes of Dykes and Barnby typically were written to accompany specific hymn poems. The harmony was in the nineteenth century manner, and every effort was made to wed the setting directly to the words. Typical of Dykes's style are "St. Andrew of Crete," for Neale's "Christian, Dost Thou See Them?" with its striking shift from the minor of the first eight measures to the major in the second half; *Vox Dilecti,* a similar treatment for Horatius Bonar's "I Heard the Voice of Jesus Say"; and the universally beloved *Lux Benigna,* for Cardinal Newman's groping plea in "Lead, Kindly Light." Barnby's essentially similar method is illustrated in *Laudes Domini* ("When Morning Gilds the Skies"), and in the evening "Merrial," with its soprano monotone on E announcing "Now the Day Is Over."

The younger generations of the Wesleys carried the family tradition over from the writing of hymn texts to the composing of church music. Charles Wesley's two sons, Charles, Jr. (1757–1834), and Samuel (1766–1837), were organists respectively at Marylebone Parish Church and Camden Chapel. Charles is best known today for "Lystra" ("Father, Whate'er of Earthly Bliss"), and Samuel for "Doncaster" ("O Bless the Lord, My Soul"). Samuel Wesley, though he became a Roman Catholic, campaigned eagerly for appreciation of the works of the Lutheran Bach. Samuel Sebastian Wesley (1810–1876), the son of Samuel, was organist at the cathedrals of Hereford, Exeter, and Gloucester, and by some is regarded as having been the most distinguished English church musician between Henry Purcell and Charles Villiers Stanford. He is represented in modern hymnals by such universal favorites as "Alleluia" ("Praise the Lord: Ye Heavens, Adore Him") and "Aurelia" ("The Church's One Foundation").

More recent developments in English hymnody have included not only a revival of interest in continental European materials, but also a greatly increased use of British melodies of folk origin. The vigorous *Ton-Y-Botel*, now joined inseparably to James Russell Lowell's "Once to Every Man and Nation," and the majestic "Llangloffan," admirably suited to G. K. Chesterton's "O God of Earth and Altar," are typical of our debt to Welsh sources. "Gosterwood" and "Selma" are from traditional melodies respectively of the Isle of Man and the Isle of Arran. "St. Patrick" and "Deirdre" (coupled in the noble "St. Patrick Hymn") are ancient Irish, and "Forest Green" and "Monks Gate" are characteristic of the English folk songs arranged by Ralph Vaughan Williams for *The English Hymnal* of 1906.

HYMNS IN AMERICA

Just at the end of the eighteenth century Oliver Holden, a carpenter and builder in Charlestown, Massachusetts, began the story of distinctively American hymnody with his *Union Harmony* (1793). Of the twenty-one tunes which he personally wrote for this collection, "Coronation" ("All Hail the Power of Jesus' Name") is the oldest American hymn setting in general use today. The pattern of American church music was most decisively affected by Lowell Mason (1792–1872), long president of the Boston Händel and Haydn Society and founder of the Boston Academy of Music. His *Carmina Sacra* went through thirteen editions between 1841 and 1860, and is said to have sold more than half a million copies. This compilation included 423 hymns and anthems, and eighty-two chant settings. Prefixed to the tunes is a thirty-three page introduction entitled "Elements of Vocal Music," along with an "Explanation of Musical Terms" and a page "On Chanting."

Indefatigably Mason borrowed, arranged, and composed; and in some cases it is difficult to learn the true history of the tunes in the forms in which he published them. "Antioch," for example, the inescapable setting for "Joy to the World," Mason noted as being "from Händel," but aside from the first four notes (those of "Lift up Your Heads" in the *Messiah*), it is impossible to find the theme certainly in any of Händel's known works. "Hamburg" ("When I Survey the Wondrous Cross") similarly is indicated as "from a Gregorian Chant," but it is rather a melody approximately in the Gregorian style than a direct borrowing. "Mendebras" ("O Day of Rest and Gladness") is said to be from a German melody, but no one as yet has found its source. "Missionary Hymn" ("From Greenland's Icy Mountains"), "Harwell" ("Hark, Ten Thousand Harps and Voices") and "Watchman" ("Watchman, Tell Us of the Night") are famous examples of Mason's own compositions for specific hymn texts.

American parallels to the work of the English hymn and tune writers appeared in considerable quantity during the nineteenth century. A notable pairing of father and son is that of George Washington Doane (1799–1859) and William Croswell Doane (1832–1913), Episcopal bishops respectively of New Jersey and Albany. To the father we owe "Softly Now the Light of Day" and "Fling Out the Banner," and to the son the Albany bicentennial hymn (1886) "Ancient of days." The tune for this last was composed by J. Albert Jeffrey, organist in Bishop Doane's cathedral. The Quaker Whittier (1807–1892) wrote devotional verse which rapidly was appropriated to the hymnals, including "Immortal Love, for Ever Full," "Dear Lord and Father of Mankind," and "O Brother Man, Fold to Thy Heart

Thy Brother," which are parts of the poems "Our Master," "The Brewing of Soma," and "Worship."

Edmund H. Sears (1810–1876), nominally a Unitarian but believed to have accepted Swedenborgian views, wrote "It Came upon the Midnight Clear," and Uzziah Burnap immediately arranged Richard S. Willis's "Study No. 23" to serve as its tune. Phillips Brooks (1835–1893) wrote "O Little Town of Bethlehem" for his Sunday school at Holy Trinity Church, Philadelphia. Again the tune, "St. Louis," was provided for the occasion by the church organist, Lewis H. Redner. Washington Gladden's "O Master, Let Me Walk with Thee" was first a devotional poem written in 1879 for his magazine *Sunday Afternoon*, but it appeared in *Songs of Christian Praise* in 1880, and has captured Canon Smith's "Maryton," written in 1874 for "Sun of My Soul," as its permanent companion.

The Methodist Frank Mason North, when corresponding secretary of the New York City Missionary and Church Extension Society, wrote "Where Cross the Crowded Ways of Life" in 1903 for his house organ *The Christian City*. It was seized upon by the editors of *The Methodist Hymnal* of 1905, and has passed into general use. The tune, "Germany" or "Gardiner," is another of those alleged borrowings from a classical composer, in this case Beethoven; but its first publisher, William Gardiner, said twenty-three years after its publication (1815 to 1838), "It is somewhere in the works of Beethoven, but where I cannot point out."

GOSPEL SONGS

A wholly independent development, consciously and pronouncedly free from the historical scholarship of nineteenth century hymnody, was that of the gospel song. It took its rise from some of the more sentimental hymns of Charles Wesley, and attained its first great popularity with the evangelistic work of Dwight L. Moody (1837–1899) and his musical associate Ira D. Sankey (1840–1908). The gospel song was an authentic expression of the highly individualist religion of the American frontier, and it used "singable" melodies of the general type of the popular songs of the day.

The early gospel songs were intensely personal in their feeling, but they dealt largely with essential values of Christian faith and experience. Fairly typical of this period are Joseph Scriven's "What a Friend We Have in Jesus" and such writings of the blind Fanny Crosby as "Safe in the Arms of Jesus." Later, with the dominance of Charles H. Gabriel and E. O. Excell, the verse became more banal, the doctrine dubious, the sentiment vapid, and the tunes scarcely distinguishable from those of the dance hall. (Note, as a fairly recent example, the identity of "The Old Time Religion" with "Give Me One Dozen Roses.") Almost every one of the gospel songs was supplied with a refrain, which was sung to what can only be called a jazzed accompaniment on the piano, and often in triumphant barbershop harmonies.

In extremely high proportion these pieces were didactic or hortatory in tone, rather than being in any sense expressions of worship: "Brighten the Corner Where You Are," "Get Close to Jesus," "If Your Heart Keeps Right," "Let Jesus Come into Your Heart," "The Victory May Depend on You." Another marked characteristic was a strong emphasis on the second coming, in harmony with the premillennial theology which was preached by most of the revivalists: "Jesus Is Coming to Earth Again," "Jesus May Come Today," "O Some-Day, with Trump of God and a Shout." In one collection of these materials, used in the Billy Sunday campaigns, forty-five of the first hundred pieces are couched in the first-person singular, and twenty-three more in the second-person singular. Only two of the hundred are addressed to God, and three to Jesus. It is needless to say more as to the total lack of interest in worship, and of any sense of a true Christian community, in such a volume as this.

Happily the vogue of the unauthorized "little book" of gospel songs at evening services and in young people's groups seems to be nearing its end, at least in the major American denominations. Reputable hymnals for young people, less bulky than the large collections and omitting those concerns which are unlikely to arise at the young people's meeting, have been issued by most of our Churches in recent years; and they should by all means be substituted for the heresies of the revivalists and the sentimentalists in every church where the change has not already been made. Let none say, "But they like 'In the garden.'" Have we no responsibility for developing decent literary and musical taste, to say nothing of true Christian faith? And what really are the youngsters thinking when they sway in unison while in close harmony they croon, "And he walks with me and he talks with me"?

CONCERTIZED RELIGIOUS MUSIC

In following the course of hymn writing and singing from the sixteenth century, we have turned aside from the history of what may be regarded as major compositions for religious purposes. Great Masses were composed from the beginning of the polyphonic period, one of the earliest being that of Guillaume de Machaut for the coronation of Charles V of France in 1364. The *Missa Papae Marcelli* of Giovanni Pierluigi da Palestrina (1526–1594), written under the authority of the Council of Trent in 1562, commonly is regarded as being the climactic achievement of Roman liturgical polyphony.

Johann Sebastian Bach (1685–1750), though a devout Protestant, wrote his tremendous Mass in B minor as a "candidate" piece when he was applying for the post of court composer to the King of Saxony. Haydn and Mozart both composed many Masses, which are better known today through long-playing records than ever they were through church use. Beethoven also wrote two Masses, the famous *Missa Solemnis* in D, and an earlier Mass in C. Hector Berlioz in 1837 produced his staggering Requiem, as a memorial for French soldiers killed during the Algerian campaigns. Verdi in his old age wrote a Requiem too, in honor of his friend Alessandro Manzoni, the author of *I promessi sposi*. In our day Igor Stravinsky and François Poulenc have given us brief and striking Masses in the modern idiom.

A parallel development, chiefly Protestant in its orientation, was that of the oratorio. One needs but to mention the *St. John* and *St. Matthew* Passions and the *Christmas Oratorio* of Bach, the *Messiah* and the *Judas Maccabaeus* of Händel, *The Creation* of Haydn, and the *Elijah* of Felix Mendelssohn-Bartholdy, to suggest the wealth of inspiration that is available here. The German Requiem of Johannes Brahms also is properly speaking an oratorio, for its text is biblical rather than liturgical. Nineteenth century English efforts in the same genre, though much admired in their time, now are largely forgotten. Among those occasionally sung today are Sir Arthur Sullivan's *The Prodigal Son* (1869), Alfred R. Gaul's *The Holy City* (1882), and Sir John Stainer's *The Crucifixion* (1887). Sir William Walton has revived the form, though in pronouncedly modern style, in his *Belshazzar's Feast* (1931).

Recently distinguished composers have turned their attention to the service of the Jewish synagogue. Notable settings are those by Ernst Bloch (1935) and Darius Milhaud (1949), both designed for the ritual as it is followed by the Reform groups in the United States, but the former with an English text and the latter chiefly in the Hebrew. These are available now in excellent recordings, and their close study will abundantly repay anyone who is interested either specifically in Jewish worship or generally in the return to religion in modern music.

The final word on this point, however, must be largely negative from the standpoint of regular and congregational worship. Magnificent as many of the Masses and oratorios are, they simply are not church music in any significant and practical sense of the word. True, a choir now and then may "get one up" and present it as a concert achievement in lieu of the regular service. By sheer bulk almost all of them are disqualified from use *in* the service, even if they were not ruled out from the typical church by the great demands they put upon the musicians.

So much attention to performance, and in many cases so great a departure from true liturgical feeling (think of Berlioz' four brass bands!), forbid any genuine realization of the sense of worship. It was in recognition of the fact that Pius X called for the replacement of the concert Masses by plainsong and by the more rigid types of polyphony. From the religious point of view it can not be doubted that the Pope was right, and that his ruling was long overdue.

USING OUR HYMNALS

Chants, psalms, chorales, hymns: all these are included in our heritage of worship, and all will help us to sing unto the Lord with clear voices and glad hearts. The typical standard hymnal of today is a practical safeguard against the possibility of using anything extremely bad; but it is not in itself a guarantee that we shall use all we might of the thrillingly good. Conservatism, timidity, and plain laziness limit too many of us to the using of only a few, and those not always the best, of the hymnal's myriad treasures.

A first step toward stirring interest in the full employment of the book well may be that of calling the people's attention to the always present, but generally ignored, data printed at the head of each hymn. Here are the names of author and composer, and commonly their dates, or else the date of writing or first publication. Here also is the title which identifies the particular tune as a piece of music, and a syllable count which (used with caution as to where the accents fall) will facilitate the interchange of tunes when this is desired.

Immediately much of the wondrously varied wealth of our heritage will become apparent. Here are Jewish psalms, early hymns of the Greek and Latin churches, songs of the Reformation days, stately reflections of the sober, ordered mood of the Church of England, intense expressions of Pietist devotion. Here are Romans and Anglicans, Quakers and Moravians, Unitarians and Independents, Baptists and Methodists, Lutherans and Calvinists. Here is folk material from many a land, along with the authorized plainsong of the ancient Church; and here too are the names of the most famous poets and composers, coupled with those of carpenters and statesmen and civil engineers. Nowhere more than in its singing has Christianity been truly catholic; and the awareness of the unity of the faith grows rapidly as we learn to sing our faith together.

Many who are affected by current trends in musical taste will find themselves using relatively high proportions of early material, and of very recent compositions, rather than being content only with nineteenth century types of expression. Romanticism had its day with hymns and tunes as in all of literature and art; and this is romanticism's day no longer. It scarcely is to be doubted that to our ears "Winchester New" (1690) is a better tune for "Ride on in Majesty" than is Dykes's "St. Drostane" (1862); or, in the other direction, that Ralph Vaughan Williams's *Sine Nomine* (1906) is greatly superior to Barnby's "Sarum" (1868) for Bishop How's "For All the Saints."

There is reasonable doubt, too, whether we shall remain content with all our borrowings from the secular works of the great composers. Edward Hodges's arrangement of the "Hymn to Joy" from the fourth movement of Beethoven's Ninth Symphony, with the words of Henry van Dyke, probably is legitimate, since Schiller's poem is one of glad praise even though cast originally in pagan terms. The "St. Anthony Chorale" of Haydn was given that name because of the churchly quality of the theme in his *Divertimento* in B-flat minor, and the "Emperor" Quartet's *andante* will not be withdrawn from Newton's classic hymn of Zion, even though in a different mood and tempo the tune is that of *Deutschland über alles*. Much less defensible are the borrowings from Weber's fairy tale *Oberon* for "Softly Now the Light of Day," and from his magic-bullet story of *Der Freischütz* for "My Jesus, as Thou Wilt." Nor is Sibelius' nationalistic *Finlandia* a natural setting for either "Be Still, My Soul" or "Through Love to Light." (One remembers gospel songs done to Freddy Martinesque arrangements of the sextet from *Lucia* and the quartet from *Rigoletto*.)

Preferences will develop, naturally and legitimately, as acquaintance grows. The important first step is to use our hymnals consciously and carefully to vary our experience and to deepen our appreciation. The question of difficulty takes care of itself, in today's almost universal training of the American people to read music, and in a reasonable time spent in choir rehearsing of new selections. The question of prejudice can be disposed of by intelligent and informed leadership. It certainly is not necessary to abandon the noble hymns that already we know best, and have come so dearly to love. It is highly necessary, if our singing is to be in fullness of both spirit and understanding, that we shall come to know many of the great and meaningful hymns, old and new alike, that up to now we have missed.

"And our mouth shall show forth thy praise." This is a communal pledge, and it requires communal fulfillment. The songs of the Church are to be sung by all her people, not by a few specialists on their behalf. This disposes at once of a priestly monopoly of chanting, and of a choir (and a fortiori a quartet or solo) monopoly of anthems. The function of the individual cleric here, or of the cantor, is simply to make possible antiphonal usages that will express authentic religious feelings in a truly responsive mood. The function of the choir is to lead and support the congregation's singing of praise, never to perform for the congregation's passive enjoyment.

To sing worthy texts to worthy settings, and to sing them well, is the immediate objective of music in the service. To sing worthily the praise of God is the ultimate aim. Those who will learn of the tradition, who will use their minds and consecrate their skills, will attain to good music. Beyond this, and hereby, they will find themselves coming into the presence of God with the voice of joy and praise, in the multitude of them that keep holyday.

VIII

LET US PRAY

"PRAY WITHOUT CEASING," St. Paul urged his friends in Saloniki. This we ought to do, and if we will we can, every moment of our waking lives. But if it is important to pray the while we are doing other things, it is not the less important that we should set aside times and opportunities to pray when we are not cumbered by doing anything else. Prayer, as the human spirit's approach to God, merits sole attention as well as incidental.

The house of God is the house of prayer, and the service within it is our praying to him. All that we do in the service is prayer: for praise is prayer, and so is confession; and so, if we use them aright, may be the lessons and even the sermon. Again, however, the centering of our attention on prayer specifically as such is critical to our full realizing of God's nearness to us his children. The means which have been used toward this end, and those which we may find serviceable for ourselves, claim now our attention.

PRAYER IN THE OLD TESTAMENT

Prayer marks the religion of the Old Testament from the earliest recorded beginnings. And from the beginning it is patent that prayer was understood to involve much more than man's petition for something he thought he wanted. Long before any of the patriarchs is quoted in address to God, the Lord speaks directly to them and reveals his will for them. There are several two-way conversations be-

127

tween God and Abraham, one of these being the discussion about the fate of Sodom and Gomorrah: in which, it will be remembered, the outcome is a compromise between divine annoyance and a human plea for mercy. Abraham prays also for the Philistine king Abimelech, and thereby secures his healing and that of his household.

Isaac prays for direction in his choosing of a wife, and Jacob for escape from the quite reasonably expected vengeance of Esau. In the wilderness Moses debates with God about his own fitness to lead Israel, and long afterward about the fitness of Israel herself to be spared from destruction. In similar vein Joshua and the Lord discuss what is to be done after the defeat of the Israelite army at Ai, and Gideon secures guidance for his tactics in the battle of Jezreel.

All these are individual prayers, though few of them relate to purely individual points of concern. While unquestionably prayer was included in sacrificial worship from the earliest days, and indeed was its primary motive, public prayer as such receives singularly little mention in the accounts of the wilderness years under Moses and Aaron. The early tale of the brazen serpent includes the statement that "Moses prayed for the people" at their request, but offers no quotation of his words. In Deuteronomy 26:12–15 a form of public prayer seems to be provided following the injunction, "Then shalt thou say before the Lord thy God." This, however, is a seventh century passage, and it may not be treated as evidential for Mosaic times.

At the end of the period of the Judges Samuel gathers all Israel to Mizpeh, that he may "pray for them unto the Lord." While the sacrifice of a lamb is specified, no words of the accompanying prayer are quoted. In the disputed matter of choosing a king we hear the Lord's words on the issue, but not Samuel's. After the battle with the Moabites Samuel's prayers secure first a thunderstorm, and then a conditional promise of mercy. Yet again no phrasing of the prayers is supplied.

In decided contrast is Solomon's prayer at the dedication of the Temple, a long and eloquent recitation of God's glory and an intense plea for his continuing favor. The king speaks in anticipation of prayer being made "toward this place"; but this seems to be symbolic only ("Thou hast said, My name shall be there"), for the recurring petition is,

> Hear thou in heaven thy dwelling place:
> And when thou hearest, forgive.

The narrative section of the book of Isaiah, paralleling II Kings 19f., cites two prayers of the later king Hezekiah: one in the Temple, for the nation under the threat of Assyrian conquest, and the other in the palace, for his own recovery from illness.

The Psalms are hymns and prayers at once, mingling praise and aspiration and petition even as they are mingled in life. Such Psalms as 60, 79, and 80 are clearly national:

> O God, thou hast cast us off,
> Thou hast scattered us . . .

> O God, the heathen are come into thine inheritance;
> Thy holy temple have they defiled . . .

> Give ear, O Shepherd of Israel,
> Thou that leadest Joseph like a flock.

Psalm 51, on the other hand, is one of individual confession:

> Against thee, thee only, have I sinned,
> And done this evil in thy sight;

yet the public use of this personal plea in the Temple service is decisively indicated by the heading, "To the chief Musician."

Daniel is represented as carrying on the practice suggested in the words of Solomon:

When Daniel knew that the writing was signed, he went into his house; and his windows being open toward Jerusalem, he kneeled upon his knees three times a day, and prayed, and gave thanks before his God, as he did aforetime.

The prayer of Daniel quoted in 2:20–23 is a thanksgiving and ascription of praise rather than a petition; and so also is the *Benedicite*, which the Alexandrian editors of the Greek text thought fitting to assign to the "three Hebrew children" in the fiery furnace.

I Maccabees, recording the historical events of the period in which the book of Daniel was written, thrice reports that the Maccabean generals prayed for their cause before joining battle, and it quotes from a prayer of Judas Maccabaeus at Bethsura. This again is thanksgiving as well as request:

> Blessed art thou, O Saviour of Israel . . .
> Let all those that know thy name praise thee with thanksgiving.

Several prayers are included in the apocryphal book of Ecclesiasticus, 23:1–16 being personal, 36:1–17 national, and 50 the account of a national thanksgiving service in the days of the high priest Simon. Included in this last is the source of Martin Rinkart's hymn *Nun danket:*

> Now therefore bless ye the God of all,
> Who only doeth wondrous things everywhere.

Finally, Chapter 51 is an individual prayer of Jesus the son of Sirach, beginning and ending with thanks and praise to God.

PRAYERS IN LATER JUDAISM

The tradition of prayer thus was firmly established among the Jews before the destruction of the Temple in A.D. 70. The precise fixing of the forms of prayer followed very soon upon this religious and national tragedy, as an effort to maintain the heritage unmodified by alien forces, attitudes, and practices. The daily litany of prayers, called "The Eighteen Benedictions," became with the *Shema* ("Hear, O Israel") the core of the synagogue service. For use in the Jewish home there were developed the *Kiddush* (Hallowing) for the beginnings of the Sabbaths and festivals, and the *Havdolah* (Separation) for their close.

Jewish prayer is primarily and essentially communal. "Wherever ten persons pray," said the Rabbi Yitzchak, "the divine presence dwells among them." The Eighteen Benedictions, though introduced in the first person singular,

> O Lord, open thou my lips,
> And my mouth shall declare thy praise,

all are couched in the first person plural:

> Blessed art thou, O Lord our God and God of our fathers . . .

> We will sanctify thy Name in the world
> Even as they sanctify it in the highest heavens . . .

> Forgive us, O our Father, for we have sinned;
> Pardon us, O our King, for we have transgressed . . .

> We give thanks unto thee, for thou art the Lord our God,
> And the God of our fathers for ever and ever.

Personal supplications were added to the service as time went on, but these also were phrased in plural form. The litany for the Ten Days of Repentance, from Rosh Hashanah (New Year) to Yom Kippur (the Day of Atonement), consists of forty-four petitions each introduced by *Abinu Melkenu*, "Our Father, our King!" The concluding adoration gives voice to the universal plea,

Let all the inhabitants of the world perceive and know that unto thee every knee must bow, every tongue must swear allegiance;

and it ends with the congregation chorusing the triumphant lines from the book of Zechariah,

And the Lord shall be king over all the earth:
In that day shall the Lord be One, and his Name One.

The mourners' *Kaddish* (Holy), a standard supplement to the Sabbath services, is yet another expression of communal spirit. Those who commemorate their own loved ones stand in the midst of the congregation, and themselves declare their hope and faith:

Blessed, praised, and glorified, exalted, extolled, and honoured, magnified and lauded be the Name of the Holy One, blessed be he; though he be high above all the blessings and hymns, praises and consolations, which are uttered in the world; and say ye, Amen.

There is in the *Kaddish* no direct reference to death, nor to the hereafter. The whole attention is centered rather on the eternal glory and the eternal goodness of God.

Reform Judaism has shortened and simplified the traditional service, and has greatly reduced the use of the Hebrew language in it. Nevertheless the historic pattern has been retained, and more importantly the basic mood has been preserved. Many Christians, when first they attend a Jewish service or read a Jewish prayer book, will be surprised to find that the prayers contain so much of general praise and so little of detailed petition. Devotion and consecration are here, indeed; but scant encouragement is given to the quest for individual favors.

In the synagogue man is engaged in blessing God for his greatness and goodness, and so man has little time left to dwell on his personal needs and wishes. As we seek to pray aright within our Christian heritage, we shall do well to take account of this Jewish concept of prayer as being primarily adoration rather than request. "Seek ye first the kingdom of God, and his righteousness, and all these things shall be added unto you." This is at once authentic Judaism and authentic Christianity.

PRAYER IN THE NEW TESTAMENT

Jesus lived ever in the spirit of prayer, but also he prayed specifically and directly. St. Luke, who seems to have taken a special interest in the matter, records Jesus' praying at his baptism, "all night" before the choosing of the Twelve, before the Transfiguration, and long in the garden of Gethsemane. Our Lord prayed also for his disciples, in particular for the wayward St. Peter, and from the cross for his very executioners.

In his teaching Jesus stressed preparation of spirit as a necessary condition of true prayer: humility in the parable of the Pharisee and the publican, forgiveness of those who have injured us, sincerity rather than display, and most of all faith. That he guaranteed "Yes" answers to specific requests seems superficially to be suggested in several Gospel passages; but "in my Name" surely means "in my spirit," and so rules out anything that is less than worthy of God's will for us. This is made explicit in the assurance in I St. John 5:14, "If we ask anything according to God's will, he heareth us." Since the avoidance of the cup of suffering was not granted to our Lord in Gethsemane, it ill behooves us to claim for ourselves a greater influence upon God's purposes.

"After this manner therefore pray ye," said Jesus as he gave the words of what the Church knows as "the Lord's Prayer" in the absolute. It is a tragedy that this prayer, introduced as it was by a warning against the use of "vain repetitions," itself has become through familiarity and carelessness often a vain repetition indeed, a wholly empty utterance. In this model prayer there are but three personal requests, one for daily bread, one for forgiveness, and one for deliverance in temptation; and all of these are expressed in the plural. The beginning of the prayer is praise quite in the Jewish manner, and the doxology in St. Matthew's Gospel seems to have been added to provide a kindred conclusion, no doubt with a view to use in the public service. As a representation of what is to be regarded as worthy praying, the Lord's Prayer argues yet again that the glory of God rather than the convenience of men ought ever to be the principal concern.

"Where two or three are gathered together in my name" points to the importance of united or congregational prayer. This is frequently illustrated in the book of Acts. In the early days St. Peter and St. John observe the traditional hours of prayer at the Temple. What purports to be a spontaneous prayer of the whole Christian assembly is recorded in Acts 4, after the release of these two apostles from arrest. Later the company of believers pray for St. Peter's delivery from another imprisonment, but scarcely will recognize him when he appears at the door. Prayer accompanied baptism, and also the consecration of individuals to particular types of service; and these prayers were likewise public in their nature.

St. Paul prays regularly for his friends, and bespeaks their prayers for him. Congregational prayer in Corinth seems sometimes, along with the "gift of tongues," to have degenerated into meaninglessness and disorder. Here the apostle insists on the use of intelligence alike in speaking, singing, and praying:

If I pray in an unknown tongue, my spirit prayeth, but my understanding is unfruitful. What is it then? I will pray with the spirit, and I will pray with the understanding also: I will sing with the spirit, and I will sing with the understanding also. . . . In the church I had rather speak five words with my understanding, that by my voice I might instruct others also, than ten thousand words in an unknown tongue.

Elsewhere in the Pauline writings are a number of passages which themselves are prayers, both as soaring praise (Romans 8, "Who shall separate us from the love of Christ?") and as petition (Ephesians 1, "That the God of our Lord Jesus Christ, the Father of glory, may give unto you the spirit of wisdom and revelation"; and Ephesians 3, "For this cause I bow my knees unto the father of our Lord Jesus Christ"). I Timothy, probably a document somewhat later than St. Paul's own time, seems to specify a regular "order of prayer" in the second chapter:

I exhort therefore, that, first of all, supplications, prayers, and intercessions, and giving of thanks, be made for all men; for kings, and for all that are in authority; that we may lead a quiet and peaceful life in all godliness and honesty.

Prayer is important to the author of the epistle of St. James, and is practically seen in harmony with his dominantly practical emphasis. "Ye ask and receive not," sternly he tells his readers, "because ye ask amiss." Everyone is to pray as he has need, but already the elders of the church are assigned a special and ceremonial function in the offering of prayers for the sick.

In the book of Revelation the saints are heard praying and praising God in heaven. Associated with their prayers, no doubt in recollection of the usages of the Jewish Temple, is the burning of incense on the golden altar before the throne. The hymns of this book are prayers also; and the whole concludes with the writer's simple, "Even so, come, Lord Jesus," and a benediction which is by definition a prayer: "The grace of our Lord Jesus Christ be with you all. Amen."

PRAYERS OF THE CHURCH

A very long Christian prayer, definitely liturgical in its character, occupies three "chapters" of the epistle to Corinth of St. Clement of Rome, which is to be dated just before the end of the first century. Much of its phrasing is biblical, and more largely from the Old Testament than from the New. Typical of its union of petition with praise is the close of Chapter 59:

Save those of us who are afflicted, have mercy on the humble, raise up those who fall, show thyself to those in need, heal the sinful, restore the wanderers, feed the hungry, deliver our prisoners, raise up the sick, strengthen the faint of heart: that all nations may know that thou alone art God, that Jesus Christ is thy servant, and that we are thy people and the sheep of thy pasture.

While spontaneous prayers continued to be offered in the Christian service, especially by those who were recognized to be "prophets," the forms of phrasing came increasingly to be fixed in and for general usage. The standard Eucharistic prayer as set forth in the *Didache* has been quoted in Chapter II. Brief formulas for the use of the congregation soon began to be employed: such ascriptions of praise as the *Gloria Patri*, used in the East from the second century; such exchanges as "The Lord be with you: And with thy spirit," probably suggested by Ruth 2:4; *Kyrie eleison*, "Lord, have mercy," which even in the West retained always its Greek wording; and of course the chorused "Amen" (So be it), at the close of each petition.

From these there developed litanies, used from the fourth century, in which the priest offered a series of brief prayers, to each of which the people made a uniform response. The "collect" originally was a summation of the preceding litany prayers, bringing the thoughts of the congregation together to a central theme. The Eucharistic prayer was offered by the priest only, but not until after the people had joined in the unison *Sanctus*, "Holy, holy, holy," and the antiphonal *Sursum Corda*, "Lift up your hearts." Gradually the major historic liturgies took form, regionally varying in details but alike in their essential structure, and all in their essence services of continuing prayer.

The ancient sacramentaries, compiled and expanded from the fifth to the ninth centuries, set forth both the prayers that were to be used at every celebration of the Mass, including the congregational responses, and also specific prayers for each particular Sunday and holy day of the Christian year. Out of the sacramentaries there developed the distinct Missals for the Mass itself, and the Breviaries detailing the structure and contents of the monastic "offices." In England there were several varying "uses," of which five (Salisbury, Hereford, Bangor, York, Lincoln) are mentioned in the Preface to the English prayer book of 1549. That of Salisbury, often called "Sarum," was codified in Missal and Breviary in the eleventh century, and revised in the thirteenth. The most generally used in pre-Reformation England, it greatly influenced the "one Use" established by Cranmer, and it remains a major point of reference for Anglicans of today.

The persistence of the very early prayers is indicated by an analysis of the materials in the current *Book of Common Prayer* of the Protestant Episcopal Church. Here the "proper" collects for the Christian year include six from the Leonine sacramentary, twenty-two from the Gelasian, thirty-one from the Gregorian, two from the sacramentary of Alcuin, and one from the Gothic Missal. A number of these prayers appear in modifications that belong to the Sarum use, but none of them seems to be wholly original in it. The total of sixty-two collects dating from before A.D. 1000 compares with forty-four more recent ones, of which twenty-one were composed for the prayer book of 1549, and but twelve are new contributions for the present American book.

Other forms of prayer, and special services of the Church, exhibit a similar reliance upon early materials, even though changes and substitutions have been made from time to time. It will interest Methodists to note that in their service of the Holy Communion, which is directly dependent upon the English one of 1552, two of the specified formulas are Jewish, one is from the New Testament, one is Greek, one is from the sacramentary of Alcuin, three are from the Roman Mass, and three are from Cranmer's service of 1549. (No, there is nothing newer; nor need there be.) Even within the tradition of Calvin the ancient formularies have been called back into use in our time. The 1932 edition of the Presbyterian *Book of Common Worship* listed among its contents three prayers from the Leonine sacramentary, eleven from the Gelasian, eight from the Gregorian, four from Eastern Orthodox liturgies, and one each from the Gallican (early French and Celtic) and Mozarabic (Spanish) rites, and from the writings of St. Augustine and Thomas à Kempis. The new edition of 1946, which does not indicate sources, shows even a greater dependence upon ancient materials.

Some much more recent prayers, by their sheer religious and literary merit, have made their way into general use. Of such are those which William Bright, Regius Professor of Ecclesiastical History at Oxford, appended to his *Ancient Collects* (1861), and of which four appear among the "Forms of Prayer to be used in Families" in the Episcopal prayer book of 1928: the prayers "for the Spirit of Prayer," "for Sunday Morning," "for Guidance," and the first of the two prayers "for Trustfulness." Dean John W. Suter of Washington Cathedral, official custodian of the Standard text of the American book, is the author of the prayer "for Quiet Confidence," that "for Joy in God's Creation," and the second prayer "for Trustfulness," all published in the "Family Prayer" section. Henry van Dyke (1852–1933), Professor of English Literature in Princeton University, and under Woodrow Wilson our Minister to the Netherlands, was very largely responsible for the structure of the two first editions of the American Presbyterian *Book of Common Worship;* and in the 1932 text he was credited with having written eighty-one of the prayers and adapted nineteen others.

THE PURPOSE OF PRAYING

What have all these writers, ancient and modern, been seeking to do as in turn they have set down forms of words intended for use in public prayer? Manifestly their intent has been that the people shall pray, and that they shall be guided in praying aright. This raises of necessity the question as to what prayer is for, and especially of what congregational prayer rightly may be designed to accomplish.

Prayer historically is converse with God, and psychologically it always must be more than "asking God for something." If, as the Westminster "Shorter Catechism" puts it, "The chief end of man is to glorify God, and enjoy him for ever," praise and thanksgiving stand first among both the Christian's duties and his privileges. Prayer as the community's united giving of thanks breathes through all the book of Psalms, is renewed in the "Benedictions" of the synagogue, and is the fount and origin of the Eucharistic prayer in the Holy Communion.

Petition too has its place, but one that needs carefully and clearly to be defined.

> Prayer is the soul's sincere desire,
> Uttered or unexpressed,

wrote James Montgomery. Yet we must ask whether all of the soul's sincere desires are legitimate ones; and immediately we have to acknowledge that many of them are not.

Specific prayers for external favors stand in a particularly dubious category. It often has been remarked that the Anglican prayer books contain, in immediate sequence, a prayer "for Rain" and one "for Fair Weather." The giving of either sort of meteorological advice to the Almighty surely is an impertinence, aside from the absurdity of preparing in advance to counter the one by its opposite. As my colleague Elliot Diller has put it, in California it would be sounder far to pray for wisdom in the planning of our great Central Valley project, and for strength to carry it through to its goal of providing water and power while controlling floods.

The greater truth which this reflects is that the significant petitions of prayer are those concerned not with outer phenomena, but with the inner life of man. Prayer is designed not to persuade the Lord to water the strawberries, but to energize the truck gardener to do his own work faithfully and well. Thus it is not the physical miracle which we ought to seek in prayer, but those moral miracles which the creative power of God ever will work in the hearts that are prepared, by prayer and in faith, to receive him.

The prayers for rain and fair weather, reflecting the perfectly natural but quite selfish interests of an agricultural community, happily are not typical of the historic prayers of the Church. By far the great majority of these are prayers not for outward blessings, but for inward and spiritual grace. Of this type are the General Confessions in the choir offices and in the Holy Communion, Alcuin's matchless Communion Collect, and practically every collect provided for the Church year. In all of these we find the congregation asking God so to prepare their hearts that they may perfectly love him, and worthily magnify his holy Name. This is why and how we should pray, and this is why and how the congregation should pray together.

The question properly arises as to the value of our praying for others than ourselves, in what is called intercession. There are two immediate affirmative answers, well within the range of the most naturalistic view of human psychology. One is that if sincerely we pray for our friends, and also for those who count themselves our enemies, we shall inevitably be the better qualified to serve and help them. The second is that if these others know we are praying for them, in sincerity of love and not in captious disapproval, they themselves will be encouraged to live more bravely. Past this, more things are wrought by prayer than this world dreams of; and the Christian does not exclude the possibility that the Spirit of God will enter the heart of another even as he has come into his own.

The earliest Old Testament stories remind us of another aspect of prayer which all too often has been forgotten in our day. It is that the road of prayer is one which is traveled in both directions. By prayer we draw nearer to God; and in prayer also God comes nearer to us. This means that in praying we not only speak to our heavenly Father, but also, and even more vitally, that we prepare ourselves to hear his voice speaking to us. We need therefore to express ourselves in prayer, and we need no less to provide for ourselves time and opportunities to receive the replies that God will make to us. The moments of quiet before and after the service well may be used to this end; and in the service too, if we don't insist on talking all of the time, we verily may hear the word of God in our hearts.

At this point of God's part in prayer we may find some clarification too of the problem of what constitutes a valid "answer." In a Methodist prayer meeting, many years ago, there had been numerous testimonies alleging external answers to prayer: sudden bodily healing, unexpected increments of money, providential securing of jobs. Then there rose an old lady, not formally educated but extremely wise. "We've been hearing," she said, "a lot about God saying 'Yes'

when we've prayed to him. I think we ought to remember that sometimes God says 'No,' and that that's just as truly an answer."

Prayer according to the will of God can mean no other. Even
the inner blessings we seek may not be those which he intends for
us; and if he gives us continuing problems instead of resolutions, and
a sense of failure rather than unbroken joy, we still must say, "Thy
will be done." "As may be most expedient for them," reads the prayer
of St. John Chrysostom which Cranmer introduced into the English
service from the Eastern ones. It is God alone who is qualified to be
the judge of ultimate expediency for us. The essential function of
prayer, then, is not that we should urge God to conform to our wills,
but that we should be brought readily and gladly to conform our
wills to his.

THE WORDS OF PRAYER

The prayers of the Church thus are expressions of praise for God's
worthiness, of thanksgiving for his great glory, of submission to his
will, and of dedication to his service. The prayers in their own character are not words at all. They are acts of faith and attitudes of heart.
The words of prayer, in every circumstance but especially in the
public service, are not themselves prayer, but are means by which we
are helped to pray in spirit and in truth. It follows that our choice
of words must be determined by the extent to which the words will
aid us toward our genuine, united, and personal praying.

Always it must be remembered that while the prayers are made by
the congregation, and the words are chosen for its sake, the prayer
and the words alike should be addressed not to the congregation but
to God. "That was the finest prayer I ever heard offered to a Congregational audience," said the little old lady from down the block.
The wording of too many so-called prayers indeed is patently designed to impress the congregation rather than to help it to pray; and
all too many homilies, little and large, are cast in the form of prayers
though they are wholly lacking in prayerful content. Did anyone
listen to the turgid keynote speeches, miscalled "invocations," of
which clergymen of almost every faith delivered themselves at the
national political conventions of 1952? Who was aided by those
display orations to ascend into the hill of the Lord?

The great virtue of the ancient forms of prayer is that they reflect universal human needs and truly catholic aspirations. Their very survival through the centuries attests their power in helping to make the Christian's praying real, and their wide acceptance and use reflect their validity as expressions of authentic Christian faith. To substitute for them the extempore outpourings of one individual, in one limited situation, is to endanger at once orthodoxy and catholicity. The minister's responsibility in leading the congregation in prayer is so great that he may not lightly use the time of praying in unconsidered and unguarded verbiage.

The historic prayers are well phrased, too, in terms of literary and aesthetic quality. This is no less desirable for the words of prayer than it is for those of hymns and of biblical translations. The words we use in our seeking of God are offerings to him, and they never should be other than the best we can find or devise. Since in our own limitations we are unlikely often to devise better than has the body of the Church in all its generations, we shall do more wisely on the whole to search and find than to think newly to invent.

Another advantage held by those prayers which are available in our heritage is that typically they are brief and specific, whereas the single "pastoral prayer" in many of our services is lengthy and pitifully diffuse. John Wesley counseled his enthusiastic preachers against praying extempore more than eight or ten minutes at one time. This seems to us fearfully long; and for extempore prayer it is. Yet eight or ten minutes devoted to an extended series of short prayers will hold and direct the attention of the people without difficulty, for these prayers will guide the mind in turn toward one after another of the major concerns of the Christian fellowship. Without the clear breaks provided not only in the subject matter, but also explicitly in the recurring oblations and Amens, it is much more difficult to keep the congregation truly praying in their hearts while the minister is using his voice.

It is patent that if the people themselves are to join audibly in the words of prayer, the written form again is of the essence. The congregation must have the words before it, or must have used certain forms of words so often that it can join in their use heartily and without hesitation. The traditional Protestant distrust of "canned prayers" has issued practically in forbidding the congregation ever to join together in vocal prayer except for the Lord's Prayer; and the restriction to this one brief formula produces that total neglect of its meaning which was noted above. At least the General Confession and the General Thanksgiving, or their equivalents, should be included in each regular service. Only thus can the voice of the people begin adequately to offer the people's prayer to God.

There are occasional times and circumstances, in the life of a parish or its members, or of the community or the nation, when it may seem necessary to use a form of words not provided in any prayer book. These occasions are fewer than might be supposed, as will be evident to anyone who searches the books to see what is available in them. When they do arise, they should be met by serious and careful preparation of forms which are in keeping with the historic tradition; not only for tradition's sake, but especially that the people most closely involved shall be encouraged to realize their sharing in a fellowship that always has turned to God for help and strength in all its hours of need, and that concerns itself with the special needs of its every member.

The minister who is convinced that he can do better (that is, that he can aid the congregation better in their praying) in his own words than in someone else's ought first to examine his judgment, and no less his attainment of Christian humility. If still he finds himself impelled to proceed in his own right, then he is required to proceed prior to eleven twenty o'clock on Sunday morning. To approach God personally without preparation of heart is worthless. To presume to aid the congregation to approach God, without considered preparation of the words intended thus to aid, and with the inevitably resulting disorder and repetitiousness, is neither religiously reverent nor practically sensible.

In the individually written prayer, as definitely as in the use of existing forms, the brief, direct paragraph means more always than does the wandering essay. The traditional form of the collect will repay careful study; and the practice of writing collects within that form will develop not only literary sensibility but also spiritual devotion. (As a happy by-product, it often will lead the writer to set aside his own experiments in favor of older and wiser examples.) The collect begins with an address to God, generally including a descriptive expression relevant to the specific subject of the prayer; then the petition itself, best phrased in a single sentence; and a conclusion conforming the prayer to the enduring Christian awareness that we come to God the Father through his Son Jesus Christ our Lord.

The first published ritual innovation of the Church of England was Cranmer's Litany of 1544. This survives, with only minor changes, in the Anglican prayer books of today. Here is a striking example of a fairly long form of prayer, requiring some ten minutes for its saying, which by variation of subject and pattern, and by provision of frequent congregational responses, escapes monotony and precludes inattention. A new and brief Litany for Ordinations, written chiefly by Bishop Charles Lewis Slattery of Massachusetts for the American prayer book of 1928, lends itself to general use by the omission of immediate reference to the persons being ordained. Many litanies, on various themes and of varying merit, have appeared in recent years. The form is one worthy of more study and wider employment, as an effective means toward a greater congregational sharing in the words as well as the act of prayer.

Akin to the technique of the Litany is that of the "Bidding Prayer." In this the congregation prays silently, but with recurring suggestion of themes by the minister. The example in the present American Episcopal prayer book is a relatively new composition, attributed to the late Bishop Cortland Whitehead of Pittsburgh. The usage goes back through the Church of England to the very earliest days, and appears in the intercessions in the Roman ritual for Good Friday. In this practice the periods of silence emphasize not only the worshiper's individual responsibility in corporate prayer, but also his opportunity to hear on his own part the still, small voice of revelation.

POSTURES OF PRAYER

There is significant biblical and churchly precedent both for standing and for kneeling to pray. There is none, prior to polemical anti-Romanism, for sitting. The faithful Jew of today stands rather than kneels, not because he thinks kneeling improper, but precisely because he regards it as a practice belonging to the Temple so loved and so long lost, and because he awaits that Temple's restoration before he will venture to assume the pose which was that of his fathers.

Russian Orthodoxy makes no provision whatever for sitting down during its long and involved service, except in the case of the aged and decrepit. The congregation alternately stands and kneels, and the latter without benefit of kneeling benches or hassocks. The Greek churches in America have conceded enough to prevailing fashion to install seats, but they still expect their people to kneel and stand at the appropriate points in the liturgy.

General usage among Lutherans provides that they shall stand for prayer, though in most churches they kneel for the Confession, and of course to receive the Communion. Anglican practice reproduces that of the historic Western Church, guided by the formula "Stand to speak or praise, sit to listen, kneel to pray." Methodists used to do this till not very long ago, though in recent years they seem to have been overborne by Congregationalist and Presbyterian modes of behavior.

The objection to kneeling originally was a phase of the extreme Protestant rejection of all the symbols that had been used and respected in the Roman Church. Its product has been the curious one of presuming to address God from the most casual and least respectful of the physical positions into which man can put himself. If the people of a given parish simply can not bring themselves to kneel, at least they might have courtesy and grace enough to stand when they are addressing themselves to the divine Majesty.

In practice it is necessary that the minister shall stand for some of the briefer prayers, especially when his duties require that he be standing immediately at the prayer's conclusion. Thus the first prayers of the Communion service are said standing, and only the Confession and the Prayer of Humble Access (the points of deepest humility and submission) with the minister kneeling. In the service of the Morning Prayer type the minister should kneel at his place in the chancel for the series of prayers, or the equivalent "pastoral prayer," before the sermon, and at the altar for those after it.

There is no justification for the minister's facing the congregation when he prays in the regular services of the Church. Since he is praying with the people rather than to them or at them, he should turn with them toward the altar, which for him as for them is the focal symbol of the presence of God in his own house. Thus for the minister reverently to lead the congregation, rather than seeming to differentiate himself from it, will help both him and his people genuinely to pray together to their one Lord.

The only proper exceptions to this last rule are the declaration of absolution if it is used, and a blessing or benediction couched in the "you" form. The "grace" of II Corinthians 13:14, the historic ending of Morning and Evening Prayer, is rightly said kneeling, for it unites minister and people in its final "be with us all." The Communion blessing, with its "be amongst you, and remain with you always," while it is a prayer to God, is also a word of assurance directed toward the people, and so is said by the minister standing and facing them.

In this connection it may be remarked that the Scriptures offer many forms of benediction in addition to those which commonly are set forth in the prayer books. There are also some nobly phrased blessings from the ancient Eastern liturgies, whose use would enrich the final moments of our services. A few examples from each of these sets of sources are noted in Appendix H. Often it will be found possible to end the service with a blessing which reflects the specific theme of the hour, and provides for it one last direct emphasis, the while also it bespeaks the divine grace upon the departing congregation.

Our prayer then is to God, and its words are designed to help God's people truly to pray to him. Realizing this, we may not do other than to seek to pray always decently and in order. With the Church of all the ages we offer ourselves to serve him whose service is perfect freedom. With the universal Church of today we pray for its peace and unity according to the will of our Lord Jesus Christ. With our fellow members of the local parish we confess our personal failures, and we declare our gratitude for God's continuing mercies to us.

"Let us pray" means all of this; and meaning this, it means also that each of us by the words of our common praying may be led into that personal converse with God which is the high privilege of those who love him and whom he calls according to his purpose.

> O thou, by whom we come to God,
> The Life, the Truth, the Way;
> The path of prayer thyself hast trod:
> Lord, teach us how to pray.

Our Lord has taught us in his words recorded in the Gospels, and also through the words in which his Church has prayed in his Name in all the years. To use the words aright is to rise beyond the instrumental words to the ultimate reality of the life that is hid with Christ in God. "Let us pray." This is, if we will make it so, our introduction to the absolute reality of worship.

IX

THE LESSON IS FOUND

THAT "THE THINGS which were written aforetime were written for our learning" is true only in part. They were written primarily for their first readers, not consciously for generations long afterward to come. Consequently our learning is hampered, at the outset, by the fact that the points of reference are not ours, but those of the times and circumstances in which the ancient writings took form. We have not inherited quite the same cultural settings, and we do not hold quite the same assumptions, as did the authors and the people for whom immediately they wrote. Sometimes it is easy for us to determine what their assumptions were, sometimes it is difficult, and now and then it may prove quite impossible to be sure. Always it is necessary to compare the older cultures with ours before we may hope rightly to find, in what was said, just what originally was meant.

Nevertheless the writings of former days often have spoken, eloquently and effectively, to the later generations. Israel preserved, collated, and compiled the written material which had taken form over a reach of perhaps twelve hundred years. The early Christians did the same with products of the first century of the life of the Church. The reading of the Jewish documents already had become an important part of worship in the synagogues. The Church followed this precedent, first with the sacred books of the Jews and soon afterward with the Christians' own. Thus the lesson has been found, and has been read publicly in the services, for well over twenty centuries. What may we find the lesson to be for us in the twentieth?

145

How shall we select it? How shall we read it? What may we hope to learn from it?

Briefly described, the Hebrew Bible is the surviving literature in the Hebrew language belonging to the period before the first century of our era. Its earliest fragments were folk ballads, such as the song of Deborah and David's "song of the bow." Then came prose folk tales, exemplified by the cycle of stories about Adam and Eve and their first children. As the tales were retold they were adapted to new audiences and adjusted to new points of view. Thus we have both the ninth century collection of stories from Judah, and the eighth century versions which were current in North Israel. The last retelling of the early tales which we have in our Bible is the much more sophisticated one of the priestly writers, dating from the fifth or possibly the fourth century B.C.

In the year 621 there was found in the Temple a book of law purporting to be from the hand of Moses. Internal evidence suggests that in fact it was written not very long before its discovery, and that it had been hidden precisely in order that it might be discovered. Nevertheless this book of Deuteronomy had a mighty effect upon the immediate situation in Judah, leading the young king Josiah straightway into his campaign for centralized worship in Jerusalem, with the attendant destruction of all the outlying shrines. This therefore may be thought of as the first Hebrew document to be invested with what we would call scriptural authority.

The law of Deuteronomy, produced in the seventh century, did not cover all the conditions of two hundred years later. In particular it did not authenticate in detail the Temple ceremonies as now they were being performed. Seeking to strengthen their position, the priests of this later day wrote out the rules which in fact they were following; and in conformity with the precedent of Deuteronomy they attributed these regulations to revelation in the wilderness days. Thus there was created that theoretical tabernacle which was examined in Chapter III, an imaginary background for the actual Temple of the postexilic period.

The next step was the uniting of all these strands of folk narrative and legislation into a compact and apparently unified body of material.

The product was our "five books of Moses," or "the Pentateuch." Because it was thought of chiefly in its legal character, the whole collection was called the Torah, or law, despite the fact that it contains much that is not legislation. By 250 B.C. at the latest the Torah had become the authoritative religious literature of Judaism; and always it has held the highest place alike in Jewish thought and in the usages of Jewish worship.

Much earlier in origin than the priestly parts of the Torah were a number of other works. Among these were accounts of the settlement in Palestine, and of events in the history of the Israelite and Jewish kingdoms. Some of these narratives appear to have been almost contemporaneous with the events they record, but all were reedited, probably in the sixth century, from the point of view of the authors of Deuteronomy. These are the books of Judges, Samuel, and Kings, substantially as we have them today. The book of Joshua, from the literary point of view often classified with the Torah to constitute a Hexateuch rather than a Pentateuch, shows decisive marks of having been edited by priestly hands.

There had been preserved also a number of quite unofficial writings, religious in assumption but largely political and polemical in content, and commonly reflecting minority protests against existing practices and policies in the kingdoms of Israel and Judah. Amos, Hosea, Isaiah 1–35, Nahum, Micah, Jeremiah, and Zephaniah belong to this category. The tradition of individual and independent writing was continued, though the mood was much altered, in the exile by Ezekiel and the unnamed author of Isaiah 40–55; at its ending in 520 by Haggai and Zechariah; and later in such works as the little books of Obadiah, Jonah, Joel, Habakkuk, and Malachi.

The early narrative works other than the Torah came by the Jews to be described as "the former prophets," and the polemic or didactic as "the latter prophets." It will be observed that this classification excludes prediction as a necessary characteristic of prophecy. By the middle of the second century B.C., all of the books of the prophets had become generally accepted as works of divine inspiration and religious authority. They never attained to equality with the Torah, however, and to this day they stand on a lower plane both in Jewish evaluation and in the reading practices of the synagogues.

Through all this time the writing and compiling of the Psalms of the Temple had been in progress. Other Jewish writings began to appear and circulate: the short stories of Ruth and Esther, the philosophy of Proverbs, Ecclesiastes, and Job, the diaries attributed to Nehemiah and Ezra, the priestly rewriting of the national history in the books of Chronicles, the acrostic Lamentations over the fate of Jerusalem, the visions of Daniel, the love poetry called the Song of Songs. In Alexandria the Jewish community translated all the Hebrew works into Greek, adding to them new materials in Daniel and Esther, and some wholly new books as well.

In the time of Jesus we find the Hebrew Scriptures mentioned most commonly as "the Law and the prophets," but occasionally as "Law, prophets, and Psalms." The necessary rethinking and reorganization of Jewish positions after the destruction of the Temple included a restudy of the standing of all these materials. A council of rabbis meeting at Jamnia (Jabneel) in southwestern Palestine, just before the end of the first century, debated the matter at length. Ultimately it assigned sacred value to all the Hebrew materials under consideration, though not without much dispute about Ecclesiastes, the Song of Songs, and the book of Esther. Indeed there is some evidence that certain of the rabbis were opposed to the acceptance of these works as late as the third century after Christ. The Palestinian consensus excluded all writings not extant in a Hebrew text, and so denied to the Apocrypha ("the hidden ones") a place in the authoritative Bible of orthodox Judaism.

The product, so far as content is concerned, was the Old Testament as Protestants know it today, but it was and is quite differently arranged. The first and foremost division is the Torah. The second is that of the *Nebi'im*, the prophets, divided as we have seen into "former" and "latter." Third, and on the lowest plane, is all the rest of the material, titled merely as the *Kethubim*, "books" or "writings."

SCRIPTURES OF THE CHRISTIANS

For Jesus and his contemporaries in Palestine, then, the Scripture proper included only Law and prophets, with the Psalms holding a marginal place. When in the next generation the Church found itself speaking Greek rather than Hebrew or Aramaic, it turned naturally to the Greek text which was available to it in Alexandria. The first Bible of the Christians therefore was that of the Alexandrian Jews, including in addition to the Hebrew canonical books such works as Ecclesiasticus and the Wisdom of Solomon, Judith and Tobit, and I and II Maccabees.

Following Jewish precedent, the Christians read from the Hebrew Scriptures in their services, though almost universally in the Greek language. Their special interest was in the prophets rather than in the Law, not only because St. Paul had been pronouncedly anti-legalistic, but also because in the Christian view the prophets appeared to have predicted the coming of the Christ and many of the details of Jesus' life. A technique commonly used to adjust other Hebrew writings directly to Christian use was that of allegory, as in St. Paul's deliberately reversed treatment of the Hagar and Ishmael story in Galatians 4, and later in the interpreting of the Song of Songs as referring to the love between Christ and his Church. Lack of acquaintance with the original Hebrew text gave rise sometimes to special Christian arguments based upon Greek mistranslations, such as St. Matthew's use of "virgin" instead of "young woman" in Isaiah 7:14, and the elaborate and rather labored discussion of the status of angels in Hebrews 1f., based largely upon the mistaken "angels" for "God" in Psalm 8:5.

The life of the Christian community soon began to produce its own documents, occasioned first by practical necessity rather than by any idea of creating a new body of Scripture. The earliest Christian writings we have are the letters of St. Paul, with those to the Church at Thessalonica (the modern Saloniki) the first in point of time. When writing to the Colossians, about A.D. 59 or 60, the apostle suggests that the epistle "be read also in the church of the Laodiceans," eleven miles away. Such interchange of letters seems to have led to the assembling of a body of Pauline materials, circulated first in western Asia Minor, which may be regarded as the nucleus of our New Testament.

With the passing of the generation which remembered our Lord in the flesh, it became important to set down the record of his life on earth. The four Gospels, of which that of St. Mark is the earliest, took their present form between A.D. 65 and 110. St. Mark's is thought to be Roman in origin, and to reflect the story as St. Peter had been accustomed to tell it. It provides the outline of events which all the other Gospels follow, and much of the actual text of St. Matthew and St. Luke.

St. Matthew's Gospel, associated with Syrian Antioch, devotes itself largely to proving that Jesus indeed was the expected Jewish Messiah. St. Luke's, supposed to have originated in or near Corinth, attempts to restate the record for Greek readers, and is specially concerned with the humanitarian aspects of Jesus' teaching and ministry. The Fourth Gospel, bearing the name of St. John, is a thoroughly Greek and "spiritual" reinterpretation rather than a factual narrative. In time all four of these varying literary portraits of Jesus became generally known throughout the Church, though the practically minded Romans long were reluctant to accept the Fourth Gospel's philosophical approach and mystical emphasis.

Other Christian writings soon began to appear, from various hands and representing various points of view. Some of these were respectfully attributed by their writers to one or another of the apostles, not in any conscious dishonesty but in the effort to assure circulation and acceptance for what the real authors thought the apostles would have said in a new day. Of these are notably the two letters ascribed to St. Peter, those named for St. James and St. Jude, and probably the Revelation of St. John. In other cases existing apostolic writings were revised or expanded to meet changing conditions. Examples are Ephesians, which is a generalized rewriting of Colossians, and many additions to St. Paul's authentic but brief notes to his young friends Timothy and Titus.

In the middle of the second century, according to St. Justin the Martyr, "the memoirs of the apostles or the writings of the prophets" were read at the beginning of each celebration of the Eucharist. This implies that functionally the Gospels now had been accorded scriptural status. At about the same time the pseudonymous II St. Peter explicitly puts the writings of St. Paul into the same category:

his epistles . . . in which are some things hard to be understood, which they that are unlearned and unstable wrest, as they do also the other scriptures, unto their own destruction.

The first attempt formally to create an independently Christian canon of Holy Scripture was made not by the Church itself, but by a heretic. Marcion, a ship captain of Pontus, rejected the Old Testament as being altogether false. For it he proposed to substitute writings of the Christian revelation, which he identified in ten letters of St. Paul (not including I and II Timothy, Titus, and Hebrews) and an abridged text of the Gospel of St. Luke.

The Church reacted not by rejecting this suggestion altogether, but by amplifying it to include Christian materials which themselves dealt favorably with the Jewish tradition. Thus a list current in Rome about the year 180, known to us as the "Muratorian fragment" from the name of the Italian scholar who discovered it in the eighteenth century, recognized four Gospels, the Acts, thirteen letters of St. Paul, the first and second epistles of St. John and that of St. Jude, and the Revelation of St. John. These, it will be noted, total twenty-two out of the twenty-seven books of our New Testament, leaving out only Hebrews, I and II St. Peter, St. James, and III St. John. The Muratorian canon mentioned also the Wisdom of Solomon and the Revelation of St. Peter, neither of which was to retain its place in the final formulation.

Through the third century discussion was lively and juagments were actively contested. A few books now relegated to the "apocryphal New Testament," such as the epistle of Barnabas and I Clement, once stood in high favor, and several in our present canon were vigorously challenged. The first listing which coincides fully with that of the New Testament as we know it is one made by the historian Eusebius, Bishop of Caesarea, about A.D. 325. This still is divided into a group which Eusebius describes as "accepted by all," the Gospels, Acts, fourteen Paulines, I St. Peter, I St. John, and the Revelation, and one of writings "accepted by most," St. James, St. Jude, II and III St. John, and II St. Peter. Actually the Revelation of St. John is mentioned again within a third category of generally rejected books, indicating that recent controversy about its value has very early precedent.

Not until A.D. 397 was there official action taken on the specific content of the Christian body of Scripture; and this, by the Third Synod of Carthage, technically was binding on North Africa only. Nevertheless it was generally accepted as normative, though it was not to secure formal ratification for the whole Roman Church until the sixteenth century Council of Trent. Protestants never have challenged the New Testament canon thus developed and taken for granted, as witness the reference in the Anglican sixth Article of Religion (the Methodist fifth) to "all the books of the New Testament, as they are commonly received."

PROTESTANT REVALUATION

The Greek canon of the Old Testament, including the Apocrypha, remained unquestioned until the time of Luther. The reference to prayers and sacrifices for the dead in II Maccabees 12, eagerly seized upon by defenders of the Roman views of purgatory and of the system of indulgences, was most embarrassing to Protestant assailants to those positions. In order to find a means of eliminating this from the category of authoritative Scripture, the Protestant disputants found themselves forced to repudiate the entire body of writings of which copies did not survive in a Hebrew text. Thus the Apocrypha were excluded from the Old Testament of Protestantism, five verses for internal cause and the rest by a circumstance of language. Thereby a great deal of interesting material, and some unquestionably inspiring, ever since has been effectively denied a Protestant hearing. The English Church indeed said that the Apocrypha were to be "read for example of life and instruction of manners," but Wesley omitted all reference to them when he rewrote the article "Of the Sufficiency of the Holy Scriptures for Salvation."

The Apocrypha regularly were printed in English Bibles, though placed in a separate unit between the Old and New Testaments, until early in the nineteenth century. It appears that then the British and Foreign Bible Society, anxious to economize in its beneficent work and so to spread the Scriptures more widely, decided to save the printing cost of what was considered secondary material. Commercial publishers, hearing no decided protest from the public, rapidly followed suit; with the result that a negligible number of Protestants today have even seen the Apocrypha, let alone possess a copy. The University of Chicago *The Complete Bible: An American Translation*, including the Apocrypha as translated by Dr. Edgar J. Goodspeed, marks a healthy and useful return to the practice that was normal until just over a century ago.

Protestant emphasis on absolute Scriptural authority was not nearly so uncritical in the early days as it has been in recent Fundamentalism. Luther, who rightly is credited with establishing the Bible as the authoritative substitute for the tradition of the Church, nevertheless had grave doubts about Esther ("It contains a superfluity of heathen naughtiness"), St. James (*recht ströherne:* "right strawy"), and the Revelation, which last after some hesitation he translated, but relegated to the appendix of his German Bible along with the Apocrypha. Luther also denied St. Paul's authorship of the epistle to the Hebrews, and nominated Apollos as a more likely candidate.

While John Calvin used the Old Testament as the basis for his theocratic legal system at Geneva, he declared that the Sabbath regulations had been abrogated by the Christian revelation, and that they had no bearing on the Christian use of Sunday as a day of worship. In the realm of criticism Calvin set aside the traditional authorship of a number of the Psalms, identifying some as coming from the time of the Maccabees in the second century B.C. Revising the Psalter for the use of American Methodists, John Wesley left out "many Psalms . . . and many parts of the others, as being highly improper for the mouths of a Christian congregation." Thus in practice the Protestant leaders continued what had been begun so long before, in testing the Scriptures by their inherent quality the while also they tested the quality of Christian life by the Scriptures.

READINGS IN THE SYNAGOGUE

The reading of the Torah has been one of the most solemn and significant parts of Jewish worship from the compiling of the books and the beginnings of the synagogue. The calf-skin scroll, always written entirely by hand, is taken ceremonially from the Sacred Ark, while specified prayers and scriptural verses are recited. Following the repetition of the *Shema*, the scroll is carried in procession round the synagogue. It then is unrolled, and readers are called up to take their turns in reading the sections specified for the day. In ancient Palestine the entire Torah was read through in the space of three years, but later this scheme was revised to provide for a complete annual reading.

When the knowledge of Hebrew still was general in the Jewish community, the reading was widely distributed among the men of the congregation. Later it came to be assigned chiefly to the *chazan*, or cantor, or to a special reader chosen by the congregation to represent it. Every Jewish boy, however, reads a portion at his *bar-mitzvah* (confirmation); and this reading, which marks his recognition as an adult man of Israel, is counted a high and never-to-be-forgotten privilege.

When the readings of the day are completed, the scroll is lifted up while the congregation says a paragraph beginning "And this is the Torah which Moses set before the children of Israel," and including "It is a tree of life to them that grasp it." Then the scroll is rolled up, covered with its mantle, and left on the desk during the reading from the prophets.

While the Torah invariably is read in Hebrew, and from the unpointed (vowel-less) text, the prophets most commonly are read in the language of the country. The prophetic selections are much the briefer, averaging about twenty-one verses; and they are accompanied only by one short blessing before and one after. Attention then returns to the Torah scroll, which is reverently replaced in the Ark after a number of additional prayers and Psalms.

The "five rolls," Lamentations, the Song of Songs, Ruth, Ecclesiastes, and Esther, are read in the service on specified occasions in the religious year. The book of Psalms of course provides many of the prayers and chants. Otherwise the third section of the Hebrew canon, that of "the writings," receives very little attention. Daniel, Job, and the books of Chronicles never are given place in the sequence of synagogue readings.

LESSONS IN THE CHURCH

Christian practice, as has been noted, differed first from the Jewish in emphasizing the prophets rather than the Law, and then in the adding of specifically Christian materials. The letters of St. Paul and "the memoirs of the apostles" thus early set the precedent for the use of epistle and gospel in the service of the Eucharist. By the fourth century the Psalms were distributed over the seven days of the week, for regular use in the monastic offices, and lessons for Sundays and holy days were assigned in the sacramentaries. In the late Middle Ages these lessons sometimes included, in addition to passages from the Old and New Testaments, selections from the so-called "New Testament apocrypha," and even from later martyrologies.

Cranmer's preface to the prayer book of 1549 referred to the way in which the "auncient fathers" had

so ordered the matter, that all the whole Bible (or the greatest parte thereof) should be read ouer once in the yeare . . . that the people (by daily hearyng of holy scripture read in the Churche) should continually

profite more and more in the knowledge of God, and bee the more influenced with the love of his true religion.

More recently, he protested,

this Godly and decent ordre of the auncient fathers, hath bee(n) so altered,
broken, and neglected, by planting in uncertain stories, Legēdes, Re-
spondes, Verses, vaine repeticions, Commemoracions, and Synodalles,
that commonly when any boke of the Bible was begon: before three or
foure Chapiters were read out, all the rest were unread.

The reorganization which Cranmer made provided for the reading
of almost the entire Bible within a year, at daily Morning and Evening
Prayer. Twelve holy days and three Sundays (Easter, Whitsunday,
and Trinity) were provided with lessons regarded as appropriate to
the several occasions, but otherwise the lectionary followed the civil
calendar of dates rather than the religious one of seasons and festivals.
Cranmer included lessons from the Old Testament Apocrypha, but
none from Chronicles or the book of Revelation. The Psalms were to
be said or sung in a monthly cycle. For the Holy Communion the
epistles and gospels still followed the pattern of the ancient sacramentaries, with some modifications dependent upon the Sarum use.

In 1559, under Elizabeth I, the remaining fixed feasts were provided with "proper" lessons, and a "first lesson" was set for each
Sunday of the Church year. The scheme as thus revised still is the
official one of the Church of England. Further changes were made by
the Protestant Episcopal Church in the United States in 1789, 1892,
and 1943. The present American Episcopal lectionary for Morning
and Evening prayer has abandoned the civil calendar entirely, and
like that for the Holy Communion seeks to provide materials appropriate to the respective subjects of emphasis of the ecclesiastical days
and seasons. The Psalms also are assigned in terms of content rather
than merely of sequence and date. Revision of the epistle and gospel
selections for the Communion is under consideration, and is likely
soon to be determined.

The Puritans objected in particular to Cranmer's inclusion of
readings from the Apocrypha, but also in general to being required
to adhere to any fixed scheme. The most recent Presbyterian *Book of
Common Worship* (1946), however, has swung sharply back toward
the Anglican tradition, providing a two-year cycle of proper Psalms
and lessons, and epistle and gospel selections for the Holy Com-

munion, for all Sundays, for nine other holy days, and for nine added special occasions. There is much more than a 50 per cent agreement between the Presbyterian and American Episcopal lists of Epistles and Gospels.

John Wesley preserved, and transmitted to the Methodists in America, the lectionary for the Communion, the proper lessons for Sundays, and proper Psalms for the major festivals. All this soon was forgotten on this side of the Atlantic, and early was left out of the official books of American Methodism. The 1944 *Book of Worship* supplied a wholly independent lectionary of lessons for each Sunday of the year, and for twelve other holy days, in which only a very few of the "first lessons" were from the Old Testament, the great majority being taken from the New Testament Epistles, and the "second lessons" without exception from the Gospels. This book has also, attached to the ritual for the Holy Communion, a "lectionary of suggested lessons" for twelve Sundays (Advent, Lent, Easter, Whitsunday, and Trinity) and for six festivals. Here fourteen of the twenty-eight Epistles, and nine of the Gospels, coincide with Mr. Wesley's listing of 1784, and so with that of the English Prayer Book of 1662. The coincidence with the current American *Book of Common Prayer* is even closer, the Epistle being the same in eighteen cases and the Gospel in thirteen.

Lutherans use a number of slightly varying lectionaries in their several autonomous bodies, but each of them provides for each Sunday and holy day a lesson from the Old Testament as well as epistle and Gospel selections. The Lutherans, along with the Anglicans, follow their lectionaries faithfully, whereas most of the Presbyterians and Methodists seem as yet to pay scant attention to what their leaders have advised. Aside from these four groups, American Protestantism until very recently has known scarcely anything of an organized plan for acquainting worshipers with the total content of holy writ.

The Congregationalists in 1948, however, with their *Book of Worship for Free Churches*, and the Disciples in 1953, with G. Edwin Osborn's *Christian Worship: A Service Book*, have provided for their people what so long has been lacking. The Congregational lectionary covers a two-year period, with Psalm, Old Testament lesson, Gospel, and Epistle for each Sunday of the traditional calendar, and for ten festivals and holy days. Psalms and lessons are indicated also for a number of national holidays and special occasions. The Osborn listing is more closely adjusted to the civil calendar than to that of the Church, but includes Palm Sunday, Easter, Pentecost, and Christmas. An ingenious tabulation makes it possible to vary the readings over a five-year cycle. With these now available, the great majority of Protestants in America have in their hands definite reading plans at least officially approved, if not required, by their respective denominational authorities.

SELECTION OF THE LESSONS

A lectionary may help particularly in guarding against the hackneying of a few passages while losing sight of much else of real interest and deep significance. Geared as they are to the thought sequences of the Christian year, the lectionaries that are available today offer many suggestions of appropriate passages for specific themes. Always it is worth checking to see what the appointed lessons, and the accompanying Psalms, may offer to supplement personal memory of relevant materials.

The wealth of the Bible is so great, and the time we have available for reading it in public is so little, that careful planning is of the essence. The importance of using both the Old Testament and the New in every Sunday service has been suggested in Chapter VI. Unless we do this we not only cut the learning possibilities provided by the lessons in half, but also we deny to our people either the early Christian or (as more commonly) the ancient Jewish estimate of the given problem or value. Similarly any large amount of repetition can result only in limiting experience and knowledge, by its inevitable denial of the hearing of less familiar passages.

In the nature of the case the lessons should be relevant to the theme of the day, which also will be the theme of the sermon. Ideally one of the lessons should include the sermon's text, and thereby will inform the people (and, it may be hoped, remind the preacher) of the immediate context, without which no single text can be rightly and fully interpreted and understood. Aside from lectionaries, a concordance may be useful in directing attention to related materials, and in many cases commentaries will help. No outside aid, however, can take the place of the minister's own thorough acquaintance with the Scriptures, and his persistent and daily searching of them.

It will not be seriously urged today that quite all of the Bible is appropriate for public reading in the Church. There is little edification in the genealogies of the priestly chroniclers, and there are a few tales in the early books that would be looked on with grave concern by the Watch and Ward Society if now they were to appear in twenty-five-cent softbacks. Cranmer, following Jewish usage, left out all of the books of Chronicles, and we probably would not want to restore very much. The new American Episcopal lectionary includes only three brief selections from this late rewriting of the historical records, and the several Lutheran systems no more, while the 1946 Presbyterian list of lessons includes none at all.

On the other hand, there is much in the Bible that we have not explored adequately for reading materials, and which in consequence our people scarcely know. This is particularly true of the latter prophets, who have much to say to our age of strife and confusion. The Apocrypha, too, now that we are beginning to recover from our unreasoning fear of anything supposed to be Roman, richly will repay an investigation of their vivid narratives and their reverent meditations.

Very occasionally it may be permissible to use extrabiblical materials as lessons. One legitimate type of case would be that in which the sermon dealt directly with a postbiblical Christian hero. A passage from the *Institutes of the Christian Religion,* for example, might throw much light upon the mind of Calvin, or one from the *Selected Sermons* on that of John Wesley. A sermon on the problems and significance of biblical translation well might be accompanied by a reading from the 1611 preface, quoted in the section immediately following this. Selections from the sacred books of other religions may be appropriate, in conjunction with our own Scriptures, when the sermon is to discuss a given non-Christian faith.

Caution is needed at this point, however. While in view of the rather casual way in which the biblical canon was determined, there can be no a priori reason for restricting one's self wholly to it, it is extremely dangerous to "shop around" for nonbiblical writings on general themes. Not only do they carry less of inherent authority for the listeners, but in most cases they neither convey such sound doctrine, nor employ such adequate language, as do passages readily available within the Scriptures themselves. Many of the semisecular readings heard in professedly "liberal" churches are sentimental in the extreme, and most of them must be counted ephemeral until and unless time proves otherwise. Until we have prospected much more deeply in the mines of Scriptural treasure, we ought not to content ourselves with the untested miscellany that lies scattered about the pithead.

Normally the lessons should not be long. A dozen verses clearly related in meaning will do much better teaching than will a whole chapter dealing with a variety of subjects. It is sound practice also to omit obvious irrelevancies, which occur rather often in the Old Testament because of the way in which its books were compiled and edited. In some special cases it may be found helpful to bring together two short passages on a single theme, especially when there are significant variations in treatment. Thus for example a prophetic and a priestly section might be conjoined for a first lesson, or parallel paragraphs from Colossians and Ephesians for a second.

CHOOSING TRANSLATIONS

Three centuries of usage have made the King James version the standard one for reading in our services. So strong is this habit that even the New Testament translations issued by John Wesley (1755) and Alexander Campbell (1827) have been firmly ignored by the denominations which trace their foundings respectively to these two brave and learned gentlemen. The version of 1611 has the advantage of being phrased in what we regard as fitting liturgical language, and unquestionably it is one of the greatest monuments of English literature. When its rendering is accurate, and its meaning clear, there can be no objection to its use; and so it is rightly to be retained in most cases.

There are not a few sections, however, in which this revered and beloved translation is either inaccurate, or unclear, or both. Here the principle of "a tongue understanded of the people" surely should prevail over attachment to a single form of words. Particularly in the writings of St. Paul the 1611 syntax is badly involved—almost as badly as was the apostle's own—and the seventeenth century vocabulary often conveys little of meaning to the modern mind. If St. Paul is to be for our people the vital, exciting person that in himself he was, he needs to be brought to them in terms that they more readily can apprehend.

We shall do well to remember that the translators of 1611 themselves had to reckon with strong prejudice against any sort of change. In their own preface, "The Translators to the Reader," they observed that

Whosoever attempteth any thing for the publick, (especially if it appertain to religion, and to the opening and clearing of the word of God) the same setteth himself upon a stage to be glouted upon by every evil eye; yea, he casteth himself headlong upon pikes, to be gored by every sharp tongue. For he that meddleth with men's religion in any part meddleth with their custom, nay, with their freehold; and though they find no content in that which they have, yet they cannot abide to hear of altering . . .

But how shall men meditate in that which they cannot understand? How shall they understand that which is kept close in an unknown tongue? . . . Nature taught a natural man to confess, that all of us in those tongues which we do not understand are plainly deaf; we may turn the deaf ear unto them.

This whole preface, which certainly ought to be printed regularly in our Bibles along with, or instead of, the fulsome address "to the most high and mighty prince James," well may be called to the attention of those who now regard the work of 1611 as the only authentic reproduction of the word of God.

Wesley and Campbell both realized the persisting though ever shifting problem of comprehension, and in making their New Testament versions they were trying to solve it for their own times. Our century has seen a flood of new translations, mostly of the New Testament, predicated upon the fact that the 1611 rendering sometimes is obscure and occasionally is positively misleading. Of individual efforts in this field those of Dr. James Moffatt (1912) and Dr. Edgar J. Goodspeed (1923) are the best known. Each of these has the advantage, too, of having a companion Old Testament: Moffatt's own work (1925) in the one case, and the joint enterprise of Dr. J. M. P. Smith and his associates (1927) in the other. Another admirable rendering, less well known than it deserves to be, is the compact and vigorous *Riverside New Testament* (1923) of Dr. W. G. Ballantine. Individually but with Church approval Father Ronald Knox, Roman Catholic son of an Anglican bishop of Birmingham, has made a translation of the whole Bible which ranks high in literary quality, and whose acquaintance is well worth the making.

No doubt it will be a long time before the Revised Standard Version (1946 and 1952), sponsored by the National Council of Churches, will be accepted into standard usage in our services. Immediately it will be of great help for individual reading and comprehension, and it ought both to be used by the clergy and to be recommended by them to their people. This, or some one of the other modern versions, should be introduced into the service, without hesitation or apology, whenever there is reasonable doubt about the accuracy or the clarity of the 1611 treatment of any given passage. Especially for the latter prophets, the stirring, rhythmic strophes of Dr. Moffatt often will be found to be a decided stimulus to the congregation's wakefulness and active thinking. And when the study of Hebrew and Greek regain their rightful place in the theological seminaries, perhaps we may hope that dominies again will be able to provide their own occasional renderings when no published one quite squares with their knowledge and understanding of the original.

READING OF THE LESSONS

Unless the lessons, and the particular versions, are selected carefully and prayerfully, their reading in the service of worship can not be other than perfunctory, and their effect is likely to be nil. Along with divers portions, though, there must be considered divers manners of treatment. With the choice of material and translation made, there still is the obligation upon the minister or other reader to read with understanding and conviction. This requires, for all except a genius, a thorough advance study of the passage, and if at all possible a vocal going through it to determine emphases, and to identify possible pitfalls of meaning or of sound. Such a line as "Lord, show us the Father, and it sufficeth us," can be an extraordinary tongue twister if one comes upon it unexpectedly.

Many churches have followed the old Jewish custom of calling on laymen for the reading of the lessons. This has decided merit in giving the laity a larger share in the activity of worship, and in allowing the congregation to hear a variety of voices. The only danger is that the reader may not be fully qualified, whether in understanding or in diction. Certainly the reading is too important to be assigned to an influential member of the parish merely because he enjoys the prestige it gives him, or because the parish gains prestige by having him thus on display. If a layman is to read, he must meet in full the conditions of ability, preliminary study, and seriousness of purpose. Whoever does the reading, only the minister is in a position to determine the selections; for the same reason as in the case of hymns, that only he can have an inclusive view, in advance, of how all the parts of the service will fit together.

The reading of the lessons in the service must find a middle course between the monster of dullness on the one hand and the whirlpool of overdramatization on the other. Lack of varied emphasis is deadly, but too much conscious elocution endangers real attention to the content. Above all things, the "holy tone" should be avoided. The Bible came out of man's quest for God, and always it must be heard in man's own world as it speaks to men of things divine. The reality of religious expression in the Bible can be altogether obscured, or it can be livingly set forth, depending on whether we treat the lesson as symbolic magic or as the ever vital, never ceasing revelation of God to those who seek him with the whole heart.

If the lesson is rightly read, it seldom will require additional comment at the time of its reading. Interpretative remarks tend to break the mood of worship, and belong rather to the sermon than at this point in the service. The exact reference always should be given, however, both in the leaflet and orally, so that the congregation will be reminded that this is only one small part of the great body of writings that constitute our Holy Scripture, and so that the more literate members will be able to relate this one section to its larger context. The traditional "Here beginneth the ———— verse of the ———— chapter of ————," and "Here endeth the ———— lesson," have the value of long precedent, are dignified in themselves, and in almost all cases will prove to be quite sufficient.

The Bible contains the record of truth as revealed over some fourteen centuries, and as expressed within our noble Hebrew-Christian tradition. Its contents deal with every phase of religious experience and aspiration, and its message still is a living one for those who have ears to hear. The solemn duty of the minister of the word is so to unstop the ears of the deaf, that they may hear the accents of all those who sought after God in the ancient days, and the revelations which God gave to those who sought him. "We desire that the Scripture may speak like itself, as in the language of Canaan, that it may be understood even of the very vulgar." This hope of the devout and courageous scholars of 1611 still must be the intent of the Church.

Since biblical times there have been many who have contributed to the new breaking forth of light out of God's word. The scholars have studied the problems of background and authorship, and thereby have been aided to discern ever deeper and truer meanings. The translators have made the Scriptures speak, "as in the language of Canaan," in all the tongues known to men. The compilers of the lectionaries have aided us at once to see the Bible as a whole, and appropriately to use its many and varying parts. It remains for the Church of our time to make its own selections wisely and well from day to day, and for him who is privileged to read in the service to do his reading at once in respect for the word and in eagerness to serve the people.

"From a child thou hast known the holy Scriptures, which are able to make thee wise unto salvation through faith which is in Christ Jesus." We have more of the Scriptures than Timothy had, for since his time the writings of the new covenant have been added to those of the old. In our day it has happened, despite our professions of devotion to the Bible and of dependence upon it, that most of our people do not know it well. The lesson rightly found, and devoutly and creatively read, yet may teach them much toward their becoming wise unto salvation through faith.

X

THAT HE MAY INTERPRET

"HOW SHALL THEY hear without a preacher?" They can worship without one, and often they should. But worship must involve understanding, and so the values involved in our worship now and then will need interpretation.

It is a striking fact that among the religions of mankind only Judaism and its descendants, Christianity and Islam, have given room to the specific interpreting of religious truth as a normal element in their services of worship. Judaism long ago lost its priests, with the loss of the Jerusalem Temple, but it has kept its rabbis. Christianity had preachers before it had priests of its own, and for many centuries it has had both, usually in the same person. Islam has no priests properly so called, but long has depended heavily upon the imam, the divinely inspired teacher or preacher.

Is this historic position of the three related religions a sound one? What is the value of preaching in the services which we hold? Has it a legitimate place in the practice of worship, and a genuine relevance to it? Can the sermon be made more worshipful, and more relevant, than commonly it has been? Is it possible for the preacher effectively to convey truth, to inspire faith, to guide behavior? Some of the answers must be sought in history, some in experiment, all in personal consecration.

A SHORT HISTORY OF PREACHING

The first preaching in Israel and Judah was not connected with the system of worship, and often was sharply antipathetic to it. Such prophets as Amos, Hosea, Isaiah, and Jeremiah repudiated the Temple sacrifices as being needless in approach to God and dangerous to the welfare of man. The only one of these to speak in the Jerusalem Temple did so without permission. On that occasion Jeremiah did not get beyond the outer gate, and as soon as he had spoken he had to flee for his life.

A decisive change occurred, however, as soon as Jerusalem had fallen to the Babylonians. Ezekiel certainly wrote, and presumably spoke, of the promise of a new and finer Temple to be built in place of the old one. The devout and sensitive prophet of the exile, whom we know as the second Isaiah, trusted that under Cyrus a new foundation for the Temple would be laid. When in 520 the Jews were allowed to commence their rebuilding, the prophets Haggai and Zechariah urged the work forward with all the eloquence at their command. "Malachi," the anonymous "messenger" of two centuries later still, urged loyalty to the Temple cultus as essential service to God.

The difference between the early prophets and the later ones clearly is that between the negative criticism which is permissible, and which may be very healthy, in the case of a going concern, and the affirmative devotion which is the only right answer in times of travail. With the political state of Judah destroyed, only the religious institution was available to serve as a rallying point for a beaten and discouraged people. The prophets of these later days therefore made common cause with the priests, and the two groups together performed the miracle of preserving Jewish identity and unity against all the pressures of the conquering empires and the confusions of the surrounding world. Incidentally we should observe that it was through the labors of the priests and scribes that even the bitter reproaches of the earlier prophets were copied out and made available for later generations.

It was in the synagogue rather than in the Temple that preaching became a standard part of Jewish custom. One of the reasons for this was the deliquescence of Hebrew as a spoken language, requiring that the more learned should provide interpretation of the Scriptures in the local vernacular. Significantly it is in Alexandria, the greatest Jewish center in the Greek world, that we find Philo Judaeus (30 B.C.–A.D. 50) describing the sermon as a regular and important feature of synagogue life:

Innumerable schools of practical wisdom, self-control, manliness, uprightness, and the other virtues are opened every Sabbath day in all cities. In these schools, the people listen with the utmost attention out of a thirst for a refreshing discourse, while one of the best qualified stands up, and instructs them in what is best and most conducive to welfare, things by which their whole life may be made better.

At first it seems that this preaching was prophetic in the sense that it was performed by anyone who had the urge, and to whom the people were willing to listen, without reference to formal assignment or any kind of ordination. Philo says explicitly that "any one of the experienced" might assume the responsibility. Not until well after the beginning of our era did the term "rabbi" ("my great one") become a specific title rather than merely a polite form of address.

It was on this informal basis that Jesus, spending a week end in his home town, was invited to speak in the synagogue of Nazareth; and St. Mark tells us that he taught in many other synagogues as well. Jesus also exercised his prophetic ministry elsewhere, on the hilltop and beside the lake, as had his precursor St. John Baptist at the ford of the Jordan. Similarly St. Paul taught in the synagogues as he had opportunity, but also on the Areopagus in Athens and at the philosophical school of Tyrannus in Ephesus. Most significantly for our present interest, Jesus and St. Paul both spoke in select gatherings of those who already were followers of the way. Our Lord's blessing of the bread and the cup at the last supper, associated with his farewell discourse to the disciples, at once followed existing Jewish practice and set definitely the Christian pattern of uniting instruction with worship.

The freedom of anyone to speak as he felt moved led to excesses in the services at Corinth. Here St. Paul indicates that in his judgment there often was more warmth than light. "If all . . . speak with tongues," he asks,

and there come in those that are unlearned, or unbelievers, will they not say that ye are mad? But if all prophesy, and there come in one that believeth not, or one unlearned, he is convinced of all, he is judged of all.

The apostle sets it down as a rule that there shall be no speaking in tongues "if there be no interpreter." "God is not the author of confusion," he concludes, "but of peace . . . Let all things be done decently and in order."

As early as the writing of I Timothy, perhaps about the end of the first century, a bishop is expected to be "apt to teach," while this qualification is not mentioned for a deacon. Gradually the volunteer prophet gave way to the authorized spokesman, and in time the preaching function came to be reserved almost wholly to the bishops. In the city of Constantinople St. John Chrysostom, "the golden-mouthed" (347–407), was so called because of his widely famed eloquence as a preacher. In the West Chrysostom's slightly younger contemporary St. Augustine (354–430) brought his pagan training in rhetoric into the service of his newly found Christian faith.

Pope Gregory I (540–604) left behind him a collection of homilies; but already in his time preaching was uncommon in the Roman Church, and soon afterward it fell into almost total eclipse. It was revived by the later monastic orders, chiefly the Franciscan and Dominican. So much has been said about St. Francis preaching to the fishes that many have forgotten how vitally he appealed to men and women. The symbol of Dominican membership, O.P., stands for *Ordo Praedicatorum*, "the order of preachers." To this day Dominican preaching is outstanding in its scholarship and logical clarity, if sometimes a shade subtle for the grasp of the average congregation.

The first stirrings of the Reformation mood are to be discerned in preaching movements. The "poor preachers" of John Wyclif (1320–1384) heralded a new day in England, even though its clear dawning was long delayed. John Hus (1369–1415) secured his fame and his martyrdom as preacher at the Bethlehem Chapel in Prague. Girolamo Savonarola (1452–1498) was duly authorized to preach, for he was a Dominican monk, and orthodox save that he liked to do as he pleased; but he was too successful to remain in favor with the authorities, and after transforming the life of Florence he lost his own life at the stake.

Luther and Calvin made mighty use of the preaching technique, as did both their immediate followers and their subsequent inheritors. The English Church, whose break from Rome had been more largely administrative than ideological, laid less stress on preaching than did the Lutheran and Reformed groups. Cranmer was anxious that the people "continuallye profite more and more in the knowledge of God," but he wanted them to have duly authorized instruction. "After the Crede ended," says his 1549 rubric in the Communion service, "shall folowe the Sermon or Homely, or some portiō of one of the Homelyes, as thei shalbe hereafter deuided." One book of twelve such homilies, three or four of them written by Cranmer himself, had been published in 1547, and another volume followed in 1563.

It may be that the provision of the official homilies tended in itself to discourage independent thought and expression on the part of the clergy. These ready-made sermons, too, no doubt wore pretty thin with frequent repetition, and in circumstances increasingly different from those under which they had been written. Certain it is that preaching in the Church of England had fallen into sad decay by the time the Wesleys appeared on the scene, just before the middle of the eighteenth century. The "Latitudinarianism" of such men as Archbishop Tillotson (1630–1694) and Bishop Burnet (1643–1715) was an enlightened creed, but it was far from being an energizing one; and the clergy followed the lead of their official leaders.

The "rotten boroughs" of the eighteenth century House of Commons were fully matched by the failure of the Church to create any new parishes in the rapidly growing industrial centers, or to take any interest at all in the spiritual and social welfare of miners and factory hands. Rectors frequently were absentees, and their vicars and curates often were both ignorant and lazy. It was in 1734, just before the Wesley brothers left Oxford for Georgia, that "The Vicar of Bray" satirized the total lack of principle which evidently was thought to characterize the clergy of the time.

The enthusiasm of the Wesleys and of George Whitefield was more than the Church could readily absorb. By their very devotion to the Church these young men were driven to defy its unconcerned authorities, and to preach outside it when they were not welcomed to preach within. Whitefield was the first to preach in the open air, at the Kingswood Colliery in Bristol, three miles away from the nearest parish church. Six weeks later, and at first very reluctantly, John Wesley joined him. Says the historian John Richard Green,

On the rough and ignorant masses to whom they spoke the effect of Whitefield and his fellow Methodists was mighty both for good and ill. The preaching stirred a passionate hatred in their opponents. Their lives were often in danger, they were mobbed, they were ducked, they were stoned, they were smothered with filth.

But the enthusiasm they aroused was equally passionate. Women fell down in convulsions; strong men were smitten suddenly to the earth; the preacher was interrupted by bursts of hysteric laughter or of hysteric sobbing. All the phenomena of strong spiritual excitement, so familiar now, but at that time strange and unknown, followed on their sermons; and the terrible sense of a conviction of sin, a new dread of hell, a new hope of heaven, took forms at once grotesque and sublime.

The earlier venture of the Wesleys in Georgia had failed, but Whitefield's preaching tour in America in 1739 and 1740 touched off the spectacular revival of religion known as "the Great Awakening." American preachers imitated Whitefield's dramatic and emotional style, and the New England clergy are said to have been "all on horse-back during the summer of 1741." Gilbert Tennent of New Jersey, rather than the sober and logical Jonathan Edwards, was the leading exponent of the "hell-fire and damnation" technique, though Edwards rather uneasily allowed himself to be drawn into the movement for a time.

TOO MUCH PREACHING

The roll of the great American preachers since Edwards is at once too long and too familiar to be rehearsed here. At the same time there were far too many preachers who were not great, especially in a culture which assumed that preaching was the primary reason for the services of the Church. The initial Puritan distaste for ritual, coupled now with the evangelistic fervor of the Methodists, made the minister's function that of pulpit orator almost to the exclusion of all else. The scholar and the shepherd of souls scarcely could rise to preferment unless they happened also to be endowed with eloquence. The very fact that the word "preacher" ceased to refer to one assigned to perform a particular duty in a particular service, but became rather the accepted title of the American clergyman, demonstrates how completely preaching had secured not only the center of attention, but practically all attention.

Preaching thus bulked too largely in American religious life. There was too much preaching in the single service as well. The practice of extempore utterance, popularized by the example of Whitefield, superseded the laborious preparation which had been the method of Jonathan Edwards; and it made, as always it does, for extreme prolixity. Sermons of two or three hours' duration were not uncommon in the early nineteenth century, though the speeding up of the general American tempo brought about some reduction later. The consequence of the centrality and the length of the sermon inevitably was that other parts of the service were sacrificed to it, some by being treated casually and many by being omitted altogether.

This, combined with the old fear of ceremony, brought about the truncated and perfunctory practice of worship which has survived so far into our time. Wesley, who assumed that the service would include the whole of the Communion or of Morning Prayer, as well as the sermon, nevertheless urged that all should be completed within the space of an hour. The American Methodists, commonly using much less than half as much worship material as Wesley had prescribed, seldom came near to finishing in anything like that time. In common with almost all other American Protestants, they went to the church to hear So-and-So preach; and anything else that happened in the service was of little interest either to them or to So-and-So himself.

There is a very nice line here to be drawn between the two historic extremes. The almost total lack of preaching in medieval Rome and in eighteenth century England left the people without religious interpretation and enlightenment. The plethora of preaching in America scarcely enlightened the people either, for commonly it substituted reiteration for interpretation. Robbed of the traditions of worship, belabored by emotional appeals and angry threats, devout Americans saw the Church only as a mechanism for the saving of their individual souls, while skeptical minds regarded it as a crowning demonstration of human stupidity and cowardice.

Better preaching, real preaching, would have helped both parties. Without preaching, indeed, no clarification could be made, nor can be. The critical distinction between useful, necessary preaching, and the useless and destructive sort, stands in whether the sermon is a genuine attempt to interpret religious truth, or is regarded as an end in itself. Instrumentally, sermons are integral to the people's adult understanding of the Christian faith. It is only when the sermon ceases to be an instrument, and the minister fails thus to be truly a servant, that sermonizing does (as so long and so widely in America) more harm than good.

Certainly it is not necessary that there shall be a sermon, or any surrogate for it, in every service that is held. A congregation rightly habituated to the worship of God as the normal way of approach to him will worship gladly, and sometimes with a perfectly natural and proper sense of relief, when knowing that there is to be no sermon at all. Weekday services in general should be services of devotion only, without the intrusion of any remarks by the leader of the worship.

At least once a week, however, and therefore most conveniently on Sunday morning, the minister owes it to his people to share with them some fresh insight into Christian truth. This is not too much preaching for the parish to hear. If preparation is careful and serious, this is about as much as the average minister can hope to do adequately.

SERMON SUBJECTS

"Woe is me if I preach not the Gospel!" The subject of every sermon must be the Christian faith and life. There is no time available to spend on anything less important. The Gospel, however, is that of the entire saving of mankind, the Christian faith relates to all of truth, and the Christian life claims every activity of man. Within the generalization, therefore, there is room for more variety of choice than any one preacher can encompass in a lifetime.

The negative restriction nevertheless is real and important. Sermons may deal with all kinds of problems, but they must deal with them under the judgment of Christian values. Politics certainly may be mentioned, and political views openly expressed; but the people will quickly catch the difference between a sermon which subjects politics to the scrutiny of Christian thought, and a stump speech that merely subjects the congregation to a political point of view. Current books may be reviewed, but not in competition with the book page or the radio commentator. Unless the book itself conveys Christian teaching, or its oral reviewer presents Christian teaching in his treatment of it, it has no place as the subject of a Christian sermon.

There is so much to be said affirmatively and specifically for God and his Christ that in any event political issues and current literature have very little claim to pulpit time. The frequency of their appearance in newspaper announcements simply indicates how unready or unwilling some of our modern clergy are to deal with matters of eternal significance. What the Church has to offer, that the men's and women's clubs do not, is the everlasting Gospel of our Lord. This is what the sermon must offer, regularly, avowedly, and without apology or camouflage.

It follows that the great truths of the Gospel must frequently and straightforwardly be set forth, and in their own right rather than as footnotes to a discussion of current affairs. Theology therefore is not to be avoided, and it need not be diluted except as its more technical verbiage may require simpler definition. Men and women not only need to hear about God, and his revelation in Christ Jesus, and the meaning and means of redemption. Today they know their need, and they want to hear; nor are they lacking in ability to understand that which most concerns their eternal destiny. It is sad indeed that the presumably well trained theologians who occupy the pulpits of our major denominations so commonly leave the great Christian doctrines to the revivalists, while they offer to their own congregations only polite and sentimental moralizings. The rise of neo-orthodoxy offers some hope at this point; but not only the followers of Karl Barth and Reinhold Niebuhr are called to preach essential Christian truth from the Christian pulpit.

The Christian year, with its systematic outline of the life of our Lord and its orderly provision for emphasis on one major aspect after another of the Christian faith, is an immediately available guide to specific sermon planning, and it is one of the best. Practically all of us now make contact with the Church calendar at least at Christmas and Easter, and an increasing number of churches are noticing it in Lent. There is much yet to be gained by recognizing also Advent and Whitsuntide, the Epiphany and the Transfiguration and All Saints' Day, and such feasts as the Conversion of St. Paul late in the winter and the Nativity of St. John Baptist at midsummer.

Within the calendar, and in conjunction with it, the lectionaries are fertile sources of sermon ideas and texts. With two lessons each for Morning and Evening Prayer, and the collect and epistle for the Communion, there scarcely can be a Sunday whose specified materials do not challenge the preacher to seize upon some aspect of

Christian teaching therein reflected, and to expand and clarify it for himself and his people. There are also the lessons for weekdays, if the Sunday ones do not immediately commend themselves; and this brings each week's own supply of possible material to a minimum total of eighteen passages of Scripture. Is any one then really hard up for sermon ideas, and actually forced into a rehashing of yesterday's headlines?

Lectionaries aside, the body of Scripture itself is an inexhaustible treasury of preaching material. No little of the current popular ignorance of the Bible is to be traced to the recent paucity of sound biblical preaching. The old notion that the business of the sermon is to "explain a text" has much to commend it. The sermon which explains a passage of Scripture both in the light of its historical setting and of its present application is the true sermon of our great tradition, and it is the most likely to bring eternal truth to bear on the life of our people today. He who "can't find a text to fit the sermon" is rightly to be suspected of failing to find a sermon to fit genuine human need.

The consciousness of that need can be investigated, and often accurately determined, by asking the congregation itself to aid in the choosing of subjects. The inclusion of a post card with each leaflet for a few Sundays is worth trying, to find out what questions the people have in mind. This has reference not at all to the cheap sort of topical question, often faked, which some sensationalists have handled in haphazard half-dozens on Sunday evenings. If the layman seriously is challenged to say what he wants to hear seriously discussed, he is not likely to ask for the trivial. When he does, he properly may be ignored. One man's experience with this technique is that he has found himself obliged to handle questions so profound and penetrating that he might not have ventured to raise them himself, and issues so difficult to treat aright that he has had to take weeks for preparation in new reading and hard thinking.

While the cycle of the Christian year inevitably results in a kind of series of topics, more or less closely knit, there sometimes may be value in scheduling a special series on a number of connected themes. Such a sequence should not be too long, and each of its individual sermons must be so designed that it will have meaning for the hearers of the one sermon only. The objective of the series pattern is to clarify important relationships in Christian history and thought; but often it will have the incidental effects of creating special interest and promoting more regular attendance.

Subjects and titles are not necessarily the same, but they ought to stand in a recognizable relation. A counsel of perfection perhaps might be to announce no sermons in advance, on the ground that people ought to come to the service of worship without reference to any particular sermon theme. We must admit, however, that people usually want to know what the day's subject is going to be; and it may be argued that they are entitled to know the theme in advance, for their own spiritual preparation, if the theme be that of the whole service and not of the sermon only. Advance announcement also provides at least a minimum guarantee that the preacher will have done some advance thinking about the responsibility that he has accepted.

The first requirement for an announced sermon title is that it shall represent adequately the actual subject to be discussed. The second is that it shall be dignified. The third is that it ought not to be dull; but this is a lesser requisite than are the other two.

It is notorious that many sensational sermon titles have all the sensation in the title, and none in the sermon. This is plain fraud, of the kind for which we are accustomed to blame Hollywood. It is true also that too many titles, patronizingly designed to appeal to the multitude, are flippant and cheap. This is unworthy of the seriousness of the Christian religion. Dullness is more often honest, and usually it is not lacking in dignity; but it is not a necessary characteristic of reputable thinking and straight speaking. A topic worth thinking about, and preaching about, surely can be described in a few words which are at once vivid and accurate.

THE PREPARING OF SERMONS

An adequate, balanced service of worship, including enough of praise, prayer, and lessons to have real meaning, and to allow the congregation full and meaningful participation, scarcely can be completed in less than forty minutes. The sermon never should occupy more than half as many, making an hour's service in all. This limitation is not only because "no souls are saved after the first twenty minutes," though that probably is true. It is also because the sermon, as one man's own effort to provide enlightenment, always must be subordinated to the corporate voice of the Church historic and present.

Twenty minutes indeed are too much, far too much, unless they are well used. It is inexcusable for any man to ask so many people to listen to him so long, unless he has made every effort in his power to ensure that each minute of the twenty shall count toward a total experience of enlightenment and inspiration. He is most unlikely to achieve anything of the sort unless every minute is thought through in advance, and planned in detail, and adjusted rightly to serve its part in the whole. An old and thoughtful English bishop remarked on his impression that "when the Holy Ghost speaks extempore, he usually talks nonsense." Those who have suffered often under extempore sermons know how right he was. And there is no reason to suppose that the Holy Ghost is less available in the unhurried quiet of the study than he is amid the countless pressures of Sunday morning.

Adequate preparation for the precious twenty minutes necessarily involves the full writing out of the sermon's text. Indeed it involves writing it out several times, till all the parts are in balance and all the transitions smooth and meaningful. It also requires at least a first writing long enough before the scheduled delivery to allow adequate time for cooling and reconsideration. To leave the work till Saturday is at best to preclude adequate revision, and at an easy worst to be prevented by some emergency from getting the preparation done at all.

Whether the preacher actually shall read the script from the pulpit depends upon his own personal tastes and skills. It is better frankly and openly to read, than to memorize and obviously recite a memory piece. It is lamentable, however, to read without looking at the congregation, and it is tragic to peer at the page and stumble over the wording.

With or without the script before him in the pulpit, the preacher should be able to see the people and to be aware of their reactions from moment to moment. He should no less have the entire structure of the sermon, and its entire phrasing, clearly in his mind. The safest way, and in general the most effective, is to read without seeming to; and this is a technique which can be learned by anyone who cares to make the effort. A minor but useful device is to slide completed pages from one stack to another, rather than visibly turning them. I am not suggesting that the minister should pretend he is not reading; but he should not call attention to the fact of reading at the expense of attention to his message.

If it be argued that all this insistence on detail of preparation takes insufficient account of the immediate emotional impact of preaching, the reply is that the sermon's particular function in the service is not primarily emotional, but interpretative. "Let him that speaketh in a tongue," urged St. Paul upon his emotional friends at Corinth, "pray that he may interpret." The fitting and needed emotions of Christian worship: humility, reverence, penitence, wonder, exaltation, gratitude, devotion, self-consecration: these belong to the acts of worship themselves. The sermon rightly may seek to evoke and to stimulate these emotions, but most of all its purpose is coherently and constructively to guide them. Whether the sermon is to stimulate or to guide, however, it will not do so the better for being unprepared.

There are inescapable human differences in originality and imagination, and so there will be differences among preachers as to the amount of their direct dependence upon other preachers and writers. If the sermon is immediately and totally derivative, the original author certainly ought in common decency to be given a credit line. ("Spurgeon said" is reported to have been one man's invariable and perfectly accurate opening.) Brief quotations are permissible if they are relevant and are credited, but a sermon with meaning has to be something other than a mosaic of quotable lines of prose or verse.

Not often is material written by one man, for one group of hearers, under one set of circumstances, totally applicable as coming from another man to other people at another time. Syndicated sermon outlines, being wholly routine, conventional, and geared not to offend the average mind, are an abomination; and books of sermons, even of good sermons, are more use for secondary stimulus than they are as supplying finished products. A man who has been accepted as a minister of Christ should be able to do his own thinking, and forthrightly to speak from his own mind and heart.

Again let it be said that he can not do this adequately unless he pays the price in both general and specific preparation. The excuse of being too busy is no excuse at all. Busy with what? What is there more important, as a minister's individual contribution to the Christian cause, than "the opening and clearing of the word of God"?

Granted, a death in the parish, or some other personal tragedy in the life of one of its members, takes immediate precedence over all else. But this is not a reason against preparing. It is simply a reason for being prepared so far in advance that no sudden crisis can prevent the sermon's full readiness on Sunday. As to busyness, no cleric of our time works nearly so hard, or preaches nearly so often, as did John Wesley. In fifty years he preached not less than forty thousand sermons, perhaps as many as fifty thousand. Yet he wrote his sermons out, and published them; and they stand today as models of ordered thinking and compelling conviction.

Wesley, of course, used his prepared sermons many more times than once each. In order to be able to do so, he had to generalize the approach so that they would fit more than one congregation. Bishops today do the same thing. It always is risky, however, to delve in the barrel. Not long ago one bishop, who rather fancied himself as a literary man, preached a favorite sermon of his in which he used the tragic story of King Lear as the principal point of reference. Unfortunately he preached it on this occasion, with the attempted aid of an interpreter, to a congregation of Chinese. It was not difficult to understand why the interpreter fumbled, and why the people looked utterly bewildered.

The parish minister has the advantage of writing in full acquaintance with his own people, and so in awareness of their knowledge, their thinking, and their dominant attitudes. He therefore can use his sermons to bring basic Christian truth immediately to bear on local and current needs, and he should. This means, however, that he ought to exercise special care when he is invited to preach somewhere else.

What was fully appropriate on one date for one body of hearers may miss the mark badly not long afterward and not far away. If a sermon is to be reused at all, it must at least be thoughtfully reexamined, and some parts of it almost certainly ought to be rewritten. A work of art, once completed, rightly is presented to more than one public without change. The service is a work of art, but the sermon usually is not and may not pretend to be. The congregation's hearing helps to make the sermon a success or a failure, and so the specific congregation always must be considered as the sermon is being given its specific form.

THE HEARING OF SERMONS

Much of this chapter no doubt has seemed to be addressed to the preacher only; and in this area he does have the first and the gravest responsibility. It may have been well for members of the congregation to listen in on some of the hints to him, and so to gain new realization both of the minister's obligations, and of his problems, in the matter of preaching adequately. But since the congregation does have a vital share in determining the usefulness of the sermon as a factor in the total service, it is required to face some problems and to accept some obligations on its own account.

Manifestly the first requirement, if the people wish to benefit by the hearing of sermons, is that they should come to the services, and regularly. The best possible use of the sermon's twenty minutes, whether in writing, delivery, or listening, can provide only one tiny glimpse of one small aspect of the vast panorama of Christian values. The minister's most careful efforts to provide a systematic correlation of these values is defeated for any individual by that individual's being present only once in a while.

The second demand is that the hearer shall listen in confident hope of hearing something important. This may be, in view of sad former experience, a hoping against hope; but it is the only way in which either a good sermon can be fully appreciated, or a feeble one in any measure redeemed. Inattention simply is deliberate wasting of the sermon time, and so of the hearer's own twenty minutes as well as of the minister's efforts made both now and in advance. The poorest of sermons scarcely can avoid including some word worth hearing. Only an affirmative will to hear the helpful word will identify it when it comes.

A third essential is that the listener shall indulge neither in fear of what is new, nor in contempt of what is old. The material of any sound Christian sermon must be largely old, for its subject matter is a historic revelation and its points of reference belong to a historic tradition. A serviceable sermon must also be in part new, sometimes in a supplying of unfamiliar data and always in a fresh arranging of the well known to give it vital force in the particular situation. Those who want only the old, and those who would listen to nothing but the new, alike and equally convict themselves of intellectual and moral laziness.

I have chosen to make here, rather than in the sections on choice of subjects or preparation of scripts, a necessary remark about honesty in preaching. It belongs here because such dishonesty as exists is based largely on fear of upsetting or antagonizing the people of the local parish. In so far as any of the laity have tried to hold pulpit utterance to nothing but the asserting of their present views, and the supporting of their favorite prejudices, the fault clearly is with the laymen. More often, I suspect, the fear is quite ungrounded in fact.

In any event the herald of the Gospel has no business to pull his punches for the sake of popularity, or even of peace. So long as he knows whereof he speaks, and so long as he speaks in love rather than in cantankerousness, he must say exactly what he thinks about the subject in hand. If he suffers for it, he suffers with countless heroes of our Hebrew-Christian past. Mostly, however, I am persuaded that he will not suffer much.

In thirty years of trying to come clean, I have found Christian people (and not only in college chapels) eagerly receptive to straight speaking alike on biblical, theological, and ethical issues. "Why didn't I hear that forty years ago?" growled an old man after a sermon on the services of biblical criticism to spiritual apprehension. The reason he didn't hear it forty years ago was not that the information was unavailable in 1913. It was only that too many ministers, then and since, had thought he and his fellows were unready to listen to some of the historic facts that have bearing upon the everlasting truth. Total honesty in the pulpit, if it be rooted in sound learning and expressed in total good will, can not be wrong and almost certainly will be helpful. There is reason to believe also that it will please the people the while it illumines them.

The minister is entitled to know the congregation's reaction to service and sermon if it has been favorable, that he may be heartened in the continuing of his work. He stands in desperate need of knowing if it has been unfavorable, that he may determine soberly how much of the fault is his own. The vague "I liked your talk" is cheering but not otherwise helpful. A real listening should have led to some coherent thinking on the part of the listener, and therefore should produce some specific and articulate response. Most preachers would be delighted, and all would be benefited, by a revival of the frank but friendly criticism which came as a matter of course from the sermon tasters of old.

The growing custom of the coffee hour after the service affords what the service itself can not, a free give-and-take between the preacher and some of those who have heard him. This is rough on the minister, after the expenditure of physical and spiritual energy which he has just made; but the values fully justify his staying vertical and awake for one hour more. In some churches, especially when a visiting preacher has occupied the pulpit, the practice is formalized into a period of public questions and answers in the parish house. This can be most illuminating, not only for the questioners as to the content and intent of the sermon, but also for the cleric as to the effectiveness of his preparation and delivery. Probably it is more useful with guests than with the local incumbent, because the guest's own basic assumptions, being unfamiliar, stand in greater need of being identified and understood.

What about pulpit guests? Normally the congregation should not want very many. The continuity of teaching, and the direct application to the local scene, both are better served if the resident minister does almost all of the preaching. Frequent invitations to outsiders on the minister's own part suggest that he is not really committed to his own teaching ministry. Demands for outsiders on the part of the congregation suggest that its members are more anxious to be entertained than to be taught.

A final and repeated hearing of the sermon may be provided not literally in hearing, but in reading. A thought-provoking sermon almost invariably raises demands for copies of the script. There is likely to be a script, for reasons noted above, if the sermon has been one really effective in provoking thought. The question is that of getting copies of it to the people smoothly, unobtrusively, and promptly. It is not difficult to mimeograph in advance, and it is possible to have a supply available immediately after the service in an inconspicuous but visible place. The coffee hour provides most conveniently for this, and a self-service scheme will avoid any awkward and incongruous money-changing in the precincts of the temple.

The pulpit is being put back where it belongs, at the corner of the chancel rather than in the center of the congregation's vision. It does belong in the Church, and in the churches, and it is not to be removed from them. Our faith is a reasonable one, and the reasoning of our faith needs regularly to be interpreted for our people. Judaism, Christianity, and Islam all have understood this necessity, and have provided for it. The sermon moreover, faithfully prepared and reverently preached, itself may become an integral and vital part of the total act of homage to God.

But the human reason is not the divine revelation, and the sermon is only one means toward Christian understanding, faith, and worship. The central place in the church is given aright to the altar, and on the altar to the cross of Christ. The preacher, standing in his pulpit at the side, is commissioned to point the central way to the altar of our worship and the cross of our salvation. May God forgive him if ever, instead of humbly and helpfully pointing the way, he allows his own person and his own words to obscure the clear and certain vision of the cross.

XI

THE HOLY COMMUNION

IT IS THE Supper of our Lord, reminding us of his last supper with his first disciples. It is the Holy Communion, which being literally interpreted is the Sacred Fellowship. It is the Eucharist, the giving of thanks to God for all his mercies, but especially for his great gift of salvation in Christ Jesus. It is the Mass, the mysterious reenactment of the sacrifice of Calvary. It is the supreme Sacrament, the outward and visible means to our inward and spiritual grace. It is the primary and the ultimate service of worship of the universal Christian Church.

Because it is so important, in history and in practice, it has occasioned much discussion and many disputes. Because it is infinitely precious to those who share in it, it often has been denied to those who would interpret the sharing differently. Because some have laid so much weight upon it, others have been impelled to discount and avoid it. Thus the symbol of fellowship has been often one rather of disunion, and in some circles the great service has become the little used one.

Not in our lifetimes shall we see all Christians gathered together at once about the table of the Lord. We may profit, however, at least to some understanding of what has gone wrong, and so toward the possibility of making things more nearly right, if we trace the story from its beginnings. Here and here, we shall see, we have diverged one from another. Is it possible that at some of these points of separation we shall find ourselves coming together again?

182

PRE-CHRISTIAN BACKGROUNDS

Long before there was a Temple in Jerusalem, or an Israelite priesthood anywhere, the tribes of the Arabian desert began the practice of eating together a ceremonial meal. This was at once a symbol of the clansmen's fellowship among themselves, and of their participating in the divine life represented in the sacred and slaughtered animal. The narrow margin between starvation and survival under desert conditions did not permit the wasting of food. It is not until much later, and under the more prosperous conditions of agricultural life, that we find the "whole burnt offering" in which the sacrifice was entirely consumed by fire. By eating rather than wasting, the desert peoples were recognizing their privation in practical terms. In the same act, however, and quite consciously, they were symbolizing their sharing in what they did have, and their necessary oneness if their company was to endure.

This desert meal, an evident communion sacrifice, passed into Hebrew and later Jewish usage in two related but distinct forms. As the annual Passover it was understood to commemorate the last of the ten plagues in Egypt, and the delivery of Israel from her bondage there. As the later *Kiddush* it became a regular prelude to Sabbaths and feast days. The central symbol of the Passover, celebrated each year in the springtime, was the paschal lamb; and this feast became, after the settlement in agricultural Canaan, also the first of the days of unleavened bread. The *Kiddush* centered on the ceremonial blessing of wine and (ordinary leavened) bread, after which those present ate and drank together. In essence both Passover and *Kiddush* were family observances, though in time they found a place also in the communal life of the synagogue.

Just as this simple kind of communion sacrifice was older far than the elaborated practices of the Temple, so it endured after the Temple rituals had come to their end. Passover and *Kiddush* persist in Judaism today. Still they are services of thanks to God, and still they are tokens of the close personal bond of those who share in them together.

The Seder, the annual Passover celebration, begins with the lighting of the festival lights in every Jewish home. The youngest at the table asks a series of standard questions, the answers to which explain the symbolic significance of the *pesach,* the sacrifice, the matzoth, the

unleavened bread, and the *moror*, the bitter herbs. The Hallel (Halle-
lujah) Psalms are sung, and the *Nishmas* prayer ("The breath of every
living being") is said. All the emphasis is upon God's mercy to Israel,
and on every Israelite's consequent obligation to serve God and to
remain a loyal member of the Israelite community. "Every Jew," says
a line in one of the service books, "should regard himself as if he personally had come out of Egypt."

The regular *Kiddush* for the beginning of the Sabbath, the Friday
evening meal, opens with the father of the household blessing God
in turn for "the fruit of the vine," for the institution of the Sabbath,
and for "bread from the earth." During the meal gay and rhythmical
table hymns are sung. The special *Kiddush* for the eve of the Passover
adds a blessing for God's special calling of Israel as his own people,
and for the giving of "holy festivals for gladness, and sacred seasons
for joy."

THE LAST SUPPER

Unquestionably it was in the Passover week that Jesus was ar-
rested, tried, and crucified. St. Mark's Gospel, followed by St. Matthew's and St. Luke's, says unequivocally that it was the Passover meal
which was eaten in the upper room: "the first day of unleavened
bread, when they killed the passover. . . . Where is the guestcham-
ber, where I shall eat the passover with my disciples?" The Fourth
Gospel, which seldom concerns itself with details of external fact,
seems in this case to offer a deliberate correction of the chronology.
The supper is placed definitely "before the feast of the passover,"
and much later that night it is said that the Jewish warders "went not
into the judgment hall, lest they should be defiled; but that they might
eat the passover."

It is difficult to escape the conclusion that here the Fourth Gospel
is historically right, and the others mistaken. Had the paschal lamb
been included in that last meal, it scarcely could have gone without
mention. Indeed its symbolism soon was seized upon to represent the
sacrifice of the Lord himself, and this may have occasioned the transferring of the date in St. Mark's account. Instead of the lamb and
the unleavened bread of the Passover, however, we find in the Gospels (as in St. Paul's even earlier record) mention only of "bread"

(not the unleavened matzoth) and "the cup." This clearly suggests a *Kiddush,* and so St. John's dating on the eve of the Passover rather than on the festival day itself.

We may think, then, of Jesus, as the elder brother in his own little family of loved ones, assuming the father's place in the familiar and beloved family rite. He took bread, and blessed it, no doubt saying what still is said by "the master of the house":

Blessed art thou, O Lord our God, King of the universe, who bringest forth bread from the earth.

And he took the cup, and gave thanks in the oft-repeated words:

Blessed art thou, O Lord our God, King of the universe, who createst the fruit of the vine.

Then, we are told, all those who were present joined in singing a hymn. This was the regular service in the Jewish household, and Jesus fulfilled the role of the householder.

But the supper that night was more than the prefestival *Kiddush,* and Jesus said more than the already ancient ritual provided. Our earliest account is not in the Gospels, but is that of St. Paul in I Corinthians 11:

I have received of the Lord that which also I delivered unto you, That the Lord Jesus the same night in which he was betrayed took bread: and when he had given thanks, he brake it, and said, Take, eat: this is my body, which is broken for you: this do in remembrance of me. After the same manner also he took the cup, when he had supped, saying, This cup is the new testament in my blood: this do ye, as oft as ye drink it, in remembrance of me.

These words of institution, which are repeated in every Mass and every Communion to this day, mark the transmuting of the Jewish *Kiddush* into the Christian Eucharist.

Thus, whatever may have been the precise date of the last supper, the sacrificial concept of the Passover is integral to the Christian Communion. Possibly St. Paul reflects his agreement with the Fourth Gospel's dating in his declaration that "Christ our passover is sacrificed for us," for this undeniably has more point if our Lord was put to death just at the time of the slaying of the Passover lamb. The Lord's supper is, and from the earliest days has been, much more than the memory of a final *Kiddush* of the Galilean brotherhood. It is rather the recognition of the ultimate sacrifice of the Lamb of God who taketh away the sins of the world.

EASTERN LITURGIES

The equivalent of the *Kiddush* in early Christian practice was not the Eucharist, but the Agape, or "love feast." This was a religious meal, but a meal it frankly was, and its emphasis was on the immediate fellowship of the company of believers. From the beginning the sacrificial Eucharist was clearly distinguished from it. The character of the Eucharist as a ceremony rather than as a social occasion is marked by St. Paul's stern rebuke to the Corinthians:

What? have ye not houses to eat and to drink in? or despise ye the church of God, and shame them that have not? . . . If any man hunger, let him eat at home; that ye come not together unto condemnation.

The meaning of the Eucharist for St. Paul is far too solemn to permit its being confused with anything gustatory and secular, "for as often as ye eat this bread, and drink this cup, ye do show the Lord's death till he come."

We have noted already, in Chapter II, that by the middle of the second century the Eucharistic prayer had begun to assume a standardized form; and one, it now will be recognized, that had obvious roots in the familiar Jewish rituals. It is interesting to observe that in the primitive rite described in the *Didache*, the cup was blessed before the bread, exactly as in Judaism; and St. Paul uses this sequence in his mention of "The cup of blessing which we bless . . . The bread which we break." In their narratives, however, the Gospels and St. Paul give the reverse order, which is the one ultimately followed in Christian procedure.

The *Apostolic Tradition* of St. Hippolytus (160–235) includes in its Eucharistic Canon the Salutation ("The Lord be with you"), the *Sursum Corda* ("Lift up your hearts"), and a Consecration prayer which is basic to those of all subsequent Christian liturgies. Its historical importance demands that it be quoted in full:

We give thanks unto thee, O God, through thy beloved servant Jesus Christ, whom in the last times thou didst send unto us to be Saviour, Redeemer, and messenger of thy will; who is thine inseparable Word through whom thou hast made all things, and who was well-pleasing unto thee. Him didst thou send from heaven into the womb of the Virgin, and being borne in her womb was incarnate and shown to be thy Son, born of the Holy Spirit and the Virgin. He in fulfillment of thy will, and preparing for thee an holy people, stretched forth his hands when he was suffering, that he might deliver from suffering those who believed in thee;

Who when he was being given over to his willing suffering that he might dissolve death, break the chains of the devil, tread hell underfoot, illuminate the righteous, set a bound (to death), and manifest forth the Resurrection, having taken bread, gave thanks unto thee and said: Take, eat; this is my body which is broken for you. Likewise also the cup, saying: This is my blood which is poured out for you. When ye do this ye make my memorial.

Being mindful then of his death and Resurrection we offer to thee the bread and the cup, giving thanks unto thee that thou hast deemed us worthy to stand before thee and act as priest unto thee. And we beseech thee to send thy holy Spirit upon the sacrifice of thy Church, which do thou in uniting it give to all the saints who partake for fulfillment of the Holy Spirit unto the strengthening of faith in truth, that we may praise and glorify thee; Through thy servant Jesus Christ, through whom unto thee be glory and honour: to the Father and the Son with the Holy Spirit in thy holy Church, now and for evermore. Amen.

The resemblance of this, alike in structure and in content, to the Consecration in the Roman and Anglican uses, will be immediately evident to every reader who is familiar with those forms.

By the sixth century three major types of liturgy had been developed in the East, known respectively as the Alexandrian, the West-Syrian, and the Byzantine. The first of these is represented by the liturgy of St. Mark and the Coptic one of St. Cyril; the second by the liturgy of St. James; and the third by those of St. Basil and St. Chrysostom. Still used in Eastern Orthodoxy, these liturgies prevail also in the so-called "Uniate Churches," those Eastern groups which have reentered into communion with Rome.

All the Eastern services are characterized by a sharp division between the Liturgy of the Catechumens and the Liturgy of the Faithful. The Divine Liturgy of St. John Chrysostom, the most widely used of the Eastern rites and the one regularly followed in the Greek and Russian Churches, will serve to illustrate the general Eastern procedure. It opens with a blessing and "the Great Litany," whose response is *Kyrie eleison*, "Lord, have mercy." There follow antiphons from the Psalms, alternating with hymns and sections of "the Little Litany." After the third antiphon, and with many introductory and concluding versicles, the "Apostle" (from the Acts or the epistles) and the Gospel for the day are read or chanted. With the sermon the period of instruction is ended, and the catechumens are dismissed by the deacon's cry, "All ye learners, go out."

At the beginning of the Liturgy of the Faithful, the choir sings the Cherubic Hymn while the priest prays privately. Then he joins in the hymn, and in the "Great Entrance" brings the bread and wine in procession from the preparation table into the nave, and thence into the sanctuary by the central "holy doors." Another litany leads to the Nicene Creed, which in accordance with Eastern doctrine omits the *filioque*, "and from the Son." An "invitation to attend" concludes with the Grace (II Corinthians 13:14) and the *Sursum Corda*.

The Consecration begins with Preface ("It is meet and right") and *Sanctus* ("Holy, holy, holy"). The prayer itself is lengthy, and complicated with responses by the lesser clergy; but it is the same in essential structure as that of Hippolytus, and those that we know in the West. The most significant difference from Roman usage is the specific invocation of the Holy Spirit for the "changing of the holy things."

The saints, the departed, and the living faithful are commemorated, the Lord's Prayer is said, and the priest breaks the sacred disk into four parts and arranges it carefully on the paten. He and the other clergy then commune. What remains of the wafer is dropped into the chalice, and those who have prepared themselves to receive the Communion are given both kinds, "the Body and Blood together," in a spoon. A prayer of thanksgiving and one of dismissal bring the service to a close. The ancient Agape now is revived in a general distribution of ordinary bread, which however has had a priestly blessing, to all members of the congregation.

All the Eastern liturgies are marked by an intense concern for corporate worship, and by a deep sense of spiritual mystery. The whole congregation is expected to take an active part, vocally and even while silent. There is no Low Mass in the East, and the language of the service is the national vernacular: now in an archaic form, indeed, but still comprehensible to those who attend. Children receive the Communion quite commonly, adults less often because of the rigorous self-preparation that is demanded of them. The Invocation of the Holy Spirit in the Consecration, as not in the Roman prayer, reflects the Eastern emphasis on the continuing divine presence; and there is in the whole service a mood of triumphant gladness not always recognizable in the celebrations of the Roman form.

WESTERN LITURGIES

Depending like the Eastern liturgies upon the primitive rite as recorded by St. Hippolytus, Western usages soon assumed distinct characteristics of their own. The major types are the Ambrosian, Gallican, Mozarabic, and Roman. The Ambrosian rite still is used in the diocese of Milan, and the Mozarabic in that of Toledo. The Gallican service, one form of which was the ancient Celtic, yielded in the eighth century to the Roman, but not without contributing largely to it. The "Use of Sarum," so largely influential in the reformers' *Book of Common Prayer*, was a local adaptation of that of Rome, and is ascribed to St. Osmund, nephew of William the Conqueror and Bishop of Old Sarum (Salisbury) from 1078 to 1099.

The Roman liturgy, substantially in its present form, was definitively set forth by the Council of Trent in the Missal of 1570. A Low Mass is spoken, most of it inaudibly, and a High Mass is sung; but the structure is one, and so also is the essential text. The Missal includes both the invariable parts (the Ordinary and the Canon) and the changing ones (the Proper).

Versicles precede the priest's Confession, which is followed by a variable Introit. Then come *Kyrie eleison* and *Gloria in excelsis*, and next the Prayer, Epistle, and Gospel for the day. The Nicene Creed is recited, and the day's Offertory, which has reference not to the taking of a collection but to the Offering of the Host and the Chalice. The priest washes his hands (the *Lavabo*), says the day's Secret Prayer or Prayers, and introduces the Preface with Salutation and *Sursum Corda*.

The *Sanctus* then is said or sung, leading up to what properly is known as the Canon of the Mass. This includes the commemoration of the living, the Consecration of the elements, and the commemoration of the dead. The Lord's Prayer is recited, and the responsive *Agnus Dei* ("O Lamb of God"). The priest receives the Communion in both kinds, and serves the people with the bread only. Variable prayers ("Communion" and "Postcommunion") and the Blessing are said, and St. John 1:1–14 is read as "the last Gospel."

The resemblances between the Eastern and the Western usages are evident. While the Eastern mood is one of mystical exaltation, however, the Roman is one dominantly of solemn recognition of the sacrifice which is renewed at the altar. The Roman liturgy, as it has been used for many centuries, lacks also the Eastern emphasis on effective corporate worship. In the Middle Ages the building of many altars in a single church, and the development of private Masses and Masses of special intent, as well as the continued use of Latin in the service after it had ceased to be a living language, greatly reduced the sense of congregational participation.

The people have had little opportunity to take part in the Roman service during the Mass itself, except for standing, kneeling, and sitting at designated points. There are vernacular prayers after Low Mass; but their placement outside the service proper, their lack of variation, and the rapid pace at which ordinarily they are said, have combined to make them seem of very little import. In general the Roman service for a thousand years has been one performed by the priest on behalf of people who are present but scarcely participating, rather than one in which the people themselves join actively in the worship of God. Real devotion there unquestionably has been, but it has been each individual's devotion directed solely toward the sacrifice of the altar, rather than the devotion of a community of believers giving thanks in one voice and one spirit.

Within the last few years, however, Rome has opened the way toward very decided changes in the conduct of the service. The "dialogue" or "community" Mass, authorized by Pope Pius XI, now has been approved for use in more than a hundred Roman dioceses throughout the United States. This provides for the congregation to say aloud the responses assigned to the server, and also the *Gloria in excelsis*, the Creed, the *Sanctus*, the *Agnus Dei*, and the *Domine, non sum dignus*. (This last in particular stresses the point that the people, as well as the priest, are offering the holy sacrifice.) A kindred usage is that in which, while one priest says the service quietly in Latin at the altar, another, standing in the body of the Church, reads the text in the vernacular, with the people making the appropriate responses. Both of these developments represent decisive change in Roman usage, and point toward practices at once more ancient (in the first ten Christian centuries) and more recent (in familiar non-Roman custom) than had been regarded as fixed in the policy of Rome.

Most recently the Sacred Congregation of Rites has been considering a general revision of the service. It is reported that the recommendations to be made will include doing away with duplications, both synchronous and repetitive; the beginning of the Mass with the Introit, as of old, with the Preparation being either eliminated or said before the public service begins; the use of only one Collect of the day; the saying of the whole Ante-Communion (through the Creed) in the choir rather than at the altar; the restoration of the ancient "prayers of the faithful" (now marked by a vestigial *Oremus*) at the time of the Offertory; the bringing of the sacred vessels and the elements at this point rather than earlier; and the excision of the last Gospel. Again it is evident that these alterations are in the direction of what we long have known as Protestant use. Some Romans, indeed, admit privately that these things would have been done long ago but for the fact that the Protestants had done them first.

PROTESTANT LITURGIES

The basic Protestant concern for united worship is reflected immediately in the character of the Confession at the beginning of the Lutheran service. This is not the priest's individual *Confiteor*, as at Rome, but a united prayer of minister and congregation. The Lutheran rite has then a variable Introit, the *Gloria Patri*, the *Kyrie*, and the *Gloria in excelsis*. The Epistle and Gospel are separated, as in the Roman practice, by a proper Gradual. The Nicene Creed and the sermon are followed by an unchanging Offertory, "Create in me a clean heart, O God." There is a General Prayer, and then the sequence of Salutation, *Sursum Corda*, Preface, *Sanctus*, and Lord's Prayer. "The Words of Institution," limited to St. Paul's phrasing in I Corinthians 11, take the place of the Prayer of Consecration. The *Agnus Dei* is sung, the Communion is received, and the *Nunc Dimittis* and a brief Thanksgiving lead to the Benediction, which is the Aaronic blessing of Numbers 6.

The Anglican story is one of largely independent development, and so of a product at some points nearer to the Roman source than is the Lutheran, and at some points further away. In 1548 there appeared *The Order of the Communion,* an English service designed for the communicating of the people in both kinds. The service in the prayer book of 1549 is captioned, "The Supper of the Lord and the Holy Communion, commonly called the Masse." It is Cranmer's abridgement, in English, of the Latin service, with the inclusion of the people's Confession and the "prayer of humble access" from the *Order* of 1548.

The "prayer for the whole state of Christ's Church" in this order followed the *Sanctus,* and led immediately into the Consecration. This latter was much the same as that in the American Episcopal service of today. The Lord's Prayer, Invitation, Confession, Absolution, and Prayer of Humble Access came after the Consecration, and immediately before the Communion. Post-Communion sentences, a Thanksgiving, and the Blessing concluded the service.

The "second prayer book of Edward VI," that of 1552, moved more decisively in the Protestant direction. The word "Mass" was dropped from the title, and "table" was substituted for "altar" in the rubrics. The Ten Commandments were placed at the beginning, immediately after Alcuin's Collect, and the Introit was omitted, the didactic thus taking the place of the devotional, and making the *Kyrie* penitential rather than joyous. This required the moving of the *Gloria in excelsis,* which became now the triumphant ending of the whole service; and reasonably enough, in view of the fact that the Liturgy of the Catechumens no longer was an effective reality. The Prayer for the Church was separated from the Consecration by the insertion between them of the Invitation, Confession, and Absolution. Most significantly, the Consecration itself was reduced to the first paragraph only of the 1549 text, concluding with St. Paul's account of the institution of the Sacrament.

The revision of the prayer book in 1662, occasioned by the restoration of Charles II, made little substantial change, and none of any consequence in the Communion. The rejection by the Parliament of the revised book of 1928 therefore has left the English service practically unaltered for the past four hundred years.

With the disestablishment of the Episcopal Church in Scotland in 1689, the liturgy which had been proposed by Archbishop Laud in 1637 became the basis for all later Scottish use. This form included the restoring of much of the 1549 Consecration. The first American book, completed in 1789, adopted the Consecration from the last preceding Scottish revision, that of 1764. The general arrangement of the American service, however, is closer to the English than to the Scottish form.

Wesley's liturgy prepared for the American Methodists was on the whole a copying out of the 1552–1662 English service. The major changes were that the Absolution was recast in the form of a prayer, and that the last paragraph of the 1549 Consecration (the "oblation of ourselves") was substituted absolutely, instead of permissively, for the final Thanksgiving. The American Methodist *Ritual* of 1944 provides two orders for the Holy Communion, both derived from Wesley's sequence but neither quite identical with it.

The basic resemblances and the minor differences among the current Western liturgies, Roman and Protestant, are exhibited in tabular form in Appendix F. What stands out clearly is that in all these rites the service is one in essence. As to elements of detail there is more of divergence between the Anglican forms of Consecration in England and America than there is between the English one and the American Methodist, and there are a number of points at which the Roman use, on the one hand, and the Lutheran and Presbyterian services, on the other, stand together in contrast with the Methodist and the Anglican. At least in the structures and the words of their orders for the celebration of the Holy Communion, all these Churches are much more nearly alike than they are different.

The Reformed Churches, being less patient with the historic rituals than were the Lutheran and Anglican, to all intents and purposes did away with the ordered Communion liturgy. Nevertheless they retained its core, in words of institution and thanksgiving which were theoretically extempore but in fact largely standard. More recently it has become evident that much of the ancient ritual is finding its way back into the services of almost all our major denominations.

When the Puritans were in control in England, the Westminster Assembly of Divines issued *The Directory for the Public Worship of God* (1644), and included in it instructions for "the Celebration of the Communion, or Sacrament of the Lord's Supper." This provided for an exhortation, the words of institution from I Corinthians 11, a prayer of "thanksgiving or blessing," the breaking of the bread, the distribution of the bread and wine, and a concluding "solemn thanks to God." Texts were supplied for all of these, though with the qualification "to this effect" for the blessing of the elements, and "or the like" for the distribution. An explanation of the words of institution was to be made by the minister "when he seeth requisite."

The order in the 1932 edition of the American Presbyterian *Book of Common Worship*, while preserving this general pattern, included within it a number of materials from the traditional liturgies: Salutation, *Sursum Corda*, Preface, *Sanctus*, and a prayer evidently based upon the Invocation and the "oblation of ourselves" which conclude the Scottish and American Prayers of Consecration. The Presbyterian revision of 1946 is almost breath-taking to one who is devoted to the ancient usages, and must be quite as much so to those who have not liked them. We find now a service which in general reproduces the Anglican, but which is closer to the Roman and Lutheran in placing the Confession and the *Gloria in excelsis* near the beginning, and in providing explicitly for the use of the *Agnus Dei*. There is a prayer based upon that "for the whole state of Christ's Church," a Consecration separated from the Words of Institution by Preface and *Sanctus* (with proper prefaces provided), and a final Thanksgiving only slightly abbreviated from that of 1549. The "Assurance of Pardon" is a verbatim transcript of the Anglican "Declaration of Absolution," including the second-person pronoun: "have mercy upon you, pardon and deliver you."

Even in the Churches of the Separatist tradition there is evidence of a return to the historic form of service. The "Service of Morning Worship with Holy Communion" in the Congregational *Pilgrim Hymnal* of 1935 uses the Communion Collect of Alcuin, the General Confession from Morning Prayer (deleting "miserable offenders"), the Lord's Prayer, and the standard English Communion Blessing. In the Unitarian *Services of Religion* (1937) the "longer form" provided for the Communion contains Alcuin's Collect, an adaptation of the ancient Eucharistic prayer of the *Didache*, *Sursum Corda*, Preface, and *Sanctus*. The "Communion Prayer," taking the place of the Consecration, includes the words of institution from St. Paul.

THE REAL PRESENCE

"This is my body which is broken for you. . . . This cup is the new testament in my blood." Whatever else is in a given liturgy, whatever else may be left out, these words are there. Sadly for the one body in Christ, it has been broken sharply, and into many segments, in dispute over what those words may mean. "Transubstantiation," the official Roman term since the Council of Trent, reflects what most of the Church had taken for granted from the beginning: that the bread and wine, consecrated in the service, had become the veritable body and blood of Christ. Rejecting this view as such, Martin Luther held firmly to what was called "consubstantiation," and refused fellowship with Zwingli because the Swiss reformer thought of the Communion in memorial and symbolic terms only.

There is some difficulty in determining just what Luther meant. "Consubstantiation," if it was designed to translate the Greek *homoousios*, would signify "identical substance" rather than "presence with." The latter represents the position of most Lutheran theologians of today. They prefer, however, not to use Luther's expression because of its ambiguity.

What was called the "black rubric," inserted into the English book of 1552 on the insistence of John Knox, declared that kneeling to receive the Sacrament did not mean

that any adoracion is doone, or oughte to be doone, eyther vnto the Sacramentall bread or wyne, there bodelye receyued, or vnto any reall and essencial presence there beeyng of Chrystes naturall fleshe and bloode.

The book of 1662 modified the last phrase to read "any Corporal Presence" instead of "any reall and essencial presence"; and thereby it marked the real and essential distinction.

There is no "black rubric" either in the Scottish or in the American service, and surely there can be none of the 1552 variety in a genuine Christian faith. The bread indeed remains bread, and the wine still is wine. The "Corporal Presence of Christ's Naturall Flesh and Blood" has not been known on the earth since the Ascension. But ultimate reality is spiritual, not physical; and the real presence is not for a moment to be confused with the corporeal.

The cup of blessing which we bless, is it not the communion of the blood of Christ? The bread which we break, is it not the communion of the body of Christ?

To deny the real presence of the Christ in the Communion of his body and blood is to deny the faith of the Church from St. Paul's time on. It is no less to repudiate the living experience of millions who have met their Lord face to face, and have touched and handled things unseen, in the physical act of eating and drinking the holy gifts of the altar.

The Communion is a memorial indeed, the one which God's Son has commanded us to make. But it is not a memorial only. It is also a present reality, in which those who "worthily receive the most precious Body and Blood" are made "one body with him, that he may dwell in us, and we in him." Of course this is a miracle; but it is not a material miracle, which could be of no importance. It is a spiritual miracle, which matters infinitely. And those who have said the Prayer of Consecration, and those who have received the consecrated elements, know how real the miracle can be; how real it is for them when their hearts are duly prepared to experience it.

This is the doctrine of St. Paul. It is the historic faith of the universal Church. It is what all the liturgies say, in the words of institution if no otherwhere. It is what the people of Christ have known for themselves, from ancient Corinth to modern San Francisco. Is the Christ not really present? Do we not receive him? If not, the fault is neither his nor the Sacrament's. It can but be our own.

THE SACRED FELLOWSHIP

So sacred was the mystery of the Word made flesh, and the expression of that mystery in the Holy Eucharist, that the primitive Church denied admission to pagans, and so to anyone who was not a complete initiate. The catechumens were instructed in the earlier part of the service, but they were dismissed before the actual celebration began. It followed that any defection on the part of a Christian, moral or ideological, excluded him also. Thus the mark of dismissal from the fellowship was excommunication, withdrawal of the high privilege of sharing in the Communion.

Excommunication was a weapon of the Church against heretics, and mutual excommunication took place between contending groups of comparable strength. Thus East and West came to the parting of the ways, factually as organizations and symbolically in the loss of access each to the other's altar. Thus also Rome excommunicated dissident individuals, and ultimately the great companies of the sixteenth-century Protestants. These reacted in kind, so far as their influence went; and so it came about that the right to commune went with the recognizing of membership in a particular body of Christians. There was no longer one body of Christ to which all could turn, and in which all could be members together.

There had been a decided loss of fellowship, too, in the rarity of individual communions in the late Middle Ages. Specifying that the people should "sit about the table, or at it," the Puritan directions of 1644 seem to be reminiscent of the Agape, the ancient love feast, in contrast with the Mass as Rome had developed it. In general the Protestant services sought to restore in the West what the East never has lost: the realization of fellowship, of true communion, among all who share in the Supper of the Lord. The giving of the Sacrament to the people in both kinds pointed in this direction, for it erased one conspicuous line that had been drawn between cleric and layman.

The traditional mode of distribution, by the priest or minister immediately before the altar, always had brought the communicants together in physical nearness as in spiritual sharing. This unifying factor had been reduced by the fact that few of the congregation actually communicated in any given service; but it still was available for those who met its conditions. The same applies to the Orthodox, who stand to receive the Sacrament, but kneel in a group on the open floor while each awaits his turn. Anglicans kneel always to receive, as do most Lutherans. Methodists are supposed to, but some of them have been falling into Reformed and Separatist habits in recent years.

The Puritan distaste for the historic altar led to its being turned into a table, literally "with legs," to its being brought forward into the church, and to placing laymen as well as ordained clergy about it. At the same time, curiously enough, this mood soon issued in the practice of leaving the rest of the congregation far away from the holy table all through the service, even for the distribution. Thus not only was the altar made of less significance, but the coming together of the people in Christian unity ceased to be expressed in their conduct.

At once as Sacrament and as fellowship, the Communion surely ought to be administered and received reverently before the altar, rather than without effort in the pew. The act of coming forward, demanding personal decision, some expenditure of energy, and a clear declaration before the assembled company, itself contributes to the meaning of the service for everyone who makes for himself the solemn decision and the reverent change of place. The kneeling at once close to the cross, and close to one's friends, intensifies both the realization of the Lord's real presence, and the awareness of one's fellowship with these others who also love the Lord. It is time therefore that the Methodists should resume their own heritage, and the dissenters that of the earlier Church.

How long will it be before our Churches will welcome into the fellowship of the Communion all those who love the Lord Jesus Christ in sincerity? Rome and the "hardshell Baptists," at opposite poles in all matters liturgical, have been at one in making the Communion a symbol of exclusion rather than of brotherhood. Few other Churches have been quite so rigid, and some recently have made definite steps toward a formal intercommunion which may issue in a real fellowship in Christ. But we have a long way to go before we shall be able to express "one Lord, one faith, one baptism," in one gathering about the table of the Lord.

Ye who do truly and earnestly repent you of your sins, and are in love and charity with your neighbours, and intend to lead a new life, following the commandments of God, and walking from henceforth in his holy ways; Draw near with faith, and take this holy Sacrament to your comfort.

There is nothing said here about denominational affiliation or shadings of theological belief. The historic Invitation requires harder things than these: repentance, love, consecration to a new life, faith. But to those who satisfy these rigorous conditions it says, "Draw near . . . and take this holy Sacrament." Is it not time for us to take this seriously, and to welcome into the fellowship all those who in seriousness of purpose wish to enter it and share its benefits?

MINISTER AND PRIEST

The minister is the servant, at once of God and of his people. The priest is the agent who helps the people in their approach to God. The words are more different than are their meanings. Judaism had priests, has rabbis, and hopes to have priests again. Christianity has had deacons, presbyters, bishops; that is to say, servers, elders, superintendents. From the second century it called its fully ordained ministers "priests"; and the rejection of the word by some Protestants has changed none of the essential facts.

The meaning of every Christian ordination is the same. He who is accepted as a qualified minister of Christ is identified specifically in his being qualified to administer the Holy Communion. This is the precise meaning of ordination, and all else is peripheral. Even lay baptism always has been recognized in emergency, and the capacity to solemnize marriages depends entirely upon varying civil laws. But no one who is not fully ordained, whatever the steps or the procedure may be, is authorized in any Church to consecrate the sacramental bread and wine. This means the recognition of a special priesthood, whatever words may be used or avoided.

This is as it should be. The solemn duty, the high privilege, is not lightly and casually to be assigned. There must be tests of capacity, of adequate training, above all of devotion. As things stand, each Church has its own rules, and each Church will rule for itself for long enough to come. That does not alter the fact that each Church gives the responsibility only to a few, and only under specified conditions.

The apostolic succession may be debated endlessly, and mostly without profit. The realization that the laying on of hands has come down in a direct line from St. Peter is important and meaningful to many. Just how the sequence has been maintained is a matter of technical dispute; and Rome is no more benevolent toward Anglican orders than Anglicans are toward Methodist. Probably most ministers in our modern Churches have the succession by physical touch. The original Puritans and Separatists, as well as the founders of Methodism, had been ordained by English bishops; and each of the inheriting denominations has preserved a succession of its own through its own clergy. The area of controversy, then, is only that of the status of recognized bishops; and there is not likely to be any quick resolution here.

What can and must be determined positively, because it is real and vital, is the spiritual status of the appointed minister. This does not mean that the validity of the Sacrament depends directly upon the character of the celebrant, for if it did, who of us would dare to minister at the altar? But it does involve the absolute obligation of the priest or minister to consecrate himself, as sincerely and as completely as in him lies, ere he ventures upon the consecration of the holy gifts. If he fails to do this, if he arrives at the Church late and breathless, and if he regards the duty as a burden, and if he ministers perfunctorily without love to the Christ and to the congregation: then verily he "eateth and drinketh unworthily," and so he "eateth and drinketh damnation unto himself."

The priesthood of all believers excludes the character of the priest as intermediary. It by no means reduces his responsibility as minister, as servant. The Church, and all the Churches, have insisted that his particular service in the Communion is an essential one. How great then is his obligation, in helping God's family to meet the elder brother face to face at his own table. There is a miracle that happens in the Consecration, a miracle to which all those can testify who have known its reality for themselves. It is not then surprising, and it is not insignificant, that the ancient Church insisted that the minister should prepare himself in prayer and fasting.

We shall hope that no layman will partake of the Holy Communion indifferently or thoughtlessly. It is therefore the more critically important that the clergyman shall perform his part in full seriousness of intent. The sacrifice is sacred, and so is the fellowship. In the privilege that is particularly his, the minister is the agent in making the one sacrifice available to all the people. He may prefer not to call himself a priest. God yet calls on him to open for the people the way of approach to God.

TIMES OF COMMUNION

As the Mass had been the principal Christian service from the beginning, so it is evident that the reformers of 1549 expected the Communion to be the chief service of the English Church. It is in the Communion Office, and not in connection with "Daily Morning and Evening Prayer," that there is a rubric providing for a sermon. Here again Puritan influence prevailed to make the service of instruction primary, and so to reduce the great service of thanksgiving to a secondary rank. Morning Prayer and its derivatives thus became standard for the "big" service of Sunday morning, with the Communion celebrated at another and less convenient hour in Anglicanism, and only a few times a year in the nonconformist Churches.

John Wesley urged the receiving of the Communion weekly, as being essential to devout and faithful Christian living. So long as he survived, the English Methodists were instructed to commune regularly at the local parish church. Since this was not always possible (in part because Anglicanism itself had made celebrations of the Communion extremely infrequent), specifically Methodist Communion services were held with growing frequency from 1740 on. These were conducted in accordance with the rules of the English Church, save that Wesley himself seems to have followed some nonjuring practices, such as that of the mixed chalice and the use of the Invocation and Oblation as in the Scottish (and later American) rites. American Methodists, not content with shortening the liturgy which Wesley had prepared for them, quickly relegated it to the very occasional use which Wesley had so deprecated in Anglicanism; and so made it clear that they regarded preaching, rather than the Communion, as the principal means toward spiritual experience.

The revival of the Communion as central in the weekly Christian worship of God came first in America in a conspicuously nonritualistic group. Alexander Campbell, the founder of the Disciples of Christ, was persuaded that the apostolic Church had celebrated the Communion every Sunday, and he was convinced that this practice was integral to a vital life in Christ. Accordingly he enjoined a weekly observance upon his followers. In proportion to membership the Disciples therefore have probably more individual communicants each Sunday than does any other Christian body; and thereby they give to their people a privilege that most of the other Churches have made difficult to obtain, or have denied altogether.

Typical Anglican usage in America provides for the Communion at eleven o'clock on the first Sunday of each month, with other celebrations earlier on Sundays and occasionally during the week. In most parishes in England the Communion, more and more commonly called by its old name of the "Mass," recently has become the regular major service of each Sunday. The Lutherans, as has been noted, never have followed any other practice.

There is much to be said for using the Communion service, or at least the first part of it, as the standard one of general Christian worship for "the great congregation." The Communion was designed for this purpose. It is indeed a service of thanksgiving, at once solemn and joyous; and it puts the instructional item of the sermon at an early rather than at an apparently climactic point. The Lutheran addition of an Old Testament lesson would dispose of the problem of Scriptural flexibility which some have seen in the Anglican restriction of biblical material in the Communion service to the stated Epistle and Gospel.

Whether or not the Communion regularly supersedes the Morning Prayer pattern on Sunday mornings, it should be celebrated not less than weekly in every Church. This is necessary for the minister, who needs continually to be revitalized in his awareness of his sacred office, and to be strengthened for its performance; and it is necessary also for his congregation, even if as yet they do not know it. A large part of the dislike of the Communion service, and discomfort in it—a dislike and a discomfort which undeniably are common among American Protestants—is to be traced simply to unfamiliarity. People who feel this way need to be reeducated, and that will take some time. But they do need to be reeducated, and not even for their sins of ignorance should they be permanently deprived.

"This do in remembrance of me." The Church has not done it nearly often enough, or faithfully enough; and so it has denied to its people the opportunity to do it aright. Preaching about our Lord is proper, and ought not to be neglected. But we shall meet the Lord the more readily, and the more really, as we gather about his table, than ever we shall in speaking or hearing words from the pulpit.

Too many Churches have fifty-two (or 104) sermons a year, and only four Communion services. Perhaps fifty-two Communions and four sermons would do more to ensure the real presence of the Lord in our midst and in our hearts. We need not settle, however, for either-or. It is rather imperative that we shall have both-and. And it is critically important that we shall recover soon from the notion that the primary Christian service is the one we ordinarily can get along without.

"This is my body." "Ye are the body of Christ." These are the two meanings, and the inseparably related meanings, of the Sacrament of the Holy Communion. It is at once Passover and *Kiddush*, Eucharist and Agape, sacrifice and fellowship.

But for the sacrifice of Calvary, there could be for us no fellowship with our Lord, and none in him. The breaking of the bread, the pouring of the wine, renew for us his eternal sacrifice once offered. Our sharing of the Body and the Blood makes us one with him, and in him one also each with each other. For nineteen centuries Christians have known this to be true, for they have known it to happen. It is true for us too—or will be, when rightly we understand it and practice it. Let us then draw near with faith, and take this holy Sacrament to our comfort. And who will not devoutly kneel?

XII

CRADLE TO GRAVE

THE CHURCH ALWAYS has met for general worship at stated times. It also has concerned itself with the personal and family life of its people, and has marked a number of signal points in their respective histories with its "occasional services." The first commitment to the Christian life in baptism, the confirming of that commitment in the assuming of responsible membership in the Church, the establishment of a new family unit, the last farewell to a physical body: all of these belong not only to the individual and the family, but also to the entire Christian fellowship. Special forms of service therefore have been developed for these occasions; and so deeply rooted are they in our general culture that many people come to the Church for these services even though for no other.

There ought by all means to be education and moral suasion brought to bear on those who thus make use of the Church without accepting any responsibility to live and serve in it. At the same time it should be possible so to conduct these personal services that they will have true meaning and lasting effect in themselves, in addition to their possible value in recalling men and women to their general Christian obligation. Each of them marks a critical point: the first three for the individual, the last for his relatives and friends. The forms of all these services normally are short. They nevertheless can exercise great power for good, for ill, or for nullity. It is the officiant's duty to see that good shall prevail for all who are concerned.

THE ADMINISTRATION OF HOLY BAPTISM

Ceremonial washing was a familiar practice in historic Judaism, and without reference to the obscure sect of the Essenes it provides sufficient precedent for the baptizing which St. John instituted at the Jordan. Jesus submitted to baptism at the hands of the desert prophet, thus aligning himself with that prophet's ethical program and with his heralding of a new baptism in the Holy Ghost. Our Lord seems also to have encouraged his disciples to use the rite as a token of initiation into the coming Kingdom of God, though the Fourth Gospel is careful to say that "Jesus himself baptized not, but his disciples." The last command in St. Matthew 28:19 may be of dubious historicity as a word of Jesus, but unquestionably it represents the very early position of the Church.

The modern Baptists have all the better of the argument about the purpose and nature of baptism, so far as the earliest days of Christianity are concerned. Baptism was of adults, on their own initiative, and it was by total immersion. Already in the New Testament, however, there are hints of change on both points. The conversion of the jailer in Philippi, recorded in Acts 16, is followed by the immediate baptizing of his whole household. This certainly implies that children were included. Nor is there any indication that the group left the house to find a body of water sufficient for immersion. (Perhaps the jailer's house had an atrium with a pool in it; but it would be wish-thinking on either side that would create any assurance here.)

Baptism seems at the beginning to have been "in the name of Jesus Christ" (Acts 2:38) or "into the name of the Lord Jesus" (Acts 8:16). St. Paul in Romans 6 speaks of being "baptized into Christ Jesus," and in Galatians 3 of "as many of you as have been baptized into Christ." Aside from the passage in Matthew 28, the earliest known occurrence of the triple formula is in the first Apology of St. Justin, written at about the middle of the first century. Here it reads, "in the name of God the Father and ruler of all, and of our Saviour Jesus Christ, and of the Holy Ghost."

It is evident that almost from the beginning of Christian history a certain magical quality was assumed to inhere in baptism. This would be particularly natural in the Greek world, accustomed as it was to the initiatory rites of the mystery cults. St. Paul takes "baptism for the dead" for granted, and in writing to the Corinthians he uses it as an argument for belief in a future life. The late appendix to St. Mark's Gospel is slightly ambiguous as to the specific necessity of the rite. It says clearly that "He that believeth and is baptized shall be saved," but it does not refer explicitly to baptism in the contrasting clause, "he that believeth not shall be damned."

The quasi-magical view of the efficacy of baptism led in two opposite directions. On the one hand, it encouraged the baptism of infants in order to ensure their salvation if they should die before reaching maturity. On the other, with the rise of the theory that sin after baptism could not be forgiven, it tended in the case of adults to postpone the ceremony until the latest possible time. Thus for example the Emperor Constantine, taking no chances, did not submit himself for baptism until he was on his deathbed.

In the beginning a simple profession of Christian faith seems to have been regarded as enough for admission to baptism. Certainly the three thousand who are said to have been baptized on the day of Pentecost had had minimum instruction, in the single sermon of St. Peter, and they could not have been tested in any way. The Ethiopian eunuch, baptized after a travel conversation with the deacon Philip, is another evident case in point. Soon, however, it became clearly necessary to establish much more rigorous standards; and the *Didache* and St. Justin both indicate that in the second century there was required a considerable preliminary period of instruction, fasting, prayer, and confession.

The Apostles' Creed came into public use first as a brief and simple statement of the faith of the one who was to be baptized, guaranteeing as it were his basic orthodoxy. Gradually the form of the service was elaborated to include exorcisms, anointing with oil, and vesting with a white robe. The English service of 1552, largely followed in the American Episcopal rite, was a combination of materials from the Sarum use, the baptismal service drawn up by Martin Luther, and the proposals of Archbishop Hermann von Wied of Cologne (1543).

It was assumed that baptisms should take place not only in the church, but also in the presence of the general congregation. This certainly is to be desired, both for the congregation's sake and for that of the persons (candidate, parents, sponsors) most directly involved. The pledge of faith and fidelity, whether made by the individual or on his behalf by his elders, should be made with many hearing it and praying earnestly for its fulfillment.

Private baptism originally was designed only for emergency cases, in the imminent approach of death. In our time it has become too frequently the excuse for a pleasant social gathering. Adults certainly, and infants in most cases, should be baptized during a regular Sunday service. What little of inconvenience may be involved is much more than balanced by the increased seriousness of effect.

That seriousness can not be secured, however, if the baptismal service is skimped for the mere saving of time. The reading of the Gospel, the blessing of the font, the signing with the cross, the prayers for candidate and sponsors, are no less meaningful than are the questions. Whatever the tradition of the particular Church may be as to the specific procedure, the administration of Holy Baptism should be sufficiently rich in detail, and unhurried in action, to reflect adequately the deep significance of the step that is being taken.

This is either the individual's first open and public commitment to the Christian way, or the commitment of his family and their close friends to see that he shall be brought up in it. This requires advance consultation and instruction, for the candidate in the one case and for the parents and godparents in the other. It requires the minister's being assured at once of full sincerity and of adequate knowledge on their part. And it requires that the minister himself shall so carry out his duties in the service that the professions and promises now made shall be deeply felt and earnestly carried out by those who make them. Baptism used to be called "christening," "making Christian." The rite still can be used to aid in creating the reality.

ENTERING THE CHURCH

The word "church" is not to be understood as capitalized in the title of this section, for membership in the universal Church of Christ is conferred in the baptismal rite itself. For those groups which permit adult baptism only, this membership and that in the particular Church organization are granted at one time in the one act. It is interesting to note, however, that some of these denominations now encourage the use of a special service for "the dedication of infants," which clearly is a surrogate for infant baptism, as in these groups baptism takes the place of the traditional confirmation.

The baptizing of a baby, unaware of the meaning of the sacrament, does not and can not provide adequately for his personal realization of, and his hearty assent to, the pledges that have been made on his behalf. Accordingly the Church developed the rite of Confirmation, literally and precisely the confirming of the baptismal vows when the individual had reached the age of discretion, and was ready to decide and speak for himself.

Here as in so many other cases we find definite Jewish precedent: circumcision as the parallel to infant baptism, and the *bar-mitzvah* ("son of duty") ceremony at age thirteen. The Jewish boy, having been duly trained in the synagogue school, is called forward and recites a prayer "on this solemn and sacred day, which marks my passage from boyhood to manhood. In my earliest infancy," he says,

I was brought within thy sacred covenant of Israel; and today I again enter thine elect congregation as an active member, bearing the full responsibility for all my doings, and under the sacred obligation to sanctify thy holy Name before all the world.

The prayer ends with the *Shema*, and then the lad reads an assigned passage from the Torah. His father adds a blessing for the successful reaching of this critical stage in physical and spiritual growth.

Within the Christian tradition, Confirmation appears to be associated with the laying on of hands by the apostles and prophets. This was understood to convey the gift of the Holy Ghost, as in the visit of St. Peter and St. John to Samaria recorded in Acts 8. In the Eastern Churches "chrism" (anointing) follows immediately upon baptism; but in the West the two came soon to be separated, and so to reflect the difference between the infant's dedication to God in Christ, and his own considered acceptance of that commitment. The importance of this step was such that only the Bishop was considered competent to administer the rite.

The English Church, while denying the status of Confirmation as a sacrament, nevertheless continued the practice with a minimum of change. The requirement for admission to Confirmation was thus stated in 1549:

So soone as the children can say in their mother tongue tharticles of the faith, the lordes praier, the ten commaundementes, and also can aunswere to such questions of this short Catechisme as the Bushop (or suche as he shall appointe) shall by his discrecion appose them in: then shall they bee brought to the Bushop by one that shalbee his godfather or godmother, that euerye childe maye haue a wittenesse of hys confirmacion.

It was in the book of 1552 that there first appeared the beautiful Confirmation prayer, said as "the Bisshoppe shall laye his hande upon euery chylde seuerally":

Defende, O lord, this child with thy heauenly grace, that he may continue thine for euer, and dayly encrease in thy holy spirite more and more, until he come unto thy euerlastyng kyngdom. Amen.

Those Churches which have no bishops, or which, like the Methodists, have not enough bishops to make annual visits to each parish, manifestly have to leave Confirmation to the local minister. It does not matter seriously that many have dropped the historic word in favor of the literal "Reception into Membership." It does matter a great deal, however, that in so many cases this reception has become a matter of a jolly handshake rather than a solemn act of dedication.

Recently the Methodist Church has authorized officially what some of its pastors had been doing long before: that is, saying the prayer for each candidate separately, with the hand laid on his head, instead of using the former summary "Defend, O Lord, these thy children . . ." At the same time it has for some reason shortened the prayer to read only:

The Lord defend thee with his heavenly grace and by his Spirit confirm thee in the faith and fellowship of all true disciples of Jesus Christ.

The Presbyterian Church has legislated to the effect that

Where persons baptized in infancy are to be admitted into full communion with the Church, they shall be examined as to their knowledge and piety, and shall in ordinary cases, with the approval of the session, make a public profession of their faith, in the presence of the congregation.

The service set forth for this purpose in 1932 was extremely brief, and amazingly it contained no prayer except the Aaronic blessing at the end. As in the case of the Communion, however, the 1946 *Book of Common Worship* has greatly enriched the service, which now is titled "Order for the Confirmation of Baptismal Vows and Admission to the Lord's Supper." The arrangement is similar to that of the Anglican rite, and the prayer "Defend, O Lord . . ." is said for each candidate, who kneels while the minister lays his hand upon him.

The acceptance of full adult responsibility as a member of Christ's

Church merits more attention than most of the churches commonly have given it. The period of instruction, whether of younger candidates or of those of riper years, can be omitted only at the peril of building up a Church membership ignorant, undisciplined, and less than fully committed. That we have so many such members in our parishes today can be laid very largely to this account.

All who will may come; but this includes the will truly to believe, eagerly to learn, faithfully to serve the Christ in the fellowship of his people. The way toward the Church indeed should be wide and well marked. But the entry into it must be kept narrow enough to permit the scrutiny of each seeker for entrance, by those who are qualified to judge of his character and his purpose. The entry must be narrow enough, too, for the entrant to be aware that he is passing through a real portal into a really different way of life.

The second requirement is that the service, whether called "Confirmation" or "Reception," shall symbolize in due measure the compelling seriousness of the step that is being taken. The services provided in Anglicanism and Lutheranism are fixed, and because of their historic rootage are adequate toward this end. The new Presbyterian form is one full of dignity and significance. Most of the others now used need both enlargement and intensification, before they will signalize worthily the solemn act of assuming active membership in the Church of Jesus Christ. The freedom which most nonconformist communions accord their clergy will allow local enrichment of the patterns of the existing service books. Such enrichment is called for, and it should be made soberly but eagerly. What we must achieve is to mark the ratifying and confirming of the baptismal vows as an absolutely critical point in the individual's life story.

THE SOLEMNIZATION OF MATRIMONY

"A wedding," remarked a mordant florist, "is for the bride's mother." Weddings often are. A marriage may not be. Nothing associated with the Church has been allowed to become so trivial, so irreligious, so much a display and so little a solemnization, as has the typical "society wedding" of our time. And the economically underprivileged, aping those who scarcely are their betters, have fallen into their own rather pathetic variations of the same bad taste and the same total lack of religious meaning.

Marriage is a civil contract, involving property rights and other juridical matters. It stands therefore under the authority of the state, and is controlled by the lawmakers of the given political unit. Puritan insistence on the separation of Church and state went so far as to rule out any religious ceremony of marriage in early New England. The state still can, and usually does, provide for fully legal marriage without any religious sanction or ecclesiastical participation. At the same time in most jurisdictions it authorizes the clergy to serve as officers of the state by means of a service held in the church.

The minister has then a dual responsibility in the marriage service. To the state he owes meticulous observance of whatever its regulations may be, both as to the eligibility of the marriage partners and in the making out and submission of the proper records. On the other hand, he owes to the Church, and to the man and woman, a no less careful concern that the marriage shall be a true one, worthy to be blessed by the Church and fittingly blessed by its minister. The obligation to the state is the easy one to fulfill, for it is precise and literal. That to the Church, and to the bride and groom, demands much more in thought, in labor, and in love.

The fact that Jewish marriage rituals seem to have contributed nothing directly to Christian practice suggests that early Christian marriages were not solemnized in the church. This view is supported by the total lack of reference to marriage services, as such, in the early authorities. Apparently the wedding took place in the home, and with Greco-Roman rather than Judaeo-Christian elements of ceremony. The married couple later asked for the blessing of the priest; and it is from that simple blessing, given after the event, that our later marriage services have come.

By the end of the fourth century, according to both St. Ambrose and St. Augustine, marriage was regarded as a Christian sacrament. The ceremonies, little changed in themselves from their pagan origins, were transferred to the church and were associated with the Eucharist, thus leading to the development of the Nuptial Mass. A preconquest English law, of King Edmund in 946, required that "the priest shall be at the marriage, and shall celebrate the union according to custom with God's blessing, and with all solemnity."

The first English prayer books derived their "Forme of Solemnizacion of Matrimonie" primarily from the existing usages of Salisbury and York, though again with some aid from the innovations suggested by Archbishop Hermann von Wied of Cologne. This service is basic to practically all those used in American Protestantism. The Methodist version of it recently has been "modernized," and the charges to the congregation and the couple have become merely statements of the nature and purpose of Christian marriage, without providing the historic opportunities for protest. On the other hand the Methodists now have borrowed the "blessing of the ring" from the (1928) American Episcopal service. The Presbyterian service follows the same order, though with modified verbiage, and with new prayers by Henry van Dyke. The "blessing of the ring," again exactly as in the Episcopal form, was added in the 1946 Presbyterian book.

The minister's first duty with respect to a marriage is in the counseling of the engaged couple. It may be that in some cases this has been a trifle overdone, especially when the clergyman has considered himself an expert on matters sexual. In our time he may need now and then to give advice at this point; but the cases will be few, and he ought to be sure of the need before he presumes to compete with college courses, doctors, and clinics.

What very definitely is in his province is the emphatic statement of the Christian view of marriage. Those who enter upon this sacred relation casually or hastily are seeking to be "coupled together otherwise than God's word doth allow." Unless the minister is completely satisfied of the couple's full understanding of the sacred compact in which they are about to engage, and of their deep sincerity of intent, he has no further part to play in their arrangements. What is left for him is to pray for their souls, and to seek their salvation from the sins of our flippant age.

The preliminary interviews will provide opportunity for the giving of some sound, and often very necessary, advice about the plans for the wedding itself. So far as in him lies, the clergyman ought now to do his best to discourage lavish display and stupid expenditure. There need not be, even to satisfy relatives and friends, an army of ushers and bridesmaids. There is no sense in hiding a beautiful sanctuary behind a mass of hothouse flowers, and there is no real hope of disguising an ugly pulpit and choir loft. The money had much better be spent for added equipment for the new home, including a family Bible. Insistence upon the basically religious character of the service will do much to straighten out the sense of values here; and most brides and grooms will be extremely grateful for a word said on the side of dignified simplicity.

In churches in which weddings occur rather frequently, a booklet for brides will be helpful. Most brides ask the same questions, and all need to be told the same things. An inclusive booklet, handed to the bride at the first preliminary interview, also will cover the minister's occasional failure to mention some minor but none the less important detail. Our little *About Weddings in the Chapel of Mills College,* drawn up in 1950, has been much appreciated by brides and grooms, and has greatly simplified the handling of procedures. It includes sections on "the mood of a marriage," "the place and the people," decoration, music, the service, the rehearsal, documentation, photographs, an outline of schedule for the wedding day, and a personal word to the man and woman. A similar booklet, recently come to hand, is that prepared by the Reverend Howard Greenwalt for marriages in the Methodist Church in San Leandro, California.

The groom should be instructed in advance to bring the necessary legal papers to the rehearsal, so that the minister can complete all required paper work before the time set for the wedding. Groom and bride may sign the church registry at the rehearsal, since their signatures are for identification only. Thus they will not have that added item to deal with on a day which for them will be quite complicated enough in any event.

It is both illegal and immoral for a minister to allow the prospective witnesses to sign before they have seen the ceremony take place. They ought rather to be instructed to present themselves to sign papers and books, in a designated room in the church, immediately after the actual service has been completed. The minister himself also will withhold his signatures until he has solemnized the marriage.

For a number of practical reasons, the rehearsal is best held two days before the wedding, rather than on the evening just preceding. This will avoid conflict with family or bachelors' dinners; it will give the couple more open time when most they need it; and, in terms of our present culture, it is much more likely to ensure sobriety as well as leisure on the part of all present. Emphasis should be laid on the importance of attendance at the rehearsal by every "member of the wedding," including the parents of both bride and groom. In some cases absentee briefing of one person or another may be inevitable;

but it should be held to a minimum. It is scarcely possible, however, to get every young person, especially in the confusion and hysteria required by prevailing social custom, to arrive at the rehearsal on time. The minister may as well schedule ninety minutes to cover the necessary thirty. Any time he finds free at the end is simply velvet.

The religious word needs to be spoken for a second time at the beginning of the rehearsal, for all who are to take part in it. A brief prayer will help also to establish the tone as one of serious concern rather than of pagan frivolity. The mother of the bride usually will have ideas about just how things should be done. If those ideas do not conflict with the spirit of the service, they may be heeded for politeness' sake. In any case where they are at all at odds with the basic usages of the Church, or with the religious character of the occasion, they must be quickly and flatly negated. Experience suggests that it is best to permit a minimum of option in the planning of the service. The position that "This is how we do it," quietly but firmly taken, not only will speed and smooth the rehearsal, but also it is much more likely to issue in a decent, orderly, and validly impressive ceremony.

In the rehearsal all movements should be gone through, more than once if necessary. The order of the service also should be described in detail, while the members of the wedding party are standing in their assigned places. The actual words of the ceremony should on no account be used at this time. With the license secured, this would constitute a marriage; and without it, it probably would be a violation of the law. Moreover, the service will mean more to all present if its gracious language is heard for the first time when actually it is carrying its full intent.

The normal place for a wedding is in the church, or in one of its chapels. The minister's study is not a proper equivalent, even if he allows himself to perform unscheduled "quickies." For sufficient cause (but let it be sufficient) the service may be held in the family home. One place absolutely not permissible is the "funeral chapel," a setting either of gloom or of pastel sentimentality, and managed all too often by persons whose idea of wedding procedure exhibits neither religious sensitivity, aesthetic taste, nor even correct social usage. Needless to say, though I shall say it, no seriously minded minister of Jesus Christ will go through the motions of a marriage ceremony on horseback or on roller skates, in a swimming pool, or on a theater or television stage. If people want that sort of wedding, let them hire (the exact word) a civil official who knows no better than they do. The music before the service must be religious, and it need not be vocal. If there is to be a soloist, he or she should be strictly forbidden to sing musical-comedy love songs, whether by Reginald de Koven or Victor Herbert. D'Hardelot's "Because" is no better, and Grieg's *Ich liebe dich* not much. There are a number of good wedding hymns in our books, and they are worth trying. In general it will be best, however, for the organist simply to play the Bach wedding chorales, and similar works to which the congregation's mind will not readily attach words, for fifteen minutes before the service is to begin.

The minister should take his place, with the groom and best man standing in front of him at his left, before the organ changes to the march tune. If this is the "Bridal Chorus" from *Lohengrin*, it is singularly incongruous to have the clergyman enter the scene on the first notes of what everyone thinks of as "Here comes the bride." This is a banal piece of music, anyway; and its context in the opera, just before a violent quarrel between Elsa and her knightly bridegroom, has unfortunate connotations. The "Trumpet Voluntary" ascribed to Purcell, though more probably composed by Jeremiah Clarke, is an admirable substitute. Many other possibilities, all preferable to the *Lohengrin*, will suggest themselves to the competent organist.

The opening of the selected march is the cue for the bridal procession to come down the aisle. At that point the minister signs to the people to stand, and he should give them no subsequent chance to sit down. This is a service, and not a show; and respectful participation takes precedence over visibility. The procession should move slowly, but its members need not use the stagy and awkward hesitation step. Brides' fathers will be particularly thankful to find themselves excused from this aspect of their total ordeal.

As soon as the bride reaches her place the music stops, and the service begins. Her father stands not in the line of the wedding party, but one pace behind the bride and a little to her left. Thence he can step back conveniently to take his place beside his wife, when he has said his one brief line and relinquished his daughter to her new man of the house.

The minister's voice has to be used at three levels. The fullest volume belongs to those parts of the service which are explicitly addressed to the whole congregation. A medium tone should be taken for the parts ostensibly addressed to the couple, but meant for the congregation to hear. Then there is the quiet direction that will be necessary now and then, for "take her right hand in yours," "place this ring on her finger and say after me," and so forth. If anything goes wrong it can be corrected unobtrusively in a low speaking voice. Only if there is an agitated whisper will the congregation be aware of difficulty.

The charge to the congregation should be followed by enough pause to make the challenge significant. Not many clergymen ever will have to deal with an actual protest. If one is made, the procedure is to break off the service, hear the complaint in the vestry, and rule on it immediately. If it has insufficient standing, the service is forthwith resumed. If it should appear to present definitive legal reason against the marriage, the minister will have to dismiss the congregation as tactfully as possible, and proceed to render what personal help he may.

The exclusive right of a father over his daughter no longer is recognized by our society. Our present attitude may be reflected suitably in the father's saying, instead of the customary "I do," rather "Her mother and I do." (This suggestion sometimes has an amazingly pacifying effect on Mama at the rehearsal.) In a church with an adequate chancel it is permissible, after the "giving away," for the minister to lead the couple and their principal pair of attendants (no one else) up to the altar for the completion of the service.

The use of two rings now is so common that it must be allowed for. If the minister holds his hand open, to receive the ring in his palm, he is less likely to drop it than if he tries to take it in his fingers. This applies also to his giving the ring to the groom, and to the bride if there are two rings. In the latter event the "blessing of the ring" is better said twice, with "he" and "she" reversed, than in the physical clumsiness of handling two rings at once, and the grammatical madness of "they."

Ordinarily the couple ought to kneel for the blessing and the prayers. This depends to a large extent, however, on sheer physical geography. They must have something to kneel on. Failing a proper altar step, a long and substantial white cushion will serve. A big *prie-dieu*, of the type sometimes supplied by wedding-furnishings departments, is an obstruction which causes more trouble than it is worth. If neither altar step nor cushion is available, it may be best to let the couple stand throughout.

The prayers are said by the minister standing, and facing the couple and the congregation, that he may duly give the blessing. The Lord's Prayer always should be included, so that the congregation may take at least this active part in the service. After the prayers are completed, bride and groom stand for the legal declaration and the final benediction. Since the Sarum use provided *osculans eam*, we scarcely can protest the usage of the groom's then kissing the bride. The minister certainly should not kiss her then or later, unless he is a very dear family friend. (He wouldn't, if he could hear the comments that sometimes are made at receptions.)

The organ starts the march (the Mendelssohn is less bad than the Wagner) the moment the benediction is concluded. Bride and groom lead out, she on his right arm, and they are followed by the pairs of attendants in order. Often it will be found desirable to have the two pairs of parents follow, the bride's first, so that they can be comfortably out of the church ahead of the departing congregation. The witnesses, normally the best man and maid of honor, will leave the procession at the church door and go straight to the place designated for the signing of the certificates and books. They can catch up with the receiving line later; but if they don't sign now, it is improbable that ever they can be recaptured for this duty.

Marriages are not for brides' mothers, and weddings are not for photographers: though this may be news to some of them. No taking of pictures can be permitted at any time during the service. One shot of the bride and groom on their way out may be allowed, for at that time the service is over. A reputable photographer will understand and appreciate the reasons for this restriction. A disreputable one simply will have to have his feelings hurt.

Not many couples in our hurrying age will be willing to take the time necessary for a Nuptial Mass, or its equivalent. The possibility ought nevertheless to be suggested, for the receiving of the Holy Communion together on this significant day is something ever to be treasured in memory. The wine ceremony which comes at the middle of the Jewish marriage service has something of the same effect, so far as expressing the unity of the couple is concerned. I have used it twice, inserted into the prayer book service after the giving of the ring, when one of the families concerned was definitely Jewish in heritage; and in both cases, I believe, the couple as well as the minister found it entirely harmonious and intensely meaningful.

Harmony and meaning are the requisites for the solemnization of matrimony. The traditional English service is textually beautiful, and structurally it is a model of intelligent order. Used aright, it sets the seal of divine blessing upon one of the most critical decisions young men and women can take. To be used aright it must be maintained as a religious service, set forth in beauty but never smothered by secular elaboration. To ensure this, the minister will have to be a rigorous stage director as well as a reverent officiant; but he will find even his stage directing a service to God and man if he does it as in God's sight.

THE BURIAL OF THE DEAD

Christianity never has blinked the fact of death. Our secular world has and does, and seeks continually to pretend death out of existence. This is the basic and irrepressible conflict between the historic Church and the modern mortician. In a sense, perhaps, both the minister and the undertaker seek to comfort the bereaved. The minister's comforting must be real and realistic, as Christianity is; and so sometimes it will be sharply at odds with the sentimentalism that funeral directors have managed to foist upon a shoddy and unrealized Christianity.

"A funeral," said a sage old cleric, "is a classic occasion, into which the romantic may not properly be intruded." This principle, carefully thought through and fully put into practice, would improve both our funeral arrangements and our conduct of the burial office. It is romanticism to buy a needlessly expensive casket, to surround it with a massive motley of flowers, to rouge the face of the corpse, to put the body on display for admiration. It is romanticism also to sing "Beautiful Isle of Somewhere," to indulge in elaborate eulogies of the deceased (whether accurate or not), to stir up still further the emotions of those who ought rather to be calmed and quieted.

Most of this romanticism is new, and a large part of it is entirely commercial. The minister always has control over the service itself, and in many cases he can effectively counsel the family in matters relating to the undertaker's part in the procedure. Whether a coffin is to be buried, or to be burned in cremation, it ought not to absorb, for the dead, funds that are needed for the living. It follows that the "minimum rate" funeral is the only one to be approved. Gifts of flowers are pagan as well as romantic, and should be replaced by gifts to some appropriate charity. Morticians and florists already are protesting the reduction of their incomes because of the spread of this point of view. They have no case, however, till they can show some utility other than a senseless desire for prestige through display.

While he counsels the family thus toward practical wisdom in a greater reverence for reality, the wise pastor also will gain their assent to a fitting service of worship instead of an emotional orgy. A sermon has no place in the burial service. Neither has a biographical review. The family will not benefit by the preaching, and they do not need the information. The family's friends are generally in the same position; and if they are true friends they will not approve a harrowing up of souls that already have suffered the bitter pains of personal loss.

A sober and detached recognition of the fact of death, an assuring declaration of the Christian's hope, and earnest prayers to God for peace and pardon, are all that have place at this time. The Psalms, lessons, and prayers of the historic English burial office provide a framework which includes these and intrudes nothing extraneous. To Cranmer's original selection of Psalms 116, 139, and 146, and of I Corinthians 15 as the lesson, additional options have been provided in successive revisions in England and America.

Such Psalms as 90, "Lord, thou hast been our dwelling place," and 130, "Out of the depths have I cried unto thee," set the brevity and sorrow of man's life on earth against the background of God's eternal purpose, and so bring even our greatest personal tragedies back into scale. Such lessons as Romans 8 and St. John 14 declare the Christian triumph over suffering and bewilderment. Portions of Proverbs 31 may be suitable for reading at the burial of a woman of mature years. The biblical materials are wiser, better phrased, and infinitely more heartening than any personal disquisition can be. Only arrogance then will substitute the personal for, or add it to, the perduring.

As soon as we think of prayers in this connection, we face of necessity the question of prayers for the dead. Rome used them, and in relation to the doctrine of Purgatory. The Protestants therefore did not use them, and were particularly emphatic on this point. Only in the last few years have the Anglican books of Scotland and America restored such prayers, as the rejected English proposals of 1928 attempted to; and as yet no other Protestant body has taken a similar step. "In Virginia, suh," declared a member of that notably low-church diocese, "we worship ouah ancestors, and we see no reason to pray for them."

Yet unless our ancestors indeed were made perfect in this life, surely they still may be supposed to need our prayers. Any personal survival after death must be a continuance of the personality that was here, or it is not a personal survival. The foibles then, and the failings too, were not done away with the collapse of the physical body; and it does not require belief in a physical mountain of Purgatory to enable us to think of continued learning and growth, and of continued service, in whatever life may be beyond the grave.

Protestants traditionally have held it to be superstitious to pray for the dead. Is it not more superstitious to think either that our departed loved ones are beyond divine help, or that they have no further need of it? That they are in the hands of God is true. But so are we who remain in the body, and yet we pray for ourselves and for each other. The fixation of the soul's growth at that point which it had reached when the cancer supervened, or when the other car swung into the wrong lane, would be a superstitious concept of the worst sort. So also would be the sudden transformation of the soul, by physical incident or accident, into a state of total perfection. Sanity argues rather that life is continuous, and that moral continuity is not to be broken off short by any physical agency. A Christian sanity therefore will pray for all living souls, those without physical bodies as well as those which still are in the flesh.

We ought also, in the burial service, to pray in gratitude for the life to date of the one whose body now is dead, and for all the heroic lives which have taught us how nobly life may be lived. Specifically too we should pray for the bereaved family, that its members may not sorrow as they who have no hope. The Anglican books are inadequate here, perhaps because the English Church did think so largely in terms of the greater Christian community rather than of personal feelings. Some of the prayers for the family, provided in other books denominational or unofficial, may be found helpful, though too many of these are more sentimental than stabilizing in their tone.

If there is to be cremation, it is well to combine the two parts of the service rather than to go to a second chapel for a pseudocommittal in which nothing visible happens. The family have taken leave of the person now two or more days ago, and there is no need for them repeatedly to take leave of the body. The phrasing of the committal in such a unified service may be, "We commit his body to its last resting place"; and it is desirable, with cremation in view, to omit the now unpleasantly literal phrasing of "ashes to ashes."

Both families and clergy now and then must deal with the proposal for a "lodge funeral." Both are to be advised against it, for few of the lodge rituals are good, and almost always they are badly read and performed. The stuffed dove of the Rebekahs and the abbreviated aprons of the Masons add indignity to sorrow; and I recall the Eagles' introduction of low comedy on one occasion, with the misreading, "The glorious hope of an everlasting—er—immorality." If the family feel required to use the lodge service as well as the Christian one, the minister can clarify the issue by being absent from the former. His duties do not include apparent approval of secular mumbo-jumbo in an hour that should be one of serious thought and deep religious devotion. There is, of course, no reason why the lodge brothers or sisters of the deceased should not be present as a group, to share in a truly Christian service recognizing the fact of death and declaring the assurance of eternal life in Jesus Christ our Lord.

A memorial service for a person of public significance is thoroughly in order, and may include more of personal utterance and individual tribute than is fitting in the funeral itself. There has been some recent discussion of the possibility of holding memorial services only, and leaving the disposition of the body entirely in the professional hands of the undertaker. If a family sincerely wishes this, there is no final and conclusive objection from the Christian point of view; and it does have the advantage of eliminating pagan concern with the corpse.

In view of our long tradition, however, most Christians will want to hear the words of the Scriptures, and of the Church, said at the moment of their parting from all that is earthly of one whom they love. When this is done with central emphasis not on the body, but on the Christian faith, it may be done rightfully and helpfully. The minister's duty in the house of mourning is not to encourage the avoidance of fact, but to strengthen faith when faith most is needed: that is, when it is most difficult to maintain. If his own faith is secure, and his love for persons real, he will not fail to bring peace and strengthening to those who are in the valley of the shadow of death.

PERSONAL AMENITIES

In all these special contacts of individual history with the life of the Church, the minister's handling of his particular role is of the highest importance. He must take seriously not only the occasions, but also each person who is involved. Often he will have to spend long hours, and sometimes at very inconvenient hours, in personal consultation and counseling. Now and then, especially in connection with arrangements for weddings and funerals, he will find himself growing impatient. He is entitled to be impatient with stupidity and bad taste, but never with the unfortunate men and women who are afflicted by them. His security in his own trained judgment is the best guarantee of his ability to guide others aright; and his Christian love is the assurance that he will do this without giving needless offence. (I say "needless." With some people offence is inevitable, and for that reason is not to be worried about.)

Positively, there are little courtesies that will do much to ensure gratitude and genuine satisfaction. One is the simple one of being available for consultation, and for the holding of the services, without being stuffy about what no doubt is already an overfilled schedule. Another is that of learning, remembering, and using personal names, so that neither the joy of a wedding nor the sorrow of a funeral shall seem to be forced onto a mechanical assembly line.

Certificates of baptism, confirmation, and marriage are available in a great variety of prepared forms. Some of these are more adequate than others, in content and in physical design. Except at the upper price levels, the official denominational ones are in general to be preferred to those offered by private commercial enterprise. The investment in a good certificate is in any event little more than that for a trashy one, and its return in appreciation is great. Even better than the printed form, which has to be filled in with a different ink and writing, is the preparation of a little book carrying the entire service, with the personal names included directly in the text, and with a certificate as the final page.

For baptisms and weddings this ordinarily can be typed far enough in advance to permit regular cloth binding by a professional binder. The cost is small: I have been paying $3.50 for each such job for the past twelve years. And the delighted surprise of the recipients is more than full repayment for the work and the expense, even when (as sometimes happens) the wedding fee fails to equal the cash outlay. In the case of funerals the typing should be in duplicate, with the minister using the carbon in the service, and handing the original to the undertaker for him to give to the family. A funeral does not allow sufficient time for permanent binding in advance; but a sturdy cover paper, in white or violet, is fully adequate.

In the matter of fees there are certain reasonable distinctions to be made. Members of the parish obviously are entitled to preferential treatment. This means that if nonmembers wish to be married in the church, they may properly be charged a fee to cover such extra costs as light, heat, and janitor service. Such a charge manifestly would be discourteous, and therefore improper, in the case of those for whom the given church is their own spiritual home. The organist, being a professional musician, always is entitled to a specific fee; and it is advisable for the clergyman or his secretary to be sure that this has not been forgotten in the excitement of the wedding festivities.

The minister himself, being a servant of God rather than a private enterpriser, scarcely will demand or specify a fee for his own services. In the case of a wedding, which occurs on two persons' own volition, and on which a good deal of money often is voluntarily expended, it is not improper for the officiant to accept (and to pass on to his wife) whatever may be given him in token of appreciation. One exception is in the marriage of another clergyman, in which case the fee is at once turned over to the bride. Another is where there are so many marriages in the parish that the income from them would be grotesquely large. In such cases all over an agreed amount should be paid into the treasury of the local church.

Baptisms present a different situation. Here the service is one considered requisite in the Christian life, and the expenditure of effort by the minister is relatively small. Accordingly any fee which is offered should be accepted on behalf of the church rather than the individual, and should promptly be turned over to one or another of the parish funds.

Funerals, in contrast with marriages and baptisms, inevitably are sudden, and involve at once deep personal grief and (even with maximum restraint and good sense) heavy financial costs. No minister of Christ will wish personally to profit from human sorrow, whether or not he previously has known the family concerned; nor will he want his church budget to benefit from this source. The only possible consequence is to return the entire fee immediately, with thanks of course, but with the suggestion that the amount be used to meet some family need, or that it be given to some favorite charity of the deceased.

From the cradle to the grave the Church is directly concerned in the personal welfare of all her people, their joys and their sorrows, their steps of progress and their hours of crisis. It seeks therefore, by its services, to share in their lives and to aid them in their living. In every case the worship of God is integral to the observance. We praise God for the gift of children, for the dedication of young people, for the joy of human love, for the life that has been with us before physical death. We pray for strength to live aright, for enduring love and patience in the family, for eternal sharing in the communion of the saints. We commend alike the baby, the youth, the couple, and the dead, into the hands of God. Any occasion which is not dominated by these attitudes of worship is not a Christian service, and has no place in a Christian church.

For the clergyman the cure of souls ever is a weighty charge. It is particularly weighty, but it can be wondrously rewarding, on those occasions when the individual most needs specific guidance and help. One of the great joys of growing old in the ministry is the entering of one datum after another in the family Bible: the marriage, the baptisms, and then the marriages of a second generation and the baptisms of a third. There will be burial entries too, in time; and these, while they can not be gaily made, also may represent warm personal touch and genuine spiritual service.

The line between creative usefulness and substantial uselessness nevertheless is a very narrow one. Only he who loves God and humanity, and who plans and acts in intelligent devotion, will serve his people as he ought to serve. Much of the idea of the Church which the mass of the community holds is derived from its experience in these services which have immediate personal reference. It is the privilege of the servant of the servants of God to fill these times to the full with Christian meaning. It is a privilege, and a heavy responsibility as well. He who appreciates the privilege will not shirk the responsibility.

XIII

THE CHURCH IN THY HOUSE

"CHRIST IS THE head of this house: the unseen guest at every meal, the silent listener to every conversation." There used to be wall cards saying this, until the interior decorators ruled out verbiage from the domestic décor. Is it possible that what the cards said is out of fashion too? We may hope that Christian homes are not quite so uncommon as the prevailing household silence about Christian values might suggest. It is conceivable, however, that our homes might be more effectively Christian if they were more explicitly so.

The same applies to the Christian individual in his inner life. He ought to pray without ceasing; but there is some question as to whether he prays at all unless sometimes, in order to pray, he ceases from doing everything else. Our enquiry into the means and the meanings of worship can not be complete until we have considered the possibilities of valid Christian worship outside the church building. We need to worship together in the larger fellowship of the community. If truly we do this, we shall be impelled also to worship in the smaller and nearer fellowship of the household, and each of us in the secret places of his heart.

FAMILY WORSHIP

The Israelite tradition asserts the practice of family worship from the earliest days. In the Judean cycle of stories the father is the priest of the household, offering sacrifices on behalf of his assembled family.

224

Thus Noah after the flood, and Abraham repeatedly in his journey-ings, both are represented as assuming the sacerdotal function for themselves. If Woolley is right in identifying Jahveh of Israel with the household god of Abraham, the origins of our Hebrew-Christian theology, as well as of our rituals, are to be traced to their sources in primitive family religion.

Through the centuries Judaism has maintained the emphasis upon the household as a worshiping group. The *Kiddush* for the Sabbaths and festivals, and the Passover Seder, persist today as family cere-monials dear to all who take part. The father still is the leader of the worship, and he performs the ancient rituals with pride and joy. The bread and the wine, the festival lights and the Chanukkah candlestick, all serve to remind Jewish children of their heritage, and of their continuing debt of loyalty to God and to their people.

It may be argued that only the closely knit Jewish family can hope to accomplish anything of this sort under the pressures of our modern age. Per contra, it may be held that only the preserving of these prac-tices could have kept the Jewish family as closely knit as it is. Here is social worship at its very roots, in the primary social unit. The in-teraction between faith and solidarity, here present, points toward a relationship that we might covet for that larger family which is the Christian Church.

That too was genuinely a family in Jesus' day. Leaving their homes as they had their occupations, the first disciples found for themselves a new home wherever their Master was. The last supper together certainly was not the first one. Many a time before that, pausing beside a dusty Galilean path, or under the olive trees on a Samaritan hillside, Jesus must have blessed and distributed the simple, common fare. Thus it is not in the great congregational meeting, but in the immediacy of the primary social group, that we reproduce most nearly the first historic expressions of Christian worship.

The home of John Mark's mother, in Jerusalem, was at once a Christian household and a center of general Christian fellowship. The same was true of Philemon's house in Colossae. As church buildings began to be erected, the general meeting naturally moved into them; but the family's own worship at home was not therefore discon-tinued. The private chapels of the great medieval landowners reflect the persisting desire to worship God in the household; the "hedge priests" stayed alive, despite Protestant persecution, because there were those families who risked judicial process to obtain their services; and "The Cotter's Saturday Night" still speaks of the practice, on a humbler scale, but with no less of vital and united family devotion.

The "greater family" of the former days is a phenomenon of our sociological past. A few of us remember it, and its regular fulfillment of the American rubric of 1789:

The Master or Mistress having called together as many of the Family as can conveniently be present, let one of them, or any other who may be appointed, say as followeth, all kneeling.

This family assembly included usually members of three generations, and a number of servants as well. Today the typical household has two generations only, and no servants. These changes have tended to make family prayer less prevalent. Surely they ought not to have made it less important.

The "Forms of Prayer to be used in Families," as they stand in the American prayer book, derive from a group of prayers which Archbishop Tillotson wrote for the private use of William and Mary, and which Edmund Gibson, then rector of Lambeth and later Bishop of London, adapted for his *Family Devotion: or a Plain Exhortation to Morning and Evening Prayer in Families,* published in 1705. To these the 1928 American revision added a number of new optional prayers, including those of William Bright and John W. Suter, Jr., which were mentioned in Chapter VIII, and also John Henry Newman's classic, "O Lord, support us all the day long."

Many will feel that these forms, being those of prayers only, need Scriptural material for their support and completion. There is no reason why a lesson should not be added to the series of prayers; and the daily lectionary as now it stands scarcely can fail to suggest one worth reading. There are also a number of books, of private authorship or compilation but some of them with denominational approval, which provide for each day in the year a lesson from the Bible, a brief meditation, and a prayer of related content. Some of these will be found listed, with brief comments, in the final section of Appendix A.

That religious instruction is best given by experts is not to be denied. Full and precise knowledge, and developed teaching skills, are important in religion as elsewhere, and they are not in every layman's reach. The experts, however, are not numerous at best, and the total time they can give in personal contact is little. The practical option for most people most of the time is not between expert and inexpert religious teaching, but between a considerable amount of lay teaching and no teaching at all. The Sunday school may do better, minute for minute, than can the average parent. Whether it can do better or not (and some do not), it can not do nearly as much. Nor are the parents' limitations such that they must keep absolute silence to ensure against their misleading their children.

The more they know about Bible and Church, and the more they are willing to learn, the better. To a large extent, however, Bible and Church speak for themselves in direct terms; and they who will read the Scriptures and the prayers reverently are not likely to do serious damage intellectually. If a father's explanation for his reluctance to lead family devotions is that he is not qualified, the answer is that he ought to qualify himself as soon and as completely as he can. It is the correlative duty of the Church to make without cessation its "plain exhortation to Morning and Evening Prayer in families," and at the same time to provide direct help to parents in developing worship techniques and in clarifying meanings.

The time excuse, which is even more common than that of lack of capacity, is even less legitimate. We always have time for what we count important, because we subordinate other activities to it. We do not have to have three different breakfast hours, unless letting everyone sleep until the last possible moment stands first among our values. Nor are we compelled to dash from the dinner table with the last gulp of pie, unless the children have been encouraged to think Hopalong Cassidy a more real and more significant figure than the Christ. The family that wants to worship as a family will find a way to do so, whatever may be the threat of the outside world against integrated family living.

Children brought up to regard family worship as normal procedure will glow with pride as first they learn to say some of the prayers, and then to read them for the whole family directly from the book. The saying of grace before meals, so often Dad's delaying and boring mumble, becomes a coveted assignment when its meaning is made clear. Daily to provide opportunity for the worship of God, daily to give the children their own experience in praising him and praying to him, is daily to build toward Christian thinking and Christian living. What Christian father and mother will discard this chance to serve their children's lasting welfare, and their own?

A CHRISTIAN CENTER

Far to the north on the Canadian prairie, just south of Saskatoon, my father rode a circuit. I have not forgotten his preaching, in a frame and tar-paper shack, on "the church in thy house." That was the house of two young and penniless homesteaders, and their very young children. On that fifty-below-zero Sunday morning it was the church of half a dozen families of their neighbors. It lacked much that a cathedral has: almost everything but the essentials of eager people and Christian devotion. The north wind whistled through it; but even more surely the Holy Spirit breathed within it.

We shall not often have occasion, in our kind of world, to invite the neighbors to worship with us under our own rooftrees. Sometimes, however, we shall have to choose whether we shall invite them, or some other visitor, to share in our worship of God; or whether, as the custom of some is, we shall dissemble our faith in the presence of our friends. For the sincere Christian the issue is not debatable. If the time for worship has come, then worship begins and is continued reverently to its close.

Not many guests will be embarrassed, and only the pseudo-intellectuals will be captious. Almost everyone else respects genuine faith, and its open expression, whether or not he shares personally in them. In more cases than the diffident will suppose, the frank exposure of Christian conviction not only will claim respect, but also will challenge hard thinking, and quite possibly will encourage emulation. Family worship is valid in itself. Its influence may reach far beyond the four walls that the FHA has financed.

This is particularly true when there are children to carry the message, as inevitably they will, down the block (kindergarten) and through the whole subdivision (junior high). Family worship as a standard practice need be forced on no one. Rightly used, it readily becomes contagious.

The influential children in any neighborhood are those who have convictions. The occasional atheist child should have made that evident, but he need have no monopoly. Christian conviction, at whatever the age, makes its inescapable impact on all who come near it.

This is not a grandiose and impersonal dream of evangelizing the world by giving to missionary funds, benevolent and desirable as that may be. It is the plain fact that a family altar is recognizable, and may be decisively powerful, for those who only have heard of it, but who may be moved thereby to return to loyalties they long have ignored.

PERSONAL DEVOTIONS

Some of us just can't bear to be alone, but all of us have to be. The most complete extravert fails to live quite all of his life in and with other people. What we do with our solitude, sometimes physical but much more often spiritual, is a basic test of what we are in ourselves. It is also a determinant of whether we are to become, in ourselves, nobler or feebler servants of the will of God.

No one can worship totally without sharing often in worship with his fellows in the faith. Neither can one worship fully in the social group unless he worships devoutly in his own heart. The solipsist devotions of the mountain climber or the Sunday golfer rightly are suspect, for they deny the relevance of the community. The social worshiping of any churchman ought to be suspect too, if it is not associated with, and supported by, his consistent practice of private meeting with God.

Personal devotion manifestly ought to be continuous, and to be real and conscious throughout the day in the office or store or factory. It needs also to be occasionally and regularly specific, in full physical privacy if possible, but at any event in the achievement of aloneness with God himself. The means still are the familiar ones of worship: praise, and prayer, and the quest for illumination. The secondary means therefore are those we have been considering: the prayers and other writings of the historic Church, the lessons for us that are contained in holy writ.

Even more obviously than in the case of the family, the individual can find time for his active and consistent devotional practices if he really wants to. It is always possible to get up fifteen minutes earlier in the morning, and to stop secular work or play fifteen minutes sooner at night. One forty-eighth of the calendar day thus set aside is not lost time, but clear gain for all the other twenty-three and a half hours as well.

Private worship has its own peculiar advantages. It requires no advance publicizing of its schedule. Its pace is not conditioned by outside factors, nor by anyone else's reaction time. Its content fits this one person's need, for he can make of it what he will. His choice of reading is for his mind and heart alone, unfettered by another's mood or preference or vocabulary. His utterance can be completely honest and unembarrassed, for God already knows him better than he knows himself.

Nevertheless we need to work at our individual devotions with the same care, and in the same eager desire for new light, as belong to our planning for family worship or for a service in the church. There is a vast wealth of devotional literature, ancient and modern, to be explored; and it yields up its treasures readily to those who will engage in the search. Whether or not one dares to exhibit his singing voice to the congregation, he can sing in his heart as he reads over the hymns he knows, and as in his leafing through the hymnal he finds hitherto unknown ones that speak to him of truth. Whatever may be his continuing and his immediate needs, he must examine them honestly, and must seek to pray about them only as he may do so in the Name of Jesus Christ his Lord.

This last is a sound reason for making use of written prayers, as well as spontaneous petition, even in privacy. The question of literary form here is secondary, though it never is altogether negligible. The realization of the long Christian experience with problems of one's own particular sort is heartening, and acquaintance with the historic prayers will provide this. Even more importantly, the way in which the Church has prayed down through the centuries will challenge us to pray worthily on our own behalf, and will guard us from asking amiss in our preoccupation with ourselves.

A helpful habit is to drop into an open church (it matters not of what denomination) near to one's work, or when exploring on a business trip or a holiday. There is likely to be something of interest, to any enquiring mind, in architecture or decoration or signs of local usage; and the alert Christian always will be anxious to find out what his fellows do. There is sure to be opportunity, for anyone who wants it, to worship quietly where he knows that many others have worshiped; and both work and vacation will be enriched by such using of a little time. A note of appreciation left for the pastor, or mailed to him afterward, is a Christian courtesy for which the man of God will be grateful.

In every circumstance the words that may be used in worship are instruments only. They are useful instruments in so far as they help to bring us truly to worship God in our hearts and by our lives. Not many of us will worship effectively without the aid of words, our own and those of others. No one of us will worship really, alone or with others, unless we set ourselves directly to declare God's worthship, and explicitly to offer ourselves to him for his disposition of all we have and are.

The difference between worship in the church on the one hand, and in the family or alone on the other, is no more than one of external circumstance. In every case the necessary attitude is the same, and the means provided in our heritage are appropriate to all. There can be no decision as to which of the three types is the most important. We all need all of them, for our Christian life and experience are strengthened by each, and they are weakened by the absence of any one. Twice daily alone, twice daily in the family circle, two or three times weekly in the fellowship of the Church: is this too much of worship to offer to our God in gratitude for all his benefits toward us?

XIV

FORM AND CONTENT

WORSHIP INVOLVES BOTH content and form, and each ideally at its highest potential. "To worship rightly is to love each other," urged the Quaker Whittier; and the living of Christian love is indeed a declaration of God's worth-ship as it is an acceptance of his will for us. Even in human love, however, symbols have their real and proper place: the ring, the birthday and anniversary and Christmas gifts, the privately developed rituals of word and touch and glance. The public declaration of the love of God can not but have its outer forms. Our problem in preparing for God's worship, and in sharing in it, always is that of finding a form that belongs to, and as nearly as possible expresses, the meaning.

The expression never will be absolute, for our grasp of meanings itself is limited, and our ways of stating them are more limited still. We can no more praise God perfectly than we can describe him precisely. We nevertheless try more truly to apprehend him, and with this we shall strive the more adequately to glorify him. Alike in understanding and in homage we shall fail often and much; but if we earnestly seek at once to understand and to adore, we shall find the two efforts working together toward the growing achievement of both.

LITURGICS AND AESTHETICS

"Beauty is truth, truth beauty." That dictum of Keats is a romantic oversimplifying of the issue. There is much that at least passes for beauty in our world that is not true in any ultimate terms, and there is much of truth whose beauty our present thinking will find it hard to discern. A primary concern for aesthetics does not guarantee the reality of worship, and a devoutly held faith does not issue inevitably in a perfect order of service.

A perfunctory imitation of genuine worship can issue either from too great an emphasis upon the form, or from total indifference to it. The latter we have seen abundantly in the Protestant story, in cases where central interest in the preaching mission of the Church has reduced worship to a minimum, and has left the few vestiges of it haphazard and graceless. The former is illustrated all too often in the services of small Roman churches, where the priest goes through all the motions indeed, but in such a hasty and angular way as to suggest that his chief objective is to get them done with as quickly as possible. One suspects sometimes that while the Roman parish clergy have had abundant training in liturgics, many of them have had not nearly enough in aesthetics.

The view that the act of worship has a kind of magical sufficiency in itself leads easily into casualness in the way in which the act is performed. The chill impersonality of many Roman Catholic funerals, and the curious lack of warmth in some Roman Catholic marriages, arise evidently from confidence in the verbiage as sufficient without reference to human reactions. Mumbled or gabbled prayers can be justified only on the theory that the mere saying of the words, in whatever tone of voice and at whatever speed, automatically produces the desired result. But this can not be accepted if the result is seen as including real effect upon the spirit of man in his experience of contact with the living God.

Rome's recent provision for the "Dialogue Mass" seems to mark a realization of the loss that has been caused by a wholly *ex opere operato* view of divine service, and a new concern that the people shall share actively and intelligently in the offering of the Sacrifice. Rome has yet a long way to go, but so have the rest of us too. Worship is offered to God, but it is not the people's worship unless it is their authentic and fully conscious offering of themselves. Protestants will do well to consider, for example, whether their saying of the Lord's Prayer, though slower than the Roman, has fallen into anything of the same thoughtlessness that they have noted and condemned in the saying of the Rosary; and whether their hymns, though sung in English, carry any more of realized meaning than does the untranslated Latin of the Roman plainsong.

Another and contrasting pitfall of the ritualist is that of being so conscious of the aesthetic, and so devoted to it in its own right, that he neither gives, nor calls, sufficient attention to the ultimate points of reference. It has been remarked that while Roman Catholics use incense in order to worship, some Anglo-Catholics have worshiped in order to use incense. The elaboration of ornaments and gestures is neither good nor bad in itself. It is good in so far as it enhances realization of the deep seriousness of the service, and of the high glory of the Lord to whom our service is offered. It can easily become bad if it deflects the worshiper's mind from the meaning to the mechanics.

On the other hand, total indifference to mechanics can be distracting too. Jerky movements, awkward transitions, hasty afterthoughts, all get in the way of the people's approach to God. "I never noticed what you were doing" is the highest compliment this writer has received on his conduct of a service. But it takes no little preparation and consideration to make the procedure wholly a servant of the religious process. The method of necessity is an aesthetic one, but the objective stands far above both artifice and art.

This book has been principally a plea for a high consciousness of worship techniques, and this to the end that the form shall duly serve the content. Beauty will do this better than ugliness, forethought better than improvisation, order better than confusion. What must be remembered always is that beauty, forethought, and order in the service are not ends in themselves, but instruments toward our realization of God's presence among us, and in us.

RITUAL AND THEOLOGY

The details of ritual therefore can not be severed from the theological convictions of the given Church. The use or disuse of Trinitarian formulas reflects one or another Christological concept. The form of the Prayer of Consecration will depend upon the view that is taken of the real presence. The saying of prayers for the dead implies not only faith in eternal life, but also a judgment about the continuation of personal character and experience past the death of the body.

Early Protestant revisions in ritual, while they aimed at general simplification, included a number of changes clearly based on theological differences from Rome. The Lutheran replacing of the Consecration Prayer by the Words of Institution, and the drastic cutting of the Prayer in the English book of 1552, both represent rejection of anything savoring of transubstantiation. The Puritan demand for a "table" instead of an "altar" bespoke the denial at once of the sacrifice and of the priesthood. The elimination of prayers for the dead was a repudiation of the doctrine of Purgatory. The Friends' silent meeting, and their unadorned meeting houses, were efforts to declare the unmediated access to God of the individual human spirit.

Liberal modernism in the early years of this century sought to make similar alterations in the interests of its typically polite and optimistic thinking. Of such were the excision of "miserable offenders" from the General Confession, the dropping of "he descended into hell" from the Apostles' Creed, and the 1932 Methodist alteration of the Prayer of Humble Access to read "so to partake of these memorials" instead of "so to eat the flesh . . . and to drink his blood." It was in this modernistic period also that quite new rituals, largely using non-Scriptural and untraditional materials, were devised and published in great number.

It is where this suave modernism survives in the pulpit (and most of the now middle-aged clergy were trained in it) that a traditionally styled chancel is so evidently a hollow shell. There is little point in having what looks like an altar unless one treats it as an altar; and one does that only if he really believes that the divine sacrifice means more than does the sermon. A true church ought indeed to be built like a church. It is yet the faith, and not the architecture, that marks the difference between authentic worship and a sentimental masquerade. I have been pleading for a revival of historic usage. I must plead here that none shall pretend to use the historic means if he thinks to deny the historic meanings.

There are two factors, however, which in our time have opened the way toward the employing of the ancient forms, and in full faith and loyalty. One is that to a large extent we are recovering from our eagerness to discredit the traditional body of Christian doctrine. The younger graduates of the seminaries have had a more Christian training than did we of thirty years ago, and that because our devil's world has driven men to seek more basic answers than seemed enough in the 1920s.

Original sin no longer is regarded as a myth or an outworn and tiresome dogma, but as an evident and fearsome reality; and so we are the more willing to confess that we are miserable offenders. Our manifest need of salvation from our sins, individual and collective, has enabled us again to see Christ the Saviour where once we could discern only Jesus the teacher, and so to pray again "through Jesus Christ our Lord, who liveth and reigneth. . . ." The rediscovery of early Methodist views, and the realization of their cogency, have restored the doctrine of the real presence to one of the two Methodist Orders of Communion authorized in 1944: not only in the Prayer of Humble Access, but also in the Consecration. (It is good to know that Methodism was fully heretical for no more than twelve years.) Returning thus to the historic Christian faith, we find ourselves ready to return more and more to its historic expressions in worship. Only ten days before this writing, a young Air Force chaplain told me that he had come to his liturgical position because of his theological one; and this is likely to be the case with many more.

SYMBOL AND REALITY

The second aid toward using the traditional forms is a new and more accurate concept of the nature of symbolism. Both the lovers of symbol, and the professed despisers of it, went astray in thinking to equate the symbol with the reality. The symbolist became too often an idolater, and the antisymbolist an iconoclast, because neither could distinguish aright between the body and the spirit. The writer to the Hebrews knew better, seeing (in his Philonic Platonism) that the physical objects never could be more than "a shadow of good things to come, and not the very image of the things." Once freed from a mechanical one-for-one equation of symbol with reality, we may use the symbol freely and gladly to reflect such glimpses of the reality as up to now we have been given. Sharing the eternal reality with all the cloud of witnesses, we can share with them the age-old symbols too; and in that very act we shall symbolize also our oneness with them in the universal and enduring communion of the saints.

It is reality that we seek in worship, and through worship. The service of the symbol, of any symbol, is illustrated in the distinction between the words of prayer and praying in itself. The words are not the prayer, but we seldom shall pray without the use of words. Neither is the church building God's physical dwelling place; but more of us have found God, and more often, in the visible church than anywhere else. The tune may be Gregorian or Genevan, Anglican or gospel song; but our hearts sing the more joyously when we make synchronous melody with our vocal chords.

The greater our concern for ultimate reality is, the more intensely we shall want to find and use the most nearly adequate symbols for its expression and conveyance. To those who have found reality in the heritage of Christian faith, the heritage of Christian worship is the obvious source in which to look for the symbols that best will declare it. In God's house, made beautiful for the sake of his beauty, we come together to meet God. From God's word, transmitted to us through his faithful servants of so long ago, we draw the lessons that will guide us through life. As members of God's family we sing the praises and we say the prayers that the whole Christian family, which is the holy Catholic Church, has created through nineteen centuries. At the Lord's table we partake together not of physical memorials only, but of a living and continuing spiritual presence. The ritual, let it be said again, is but the means to the worship of God. Nevertheless it is the means that millions have found good, and than which it will be hard to find a better.

RIGIDITY AND FREEDOM

"Blessed art thou," reads one of the Oxyrhynchus sayings of Jesus, "if thou knowest what thou art doing." This was anent a man who was plowing on the Sabbath day, and who might or might not have thought through his reasons for disobeying the ancient ordinance. The rules of life are its guides, derived from experience and designed to preclude error. The rules of ritual, gradually developed and always in process of change, record the experimenting and the experience of the Church in many lands and in many varying cultures. It is impossible to maintain that any given ritual carries final authority in its own right, and for all people everywhere. It is surely unwise to dismiss any ritual, or to depart from one inherited, without full and careful consideration.

Neither slavish obedience to rule, nor a priori hatred of it, is fully adult. The unreflective conformist becomes a bureaucrat, and the unreflective negater an anarchist. Both he who obeys and he who rejects are obligated to know what they are doing, and why. The rule, however, being a historic and social product rather than an individual vagary, stands in the stronger position; and so the burden of proof is upon him who would set it aside. The closely organized Churches have given to their bishops, as chief pastors, the authority to permit changes in procedure for due cause. Other denominations have thought, or without thought have assumed, that local ministers or congregations can be trusted with this responsibility. It is a responsibility, and a grave one, for anyone who receives it.

The Churches which the English call "nonconformist" have here a special difficulty, and with it a special opportunity. Lightly taken, the freedom to vary the service has opened the way to bad taste, disorder, and even heresy. Seriously accepted, freedom in the planning of worship may produce enrichment which is less readily available to those whose forms are the more closely fixed. The Anglican, for example, is held principally within the limits of his prayer book. The nonconformist has free access to everything that is in that book, and equally to materials from countless additional sources.

Within the basic patterns of the Christian services there is room for great variety of content and procedure. A prayer book rightly used is not a prison, but an overflowing treasury among whose gems we are invited to choose. The searching of service books, Jewish and Orthodox and Roman and Protestant, will provide for the imaginative leader of worship a wealth of suggestion and inspiration; and thorough acquaintance with those books will help also to develop some important criteria of taste.

Reverently we can use our freedom to search, to select, and (though ever guardedly) to create. The Christian consensus is a guide we may not ignore, and which often we shall follow gratefully and gladly. The Christian leader yet is called to lead, when he has qualified himself to know where he is going. If he is Christian, he will not forget what the Christian heritage means, and what it has offered to him for his use. Let him learn well what there has been; and then he can be trusted to suggest what there ought to be.

Such disciplined freedom, operating within the main stream of the Christian tradition, already is pointing toward a new unity among those who name the name of Christ. The basic identity of all our traditional services, both of thanksgiving and of instruction, has become increasingly clear. Fear and suspicion among Christian groups no longer are compulsions to difference in thinking and practice. While

Anglicanism clearly has been moving nearer to some of the ways of Rome, Rome now shows signs of admitting some usages of the Anglicans. The Presbyterians have adopted more and more of the pre-Puritan service patterns and texts, and the Methodists have recovered much that once they threw away. In smaller degree, but quite unmistakably, all the other major Churches are turning in the same direction. Thus in our ways of worship we are today more nearly one than we have been for four hundred years. May this be a presage of our being more truly one in faith and fellowship.

The great adventure of all our life is our search for God. A vital adventure within this is our quest for means to God's worship. Too long we have neglected means that have lain ready to our hands, means created in adventurous faith, used in glad community, and tested well by time. Today our Churches have become interested in the rediscovery of Christian worship. It is not too much to hope that thereby they will be aided to new discoveries of God in Christ Jesus, and to new realization of the brotherhood of all who come to God through him. Brother Lawrence wrote of "The Practice of the Presence of God." This is our purpose in our worshiping him. May God grant that it will be the result, alike in the great congregation and within ourselves.

APPENDICES

Appendix A

SOME OF THE USEFUL BOOKS

This makes no pretension to being an exhaustive bibliography. Those who may have been interested in the subject matter of this book, however, will find more of detail in the works mentioned below. As will be noticed, I have listed chiefly the source materials of Christian worship: service books and hymnals: with a smaller emphasis on secondary treatments. In general the order within each section is chronological: Jewish, Orthodox, Roman, and Protestant in the order of origin of the several traditions.

SERVICE BOOKS

The Authorised Daily Prayer Book, ed. Dr. Joseph H. Hertz. New York, Bloch Publishing Company, 1948.

This includes the principal services of Orthodox Judaism, in the Hebrew text with an English translation and a detailed commentary by the late chief rabbi of the British Empire.

High Holiday Prayer Book, compiled by Rabbi Morris Silverman. Hartford, Prayer Book Press, c. 1939.

Full services for Rosh Hashanah (New Year) and Yom Kippur (Day of Atonement), with numerous supplementary materials, as used in Orthodox and Conservative congregations in America. Hebrew text with English translation.

The Union Prayer Book for Jewish Worship, 2 vols. Cincinnati, Central Conference of American Rabbis, c. 1940.

The standard book of American Reform Judaism. Vol. I contains the services for Sabbaths, and Vol. II those for special occasions. The psychological and cultural difference from Orthodoxy and Con-

243

servatism is illustrated in the fact that these Reform volumes are arranged from left to right, whereas those mentioned above are in the reverse order because of the primacy of the Hebrew text.

The Liturgies of SS. Mark, James, Clement, Chrysostom, and Basil, and the Church of Malabar. Translated, with introduction and appendices, by the Reverend J. M. Neale and the Reverend R. F. Littledale. London, Griffith Farran, 7th ed., n.d.

Dr. Neale first issued this work, commonly referred to as "Translations of the Primitive Liturgies," in 1859. It is a landmark of the Oxford Movement in England, as well as a reproduction of the ancient liturgical texts.

Eastern Catholic Worship, ed. Donald Attwater. New York, Devin-Adair Company, 1945.

These are the Eastern liturgies as used in the "Uniate" Churches in communion with Rome. They include the Byzantine, Armenian, Coptic, Ethiopic, Syrian, Maronite, Chaldean, and that of Malabar, with an appendix providing the English text of the Roman Mass for purposes of comparison.

The Divine Liturgy of Saint John Chrysostom, ed. Archbishop Benjamin of Pittsburgh. New York, Alumni Association of the Russian Theological Seminary of North America, 1948.

A full bilingual text, Slavonic and English, of the Russian service as used in the United States today. Includes also Vespers, Requiem, and occasional prayers. Available for purchase in most Russian churches.

The Holy Liturgy of the Greek Orthodox Church, ed. John Chrysostom and George J. Leber. Washington, Order of the Sons of Pericles (Junior Order of Ahepa), 1946.

Includes the Greek and English text of all the publicly audible parts of the Liturgy of St. John Chrysostom, with a section on "the symbolism of the Church," and musical settings for the choral elements of the service as commonly used in the Greek churches in the United States.

The Greek Orthodox Liturgy of S. John Chrysostom, arranged for use in English, transl. and ed. Stephen A. Hurlbut. Washington, Saint Albans Press, 1942.

This edition of the Orthodox liturgy is designed for occasional use in churches of the Anglican Communion. The service is somewhat shortened, and the notations are designed to inform those who are unfamiliar with Eastern practice. Appended is a comparative table of liturgies Primitive, Orthodox, Roman, and (American) Anglican.

The Sunday Missal, ed. the Reverend F. X. Lasance. New York, Benziger Brothers, 1939.

Includes the Latin and English text of the Ordinary of the Mass, along with the English of the Proper for all Sundays and holy days, and a number of major saints' days. Also has a study plan, entitled "Read Mass with the Priest," by the Reverend William R. Kelly.

My Sunday Missal, ed. the Right Reverend Monsignor Joseph F. Stedman. Brooklyn, Confraternity of the Precious Blood, c. 1942.

A simplified treatment, emphasizing the use of the "Dialogue Mass." Uses a new authorized translation of the Ordinary, and the New Testament version of the Confraternity of Christian Doctrine (1941) in the Proper.

Common Service Book of the Lutheran Church. Philadelphia, Board of Publication of the United Lutheran Church in America, rev. ed., 1929.

This may be regarded as typical for the Lutheran bodies. Lutheran practice is to include the entire ritual in the same volume with the Hymnal, and so the materials may be found readily by visiting almost any Lutheran church. Differences among the services of the various Lutheran groups are extremely slight; and at present work is well in progress toward a uniform ritual for the great majority of the Lutheran bodies in the United States.

The First and Second Prayer Books of Edward VI. With a brief introduction by Bishop E. C. S. Gibson. New York, E. P. Dutton & Company (Everyman's Library), 1910.

The entire text of the book of 1549, in the original spelling; and all those parts of the book of 1552 which differ from the corresponding sections of its predecessor. An essential for study of the history of the English services.

The Book of Common Prayer and Administration of the Sacraments and Other Rites and Ceremonies of the Church, according to the use of the Church of England.

There have been innumerable editions of the English *Book of Common Prayer*, which in its essential parts has remained unchanged since 1662. The name of the reigning Sovereign, and those of the Royal Family, of course are altered as occasion requires. Copies published before 1859 carried an appendix of four "State Services," for 5 November (Guy Fawkes), 30 January ("King Charles the Martyr"), 29 May (birthday and restoration of Charles II), and "The Accession of the Sovereign." The university presses have the exclusive right to publish the book.

The Book of Common Prayer . . . with additions and deviations approved in 1928.

This would have been the title of the revised English book had it not been rejected by the House of Commons. As "the Deposited Book" it was circulated without authorization for use, but in practice much of it has found a place in current English services.

The Annotated Book of Common Prayer, ed. the Reverend John Henry Blunt. London, Rivingtons, 7th ed., 1876.

An encyclopedic work of more than six hundred quarto pages, based on the English book of 1662. Sources of English prayers are shown in the original languages, and the Proper of each date is indicated for the Eastern, Modern Roman, Salisbury, and Modern English uses.

The Book of Common Prayer . . . according to the use of the Protestant Episcopal Church in the United States of America.

The three American prayer books were authorized respectively in 1789, 1892, and 1928. Numerous printings of the 1928 book are available. All have uniform pagination through the Prayer Book itself, though not necessarily for the Ordinal, Catechism, Family Prayers, and Articles of Religion. Recent printings include the revised lectionary of 1943.

The Oxford American Prayer Book Commentary. By Massey Hamilton Shepherd, Jr., New York, Oxford University Press, 1950.

The American equivalent to Blunt's *Annotated Book.* Full text of the American Prayer Book of 1928, except for the Psalter, with detailed historical and interpretative notes.

The Book of English Collects, ed. John Wallace Suter, Jr. New York, Harper & Brothers, 1941.

The assembled Collects from the English, Scottish, Irish, Canadian, South African, and American *Books of Common Prayer*, with notes, and an essay on the Collect form.

The Book of Common Worship Approved by the General Assembly of the Presbyterian Church in the United States of America. Philadelphia,

Publication Division of the Board of Christian Education of the Presbyterian Church in the United States of America, c. 1946.

The third and most recent text of the official Presbyterian book. Its predecessors appeared in 1906 and 1932.

The Ritual: A Reprint of Part X, Worship and Ritual, from Doctrines and Discipline of the Methodist Church, 1944. (Nashville), The Methodist Publishing House, c. 1944.

This is the revised ritual prepared by the Commission on Ritual and Orders of Worship appointed by the General Conference of 1940. It is appreciably altered and expanded from that appearing in *The Methodist Hymnal,* which is the text of 1932. The full content of *The Ritual* is reproduced also on pages 369–520 of *The Book of Worship for Church and Home,* cited immediately below.

The Book of Worship for Church and Home, With Orders for the Administration of the Sacraments and Other Rites and Ceremonies According to the Use of the Methodist Church. (Nashville), The Methodist Publishing House, c. 1945.

The *Ritual* of 1944, preceded by 389 pages of orders of service and other worship materials, and supplemented by additional materials for the celebration of the Holy Communion. Marked "for voluntary and optional use." It seems that the option was not taken up sufficiently to keep the work in print. The "Pattern for the Orders of Worship," which begins the book, nevertheless is reflected in the structure of many Methodist services of today: "The Adoration of God," "The Confession of Sin," "The Affirmation of Faith," and "The Dedication of Life." Well indexed, but with specific sources indicated only for materials which stand under copyright.

Service and Prayers for Church and Home, ed. Wilbur Patterson Thirkield. New York, Methodist Book Concern, c. 1918.

A useful compendium of prayers ancient and modern. Unevenly edited, but containing the authentic text of John Wesley's "Sunday Service" as distinct from the shortened one now appearing in the Methodist *Ritual.* Bishop Thirkield's little volume is a landmark in the story of Methodism's rediscovery of its heritage in worship.

A Book of Worship for Free Churches. Prepared under the direction of the General Council of the Congregational Christian Churches in the United States. New York, Oxford University Press, 1948.

Starting with materials closely related to those included in *The Pil-*

grim Hymnal (1935), this book goes on to provide orders for all types of services, an abounding "Treasury of Prayers," and a lectionary and calendar. There is large dependence on *The Book of Common Prayer*, and evident influence also of the Presbyterian *Book of Common Worship*. A brief and helpful treatment of "Symbolism in Worship" precedes the service texts.

Christian Worship: A Service Book, ed. G. Edwin Osborn. St. Louis, Christian Board of Publication, 1953.

This is a companion to the Baptist-Disciples *Christian Worship: A Hymnal, q.v.* below. Orders of service, in the Disciples' manner but showing considerable influence from more traditional usages, occupy the first 150 pages. Part II, "Materials of Worship," provides 415 pages of prayers, litanies, etc., most thoughtfully selected and credited with precision to their sources. Part III contains a lectionary of lessons from the New Testament and the Psalms, arranged to cover a five-year cycle.

Services of Religion . . . for use in the Churches of the Free Spirit. Boston, The Beacon Press, 1938.

The official Unitarian book, including 166 pages of worship materials, followed by a Hymnal (*q.v.*). It is interesting to compare this with the Unitarian *Book of Common Worship* of 1913, which contained nothing but fifty-two responsive readings.

ON THE HISTORY AND MEANING OF WORSHIP

Christian Worship: Studies in its History and Meaning, by members of Mansfield College, ed. Nathaniel Micklem. Oxford, University Press, 1936.

Compact and scholarly treatment of the materials, seen from a dominantly nonconformist point of view.

Liturgy and Worship: A Companion to the Prayer Books of the Anglican Communion, ed. W. K. Lowther Clarke and Charles Harris. New York, The Macmillan Company, 1932.

A practically exhaustive treatment of the history, with emphasis upon Anglican uses but including much material on the Jewish, Eastern, and Roman backgrounds. The articles are by recognized experts in the respective fields. Invaluable for the student of liturgical history, the book will prove illuminating for every reader who may pick it up.

Christian Worship: Its Origin and Evolution; a study of the Latin Liturgy up to the time of Charlemagne, by Monsignor Louis Duchesne, transl. from the third French edition by M. L. McClure. New York, Young, 1903.

Long the established classic in its field, and used by Romans and non-Romans alike. Some of the details of judgment now have been superseded in the light of further enquiries.

The Church and the Ministry in the Early Centuries, by Thomas M. Lindsay. London, Hodder & Stoughton, Ltd., 1902.

A work of most careful scholarship, thoroughly documented, by the Principal of the Glasgow College of the United Free Church of Scotland. Discusses both the worship of the primitive Church and its organizational structure.

Christian Worship in the Primitive Church, by Alexander B. MacDonald. Edinburgh, Clark, 1934.

A clear and well organized account. Originally prepared as a Ph.D. dissertation at Edinburgh University, but free from academic jargon.

The Worship of the Church, by Massey H. Shepherd, Jr. Greenwich, Conn., Seabury Press, 1952.

The fourth volume in the series The Church's Teaching, designed for Anglican laymen in America. Part I deals with "The Principles of Christian Worship," and Part II with the services of the Prayer Book. Authoritative and eminently readable.

The American Prayer Book: Its Origins and Principles, by Edward Lambe Parsons and Bayard Hale Jones. New York, Charles Scribner's Sons, 1937.

An account and interpretation of Anglican worship, with special reference to the American Prayer Book of 1928. Includes a brief but most helpful bibliography.

Art and Religion, by Von Ogden Vogt. New Haven, Yale University Press, 1921.

A cogent plea by a religious liberal for a return to the ancient worship usages of the Church.

Reality in Worship: A Study of Public Worship and Private Religion, by Willard L. Sperry. New York, The Macmillan Company, 1925.

The modern classic in the field, by the dean of Harvard Divinity

School. A remarkable blending of clear psychological insight with deep religious conviction.

The Quest for Experience in Worship, by Edwin H. Byington. Garden City, Doubleday, Doran, & Company, 1929.

More largely historical than the preceding, but directed toward the same psychological ends. "Liturgical" and "non-liturgical" types of worship are differentiated, but are seen as useful complements each of the other.

ON THE CONDUCT OF WORSHIP

A Manual on Worship, by Paul Zeller Strodach. Philadelphia, Muhlenberg Press, rev. ed., 1946.

A detailed guide for the clergy of the United Lutheran Church, but containing much that is relevant for all sharers in the Christian heritage.

The Parson's Handbook, by Percy Dearmer. London, Humphrey Milford, 12th ed., 1932.

The Dean of Westminster's indispensable guide for the parish minister. Based definitely upon the English Prayer Book, with much reference to the Sarum rite, but includes many suggestions applicable and useful in every church.

Christian Worship and its Future, by G. A. Johnston Ross. New York, Abingdon Press, 1927.

A Scottish Presbyterian lecturing to American Methodists (at Ohio Wesleyan University) on the importance of a return to the traditional uses of the universal Church. Pungent and devout.

The Public Worship of God, by J. R. P. Sclater. New York, George H. Doran Company, 1927.

Another series of lectures, these at Yale by the minister of Old St. Andrew's Church in Toronto. Practical counsel on all aspects of planning and conducting the services, with a strongly sacramental emphasis.

The Art of Conducting Public Worship, by Albert W. Palmer. New York, The Macmillan Company, 1939.

A leading Congregational minister and educator provides sensitive and informed advice, and concurrent argument for a greater use of traditional usages and materials than has been common in nonconformist circles.

ON CHURCH ARCHITECTURE AND DECORATION

The House of God: A History of Religious Architecture and Symbolism, by Ernest H. Short. New York, The Macmillan Company, 1926.
Includes treatment of non-Christian as well as Christian examples. The arrangement is by regions and periods. Numerous excellent photographs.

The Symbolism of Churches and Church Ornaments, ed. the Reverend John Mason Neale and the Reverend Benjamin Webb. London, Gibbings, 3rd ed., 1906.
This is a translation of the first book of the *Rationale Divinorum Officiorum,* by William Durandus, Bishop of Mende in the middle of the fifteenth century, with an introductory essay of more than a hundred pages setting forth the views of Dr. Neale and his associates in the Oxford Movement.

The True Principles of Pointed or Christian Architecture, by A. Welby Pugin. Bound with his *An Apology for the Revival of Christian Architecture in England.* Edinburgh, John Grant, 1895.
The *True Principles,* first published in 1841, has aptly been termed "the textbook of the Gothic revival in England."

The Stones of Venice, by John Ruskin.
Innumerable editions are available. This work can not be omitted even from a small list, in view of its ringing plea for a return to Gothic. Says Mr. Ruskin, "Exactly in the degree in which Greek and Roman architecture is lifeless, unprofitable, and unchristian, in that same degree our own ancient Gothic is animated, serviceable and faithful."

A Brief Commentary on Early Mediaeval Church Architecture, by Kenneth John Conant. Baltimore, Johns Hopkins Press, 1942.
The letterpress constitutes only 34 pages, but the plates and diagrams are remarkably clear and informative.

The Heritage of the Cathedral: a study of the influence of history and thought upon cathedral architecture, by Sartell Prentice. New York, William Morrow & Company, 1936.
Somewhat sentimental in treatment, and now and then overwritten, but packed with interesting and on the whole dependable information. Eminently readable for the architectural layman.

An Introduction to French Church Architecture, by Arthur Gardner. New York, The Macmillan Company, 1938.

This book, and the six following, are included because much of the spirit of church architecture needs to be absorbed as well as understood. To 85 pages of text Mr. Gardner adds twenty drawings and 245 very fine plates.

Mont-Saint-Michel and Chartres, by Henry Adams. Boston, Houghton Mifflin Company, 1936.

This small edition of Henry Adams's "revelation of the eternal glory of mediaeval art" includes the introduction prepared for it by Ralph Adams Cram, for the edition sponsored by the American Institute of Architects. No one ought to attempt to build a church, or perhaps even to look at one, without having seen Chartres through Adams's eyes.

Deutsche Dome des Mittelalters, by Wilhelm Pinder. Leipzig, Karl Robert Langewiesche Verlag, 1929.

12 pages of text, with 110 plates. The notes include eleven drawings of ground plans.

English Cathedrals and Abbeys, with introductions by John Pennington. London, Odhams Press, n.d.

One of the "Britain Illustrated" series, with 120 photographs and brief but significant text and notes.

England's Greater Churches, with introduction and commentary by C. B. Nicholson. London, Batsford, Ltd., 3rd ed., 1949.

A small book with minimum letterpress but magnificent photography. This and the preceding are well worth ordering from England.

American Church Building of Today, ed. Ralph Adams Cram. New York, Architectural Book Publishing Company, c. 1928.

This was published before "contemporary" styles began to appear in American church building. It reflects all that was best in the nostalgic movement of which Mr. Cram was so significant a leader. 283 plates, of which 72 represent Mr. Cram's own work.

Modern Church Architecture, by Edward Maufe. Cleveland, Jansen, foreword 1948.

Fifty illustrations of churches of contemporary design, of which only two are American (and one of these the most conservative in the book).

Church Building: A Study of the Principles of Architecture in Their Relation to the Church, by Ralph Adams Cram. Boston, Marshall Jones Company, 3rd ed., 1924.

This work, first published in 1899, brought together a series of articles which had appeared in *The Churchman.* The point of view is reflected in Mr. Cram's "To Gothic we return inevitably . . . One style, and one only, is for us; and that is the English Perpendicular."

Building the House of God, by Elbert M. Conover. New York, Methodist Book Concern, c. 1928.

Detailed advice by the director of the Bureau of Architecture of the Methodist Episcopal Church.

The Church Builder, by Elbert M. Conover. New York, Interdenominational Bureau of Architecture, c. 1948.

Dr. Conover, now director of this interdenominational agency, continues his labors for the erection of buildings at once beautiful and functional.

The Church Beautiful: A Practical Discussion of Church Architecture, by J. R. Scotford. Boston, Pilgrim Press, 1946.

A strong plea for the traditional church plan, with central altar, by the editor of the Congregational journal *Advance.* Numerous illustrations. Especially helpful are those showing "before" and "after" views of churches which have been remodeled to eliminate the center pulpit.

The Small Church: How to Build and Furnish It, by F. R. Webber. Cleveland, Jansen, rev. ed., 1939.

Detailed instructions and advice, with numerous plans and illustrations. The general point of view is Anglo-Catholic.

The Voices of the Cathedral: Tales in Stone and Legends in Glass, by Sartell Prentice. New York, William Morrow & Company, 1938.

A companion volume to *The Heritage of the Cathedral,* mentioned above. Discusses chiefly carvings and windows.

Handbook of Christian Symbolism, by W. and G. Audsley. London, Day, preface 1865.

A systematic treatment of historic Christian symbols, with numerous illustrations.

The Sign Language of Our Faith, by Helen Stuart Griffith. Privately printed, 1939.

An elementary but beautifully clear treatment, illustrated by line drawings. The author is a Pilgrim Aide at the National Cathedral in Washington.

ON CHURCH MUSIC

The History and Growth of Church Music, by the Reverend Ethelred L. Taunton. New York, Catholic Publication Society (1884).

A compilation of articles first published in the *Weekly Register.* Roman Catholic in orientation, but written prior to the *Motu Proprio,* and so no longer wholly representative of Roman practice.

Music in the History of the Western Church, by Edward Dickinson. New York, Charles Scribner's Sons, c. 1902.

A complete and beautifully balanced history by a professor in Oberlin College. Even at this early date, when the tunes of Barnby and Dykes were innovations, the plea is for a return to appreciation and use of the historic music of Western Christendom.

The Song of the Church, by Marie Pierik. New York, Longmans, Green & Company, 1947.

Historical, interpretative, and practical treatment of Church plainsong. Clear in style and authoritative in content.

Protestant Church Music in America, by Archibald T. Davison. Boston, E. C. Schirmer, 1933.

Professor Davison, conductor of the Harvard Glee Club, takes a dim view of the musical situation in the American churches. He favors plainsong, sixteenth century counterpoint, Reformation chorales, and a limited amount of seventeenth and eighteenth century material; and says very clearly why.

Music in Worship: The Use of Music in the Church Service, by Joseph N. Ashton. Boston, Pilgrim Press, 3rd ed., 1944.

A gentler and less closely documented statement of what is in essence the same point of view, somewhat apologetically presented to those who are unfamiliar with liturgical traditions.

A Dictionary of Hymnology, ed. John Julian. London, John Murray, 2nd ed., 1907.

Almost 1,800 pages of precise scholarship, and after these fifty years still indispensable for the student of hymnody.

The Hymnal 1940 Companion. New York, Church Pension Fund, c. 1949.

This scholarly work, sponsored by the Joint Commission on the Revision of the (Protestant Episcopal) Hymnal, was prepared chiefly by the Reverend Arthur Farlander and the Reverend Dr. Leonard Ellinwood. It discusses the hymns and chants in numerical sequence, and presents biographical data in a separate alphabetical arrangement. The most careful and trustworthy of the handbooks to denominational hymnals.

Handbook to the Hymnal, ed. William Chalmers Covert and Calvin Weiss Laufer. Philadelphia, Presbyterian Board of Christian Education, 1935.

A guide to the current Presbyterian *Hymnal.* Well arranged, and full of interesting material, but sometimes incomplete and occasionally inaccurate.

Our Hymnody: A Manual of the Methodist Hymnal, by Robert Guy McCutchan. New York, Abingdon-Cokesbury Press, c. 1937.

A hymn-by-hymn commentary on the Methodist book, with abundant and sometimes extremely detailed notes on authors, composers, and sources. Invaluable for the Methodist minister, and useful for all who use hymns included in the book.

HYMNALS

The St. Gregory Hymnal and Catholic Choir Book, ed. Nicola A. Montani, Philadelphia, St. Gregory Guild, c. 1920.

150 English and 130 Latin hymns, with a simple *Missa Brevis* by the compiler. Authentic within the Roman tradition, but reflects the musical unsophistication of the typical Roman parish choir in the United States.

The Lutheran Hymnal. St. Louis, Concordia Publishing House, c. 1941.

The book of the Missouri Synod. Includes 168 pages of service materials, 660 hymns, and 8 chants in addition to those printed in the service texts. Approximately 200 German chorale tunes, some of them used a number of times.

The Hymnal and Order of Service. Rock Island, Augustana Book Concern, c. 1925.

This, in contrast with the preceding, represents the Scandinavian Lutheran tradition. It includes only three settings by Bach, but many from Swedish sources, and a much larger proportion of English and American material than does *The Lutheran Hymnal.* Compare also *The Hymnal* bound in the United Lutheran *Common Service Book.*

Hymns Ancient and Modern, for Use in the Services of the Church. London, William Clowes, various dates.

The standard hymnal of the Church of England. The first edition appeared in 1861, and was followed by an Appendix in 1868. New editions, each considerably revised from its predecessors, were published in 1875, 1889 (a Supplement), 1904, and 1950.

Hymns: The Yattendon Hymnal, ed. Robert Bridges and H. Ellis Wooldridge. London, Oxford University Press, 1920.

This erudite, discriminating, and physically exquisite work, first issued in complete form in 1899, was designed for the use of a village choir of which Mr. Bridges was the precentor. The settings, all in four-part harmony, include thirteen arrangements of plainsong (of which nine are from the Sarum use), numerous Psalm paraphrase tunes, eight Bach settings, and seven new tunes by Mr. Wooldridge. Bridges wrote and/or translated the texts of at least forty of the hundred hymns included. The editors have supplied detailed notes on the text and setting of each hymn.

The English Hymnal with Tunes. Oxford, Oxford University Press, 1906.

The Preface was signed by W. J. Birkbeck, Percy Dearmer, A. Hanbury-Tracy, T. A. Lacey, D. C. Lathbury, and Athelstan Riley. It describes the work as "a collection of the best hymns in the English language . . . offered as a humble companion to the Book of Common Prayer for use in the Church." The musical editor was Ralph Vaughan Williams. There are 656 hymns, plus Litanies, Introits, and an Appendix. Forty-eight of the tunes are arranged from traditional English melodies and carols, 33 are from the works of Bach, and 16 are by Orlando Gibbons. Thirteen hymns from *The Yattendon Hymnal* were included by the editors, and thus gained general currency throughout English-speaking Christendom. These two works mark the beginning of the new day in English hymnody.

The Hymnal of the Protestant Episcopal Church in the United States of America, 1940. New York, The Church Pension Fund, c. 1940.

This book, which replaced its predecessor after only twenty-four years, exhibits the current trend toward the use of ancient and recent materials, with less emphasis upon the products of the nineteenth century. 600 hymns and 141 chants, the latter including four complete choral settings for the Communion: Merbecke (1549), Healey Willan (1928), George Oldroyd (1938), and plainsong.

The Hymnal. Philadelphia, Presbyterian Board of Christian Education, c. 1933.

A standard all-purpose hymnal, with 513 hymns and 95 chants. As is to be expected, this includes more Psalm tunes, and fewer chorales and plainsong materials, than do the Lutheran and Anglican books.

The Methodist Hymnal. New York, Methodist Book Concern, 1935.

Another good standard hymnal, including 564 hymns and 80 chants. These latter include 24 selections grouped as "Ritual Music for the Holy Communion." Worship materials include Orders of Worship, the *Ritual* as of 1932, responsive readings for fifty-three Sundays, a few festivals, and a number of special subjects.

The Pilgrim Hymnal. Boston, Pilgrim Press, rev. ed., c. 1935.

The official book of the Congregational Christian Churches. 510 hymns, 41 chants, and 157 pages of worship materials.

Christian Worship: A Hymnal. St. Louis, Christian Board of Publication, and Philadelphia, The Judson Press, c. 1941.

This hymnal is a joint enterprise of the Disciples of Christ and the Northern (now National) Baptist Convention. Responsive readings from Old and New Testaments, and six pages of other worship materials, precede the hymnal proper. The selection is somewhat less "churchly" than in the Presbyterian and Methodist books, but maintains high literary and musical standards. Some of the hymn texts have been altered in the mood of liberal modernism; and the Disciples' edition, though not the Baptist one, avoids direct reference to the "blessed Trinity" in the hymn "Holy, Holy, Holy."

Hymns of the Spirit. Boston, The Beacon Press, c. 1937.

The hymnal bound with the Unitarian *Services of Religion.* The standard of musical selection and editing is extremely high. In many cases hymn texts have been adjusted to avoid reference to Trinitarian doctrine.

The New Church Hymnal, ed. H. Augustine Smith. New York, Fleming H. Revell Company, c. 1937.

One of the best of the unofficial books, especially notable for having introduced to Americans the now beloved "Angels we have heard on high." It contains 492 hymns, 25 chants, 32 pages of worship materials, plus 53 responsive readings. Of special interest are a number of new litanies on varying themes.

The Oxford American Hymnal for Schools and Colleges, ed. Carl F. Pfatteicher. New York, Oxford University Press, 1930.

A very learned work comprising 387 hymns and 47 chants. The musical point of view is illustrated by the fact that there are forty-two chorale harmonizations by J. S. Bach. As a general hymnal this probably is beyond the present grasp of the average congregation, but it is a remarkably fine source for special materials.

The Hymnal: Army and Navy, ed. Ivan L. Bennett. Washington, Government Printing Office, 1942.

A remarkable illustration of the comity that has developed through the chaplaincy in the armed forces. Worship sections Protestant (83 pages), Roman Catholic (52), and Jewish (21), followed by a collection of 468 hymns. This last is similar to any standard hymnal, save that (no doubt in recognition of the backgrounds of many of the boys) it includes more than the usual proportion of gospel songs.

Union Hymnal for Jewish Worship. (Cincinnati), Central Conference of American Rabbis, c. 1914.

Contains 226 hymns in English, and 22 in Hebrew, with eight services for children. The Hebrew necessarily is in transliteration, in order to accompany the left-to-right sequence of the music. This book, conspicuously like a Christian hymnal, represents the Reform position in Judaism.

DEVOTIONAL

Mention should be made first of some of those devotional classics which, in a more leisurely day, were known to almost every literate Christian. Among those which should become known again are the *Confessions* of St. Augustine (354–430); *On the Imitation of Christ,* by Thomas à Kempis (1379?–1471); the *Table Talk* of Martin Luther (1483–1546); the

Treatise on the Love of God, by St. Francis de Sales (1567–1622); the *Religio Medici* of Sir Thomas Browne (1605–1682); *Holy Living and Dying*, by Jeremy Taylor (1613–1667); and *A Serious Call to a Devout and Holy Life*, by William Law (1686–1761). It is needless to list editions of these. All are in the public domain, and have been issued in many forms. Methodists in particular should become acquainted with the two last, which had major influence in determining the trend of John Wesley's thinking.

The remainder of this section lists general devotional anthologies, two anthologies of religious poetry, works of four modern poets, six small books of prayers, and five volumes arranged for daily devotions. It is tempting to add more, but one must stop somewhere.

The Spirit of Man: An Anthology in English and French from the Philosophers and Poets, ed. Robert Bridges. New York, Longmans, Green & Company, 1916.
Contains 449 brief selections, ancient and modern, topically arranged. Discerning notes by the late poet laureate.

Great Companions: Readings on the Meaning and Conduct of Life from Ancient and Modern Sources, compiled by Robert French Leavens and Mary Agnes Leavens. Boston, The Beacon Press, 1927.
A similar collection, representing a less traditional point of view, made by a former chaplain of Mills College and his sister.

Freedom, Love, and Truth: An Anthology of the Christian Life, by the Very Reverend William Ralph Inge. Boston, Hale, Cushman and Flint, (1938).
The "gloomy Dean" exhibits not only his tremendous erudition, but also his strong and stable religious conviction. Many of the selections are from little known Anglican sources.

Religious Resources for Personal Living and Social Action, by Kirby Page. New York, Farrar & Rinehart, 1939.
As is to be expected from this leader of Christian social thought and action, a large part of the book is devoted to the impact of personal faith upon social relationships. There are daily readings to cover a period of fourteen weeks.

The Choice Is Always Ours: An Anthology on the Religious Way, ed. Dorothy Berkley Phillips. New York, Richard R. Smith, 1948.
This reflects the religious position of Dr. H. B. Sharman and his associates. A large proportion of significant recent material.

Man and God: Passages chosen and arranged to express a mood about the human and divine, by Victor Gollancz. Boston, Houghton Mifflin Company, 1951.

A widely ranging selection by a leading British publisher. Particularly remarkable for its inclusion of material from Chasidic (Jewish mystical) sources.

The World's Great Religious Poetry, ed. Caroline Miles Hill, New York, The Macmillan Company, 1923.

By no means limited to Christian sources, but definitely Christian in orientation. Edited and indexed with meticulous care.

Joyce Kilmer's Anthology of Catholic Poets. New York, Liveright Publishing Corporation, 3rd ed., 1937.

Only poets writing in English, from the middle of the nineteenth century on, are represented. Catholicism is broadly interpreted, to the definite enrichment of the whole. Two groups of additions have been made, respectively in 1926 and 1937, to the collection originally made by Kilmer in 1917.

The Testament of Beauty, by Robert Bridges. New York, Oxford University Press, 1930.

The last and greatest work of the late poet laureate, and the summation of his intense Christian faith.

The Cicadas and other poems, by Aldous Huxley. London, Chatto and Windus, 1931.

These poems, written when Mr. Huxley was explicitly making his transition from futilitarianism to faith, are all too little known. Particular attention is called to "Orion."

Collected Poems, 1909–1935, by T. S. Eliot. New York, Harcourt, Brace & Company, 1936.

The early and supposedly "difficult" poems are here; but also "Ash Wednesday" and the choruses from "The Rock," which should be susceptible of apprehension by anyone who earnestly cares to apprehend.

Four Quartets, by T. S. Eliot. New York, Harcourt, Brace & Company, 1943.

"Burnt Norton," "East Coker," "The Dry Salvages," "Little Gidding." These may not yield up all their meaning on first reading, but they are worth many more readings than one. And before I leave Eliot, let me but mention the Archbishop's Christmas-morning sermon in *Murder in the Cathedral* (1935).

The Collected Poetry of W. H. Auden. New York, Random House, 1945.

Those *enfants terribles* of the middle 1930s, Auden, Spender, and C. Day Lewis, all have experienced a healthy recovery from contempt of what is old. Nowhere is this more clearly shown than in Auden's Christmas oratorio "For the Time Being."

A Manual of Eastern Orthodox Prayers, ed. Nicolas Zernov. New York, The Macmillan Company, 1945.

A publication of the Fellowship of Saint Alban and Saint Sergius, devoted to *rapprochement* between Eastern Orthodoxy and Anglicanism. It contains 82 pages of prayers, and a complete table of the Calendar of the Eastern Church.

Doctor Johnson's Prayers, ed. Elton Trueblood. New York, Harper & Brothers, 1947.

It is not widely enough recognized that Samuel Johnson was both a faithful Churchman and a devout Christian. All his extant prayers here are brought together, with a discerning and helpful introduction by Dr. Trueblood.

The Temple: A Book of Prayers, by the Reverend W. E. Orchard. New York, E. P. Dutton & Company, 5th ed., 1932.

Prepared largely for use in the evening services of a city church, these prayers will be found helpful also in personal devotional life.

Let Us Pray, by Robert French Leavens. Mills College, Eucalyptus Press, 1939.

Thirty-seven brief prayers written by Dr. Leavens for use in the services of the Mills College Chapel.

A Pocket Prayer Book and Devotional Guide, by Ralph Spaulding Cushman. Nashville, The Upper Room (Methodist Publishing House), 1941.

A small but very usable collection, including Morning and Evening Prayers, prayers for special occasions, Scriptural materials, and a few devotional poems by Bishop Cushman.

Aids to Worship: A Handbook for Public and Private Devotions, ed. Albert W. Palmer. New York, The Macmillan Company, 1944.

These are the worship materials which Dr. Palmer prepared for the *Inter-Church Hymnal* (1938). The sections titled "Personal Meditations" and "Prayers" are particularly significant for private worship.

The Cloud of Witness: A Daily Sequence of Great Thoughts from Many Minds, by the Honorable Mrs. Lyttelton Gell. London, Frowde, preface 1891.

The daily selections follow the pattern of the church year. Many of the selections are Victorian, and demonstrate that Victorianism had more to commend it than nowadays we suppose.

The Daily Altar: an aid to private devotion and family worship, ed. Herbert L. Willett and Charles Clayton Morrison. New York, Harper & Brothers, n.d.

This pioneer work of some thirty years ago has passed through twenty editions. A brief meditation, a verse or two of Scripture, a few lines of verse, and a prayer, are provided for each day of fifty-two weeks, without reference to a calendar; and also for eleven "special days," of which only three (Palm Sunday, Easter, and Christmas) belong to the traditional Christian year.

A Book of Worship for Use at Table on Every Day of the Year, ed. Wade Crawford Barclay. New York, Abingdon Press, 1923.

The arrangement is that of the civil calendar. For each day there are provided a topical verse, a Scriptural lesson, two brief selections from more recent writers, and a brief prayer.

The Upward Look: A Volume of Morning Devotions for the Family Altar, ed. Harold Garnet Black and Gaius Glenn Atkins. Boston, Houghton Mifflin Company, 1936.

Two hundred and forty-seven American Christian leaders, of a wide variety of denominations, contributed to this little book. For each day there is a brief meditation, a passage of Scripture, and a prayer.

Every Day a Prayer, by Marguerite Harmon Bro. New York, Harper & Brothers, c. 1943.

365 numbered sections, including brief meditations, quotations from an amazing variety of sources Christian and non-Christian, and brief prayers in simple, informal language. The catholicity of approach is well represented by the fact that both St. Thomas Aquinas and Martin Luther are quoted in the meditation on "Eternal Dependence." Unfortunately there is no index.

Appendix B

MAJOR VARIABLE DATES OF THE CHRISTIAN YEAR

These dates and seasons are generally recognized in Western Christianity, except where otherwise noted. R = Roman Catholic, L = Lutheran.

ADVENT

The First Sunday in Advent. The Sunday nearest to St. Andrew's Day, 30 November.

The Ember Days. Wednesday, Friday, and Saturday following 13 December. Also those following the First Sunday in Lent, Whitsunday (Pentecost), and 14 September.

Gaudete Sunday. The Third in Advent (R).

CHRISTMASTIDE   (from 25 December)

The Most Holy Name of Jesus. The Sunday between the Circumcision (1 January) and the Epiphany (R).

EPIPHANYTIDE   (from 6 January)

The Holy Family. The First Sunday after the Epiphany (R).

The Transfiguration of Our Lord. The Sunday before Septuagesima, except when there is only one Sunday between the Epiphany and Septuagesima (L).

PRE-LENT

Septuagesima. The Third Sunday before Lent.

Sexagesima. The Second Sunday before Lent.
Quinquagesima. The Sunday next before Lent.

LENT

Ash Wednesday. The first day of Lent; the Wednesday after Quinquagesima.

The Ember Days. Wednesday, Friday, and Saturday after the First Sunday in Lent.

Laetare Sunday. The Fourth in Lent (R). Known in England as "Refreshment" or "Mothering" Sunday, but not thus titled in the Anglican Prayer Books.

PASSIONTIDE

Passion Sunday. The Fifth in Lent.

The Seven Dolors of the Blessed Virgin Mary. The Friday after Passion Sunday (R). (See also 15 September, in Appendix C.)

Palm Sunday. The Sunday next before Easter, and the Sixth in Lent.

Maundy Thursday. The Thursday before Easter.

Good Friday. The Friday before Easter.

Holy Saturday, or Easter Even. The day before Easter.

EASTERTIDE

Easter Day. The Sunday after the first full moon after the vernal equinox. The earliest possible date is 22 March, and the latest 25 April.

Low Sunday, or *Quasi modo*. The First Sunday after Easter.

The Solemnity of St. Joseph, Spouse of the Blessed Virgin Mary. Wednesday before the Third Sunday after Easter (R).

Rogation Sunday. The Fifth Sunday after Easter.

The Rogation Days. Monday, Tuesday, and Wednesday between Rogation Sunday and the Ascension Day.

The Ascension Day. Forty days after Easter, and therefore always a Thursday.

WHITSUNTIDE

Whitsunday, or Pentecost. Fifty days after Easter, and ten after the Ascension Day.

The Ember Days. Wednesday, Friday, and Saturday following Whitsunday (see under Advent).

TRINITY SEASON

Trinity Sunday. The Sunday after Whitsunday.
Corpus Christi. The sixtieth day after Easter (R).
The Sacred Heart of Jesus. The sixty-seventh day after Easter (R).
The Ember Days. Wednesday, Friday, and Saturday following 14 September (see under Advent).

Appendix C

MAJOR FIXED DATES OF THE CHRISTIAN YEAR

These dates are generally recognized in Western Christianity, except where otherwise indicated. R = Roman Catholic, L Lutheran, E English, S Scottish, I Irish, SA South African, A American, C Canadian.

NOVEMBER

30. St. Andrew the Apostle.

DECEMBER

8. The Conception of the Blessed Virgin Mary (R, S, C).
21. St. Thomas the Apostle.
25. Christmas Day.
26. St. Stephen, Apostle and Martyr.
27. St. John, Apostle and Evangelist.
28. The Holy Innocents.

JANUARY

1. The Circumcision of Christ.
1. New Year's Day (S, I, C).
2. The Most Holy Name of Jesus (R) (if no Sunday falls between the Circumcision and the Epiphany, 1 and 6 January).
6. The Epiphany, or the Manifestation of Christ to the Gentiles.
13. St. Kentigern, Bishop of Glasgow (S).
24. St. Timothy (S).
25. The Conversion of St. Paul (all but R).

FEBRUARY

2. The Presentation of Christ in the Temple, commonly called The Purification of St. Mary the Virgin (Candlemas).
6. St. Titus (S).
24. St. Matthias the Apostle.

MARCH

17. St. Patrick of Ireland, Bishop (R, S, C).
19. St. Joseph, Spouse of the Blessed Virgin Mary (R, S, C).
25. The Annunciation of the Blessed Virgin Mary.

APRIL

25. St. Mark the Evangelist.

MAY

1. St. Philip and St. James, Apostles.
3. The Invention (i.e., Finding) of the Holy Cross (R, E).
6. St. John before the Latin Gate (S). Cf. 27 December.
8. The Apparition of St. Michael the Archangel (R).

JUNE

9. St. Columba, Abbot of Iona (S).
11. St. Barnabas the Apostle.
24. The Nativity of St. John Baptist.
29. St. Peter the Apostle (SS Peter and Paul, R, L).

JULY

1. The Most Precious Blood of our Lord (R).
2. The Visitation of the Blessed Virgin Mary (R, L, E, S, C).
22. St. Mary Magdalen (E, S, C).
25. St. James the Apostle.
26. St. Anne, Mother of our Blessed Lady (R, E, S, C).

AUGUST

1. Lammas Day ("St. Peter's Chains") (E, S, C).
6. The Transfiguration of Christ.
7. The Name of Jesus (S).
15. The Assumption ("Falling Asleep") of the Blessed Virgin Mary (R, S).

16. St. Joachim, Father of the Blessed Virgin Mary (R).
24. St. Bartholomew the Apostle.
29. The Beheading of St. John Baptist (S).

SEPTEMBER

8. The Nativity of the Blessed Virgin Mary (R, E, S, C).
14. The Exaltation of the Holy Cross (R, E, S, C).
15. The Seven Dolors of the Blessed Virgin Mary (R) (see also under Passiontide, in Appendix B).
16. St. Ninian, Bishop in Galloway (S, C).
21. St. Matthew, Apostle and Evangelist.
29. St. Michael and All Angels (Michaelmas).

OCTOBER

7. The Most Holy Rosary of the Blessed Virgin Mary (R).
11. The Maternity of the Blessed Virgin Mary (R).
18. St. Luke the Evangelist.
28. St. Simon and St. Jude, Apostles.
31. The Festival of the Reformation (L).
The Last Sunday in October. Our Lord Jesus Christ, King (R).

NOVEMBER

1. All Saints.
2. All Souls (R, S, SA).
16. St. Margaret of Scotland (S).
Fourth Thursday. Thanksgiving (A).

Appendix D

THE CATHOLICITY OF OUR HYMNALS

Sources of the first hundred hymns appearing in each of five current standard hymnals.

Denominational source	CONGREGATIONAL (1935)	EPISCOPAL (1940)	LUTHERAN (1928)	METHODIST (1935)	PRESBYTERIAN (1933)
Anglican	41	32	33	40	39
Baptist	2	1	0	1	1
Congregational	4	0	1	2	1
Independent	4	0	4	7	12
Jewish	0	0	0	1	1
Lutheran	9	15	21	9	6
Methodist	5	5	4	11	3
Moravian	3	2	3	2	2
Orthodox	0	5	4	1	1
Presbyterian (including Reformed)	2	0	4	11	21
Roman (including early and medieval Catholic)	10	35	22	6	6
Unitarian	11	3	4	5	5
Unknown or un-identified	9	2	0	4	2

Correlation of the hymns indexed under the letter A in the same five hymnals:

Hymns occurring in all five, 14; in four, 5; in three, 10; in two, 15; in one only, 64. This means that almost exactly one-third of the hymns occurring in any one book appear in all five, and that a somewhat smaller proportion appear in any one book only. The average frequency per hymn is 1.899.

Appendix E

SERMONS BY REQUEST

The majority of sermons in the Mills College Chapel are based upon suggestions which the students submit on post cards. The following list of subjects reflects student interests in the past few years.

SINGLE SERMONS

1948–1949: Who Made the Devil? Does God Tempt Us? What After We Die? What Religion Isn't, and Is. Why Pray? Gullibility or Faith? Is Christ a Myth? Is Religion a Racket? Catholic and Protestant. What Is Life For? Why Do We Have to Stand It? What Is Christianity For? Sight and Insight. The Religion of Robinson Crusoe. Why One God? The Holy Ghost, the Discomforter.

1949–1950: Is Worship Worth While? What Are the Christian Symbols? Why Heaven? Ideal or Practical? Evolution and Creation. Is the Beautiful Religious? Must Religion Change? What's the Use of Living? Personal God or Universal Spirit? To Whom Do We Pray? Virgin Birth and Immaculate Conception. Jesus: Prophet and Priest. Is Nature God? Do We Need Forgiveness? On Being Judged.

1950–1951: God in Men's Eyes. Is God Limited? On Kidding Ourselves. On Being Graded. The Meaning of Lent. Why Pray for Others? Love and In Love. A God for Grownups. Do We Need a New God? Three Ways to God.

1951–1952: Is Religion Necessary? Is the Bible Worth Reading? Is Prayer Useful? Is Faith Possible? The Meaning of the Redemption. How Shall We Think of Death? What Is a Saint? Taboos: Religion or Superstition? Should We Resist Evil? Is Religion Relevant to Learning? Religion and Beauty. Hindus, Christians, and God. John Calvin in 1952. When May We Compromise?

1952–1953: Can One Have a Private Religion? Revisions and Reservations. Meanings and Means of Prayer. Loving and Hating. The Seven Deadly Sins. Ourselves, Others, and God. Should We Compile a New Bible? Marriage Ancient and Modern. How Far Does Tolerance Go? Can We Be Christian Without Christians? The Seven Deadly Virtues. Where Is Jesus Now? What Comforting Do We Need? Human Experience and the Holy Trinity.

SERMON SERIES

Spring 1947: I Believe (eleven sermons on the Apostles' Creed).

Spring 1948: Let Us Join Together (seven sermons: in Worship, in Prayer, in Praise, in Learning, in Thought, in Work, in Fellowship).

Autumn 1950: Light and the Lamps (six sermons: People and the Society, Experience and the Books, Ideals and the Regulations, Attitudes and the Ceremony, Truth and the Teaching, Eternity and the Calendar).

Autumn 1951: Our Living Past (six sermons, in the centennial year, on the college's heritage in religion: Jewish, Orthodox, Catholic, Protestant, New England, Mills).

Autumn 1952: How We Got Our Bible (six sermons on biblical languages, composition, manuscripts, canon, translations, and "Is the Bible True?").

Autumn 1953: Religion on the Campus (six sermons: Religion and Scholarship, Religion and the Natural Sciences, Religion and the Fine Arts, Religion and the Humanities, Religion and Community Service, Religion MTWThFS).

Appendix F

ARRANGEMENT OF SOME CURRENT WESTERN LITURGIES

ROMAN	LUTHERAN (Missouri Synod, 1941)	CHURCH OF ENGLAND (1552, 1662)	AMERICAN EPISCOPAL (1928)	AMERICAN METHODIST (Order I in the *Ritual* of 1944)	AMERICAN PRESBYTERIAN (First form in the book of 1946)
	Hymn			Hymn	
Versicles	Versicle			Versicles	Versicles
Confession	Confession				
Prayer for Absolution	Absolution				
Introit	Introit				
	Gloria Patri			*Gloria Patri*	
		Lord's Prayer	Lord's Prayer		

272

Kyrie Eleison	Collect for Purity	Collect for Purity	Collect for Purity	Collect for Purity
				Lord's Prayer
	Decalogue with *Kyrie*	Decalogue with *Kyrie*	Decalogue with *Kyrie*	Decalogue with *Kyrie*
				Invitation
				Confession
				Declaration of Absolution
			Beatitudes	
			Responsive Scripture (Isaiah 53)	
Gloria in Excelsis	*Gloria in Excelsis*			*Gloria in Excelsis*
Prayer of the day	Collect for the day	Collect for the day		
Epistle	Epistle	Epistle	Epistle	Epistle
Gospel	Gospel	Gospel	Gospel	Gospel
Nicene Creed	Nicene or Apostles' Creed	Nicene Creed	Apostles' Creed	Apostles' or Nicene Creed
	Hymn			

ROMAN	LUTHERAN	CHURCH OF ENGLAND	AMERICAN EPISCOPAL	AMERICAN METHODIST	AMERICAN PRESBYTERIAN
Offertory	Sermon	Sermon	Sermon	Sermon	
				Hymn	
Lavabo	Offertory	Offertory	Offertory	Offertory	
Orate Fratres					
Secret prayer	General prayer	Prayer for the Church	Prayer for the Church		Prayer for the Church
					Hymn
					Sermon
					Offering
		Invitation	Invitation	Invitation	
		Confession	Confession	Confession	
		Declaration of Absolution	Declaration of Absolution	Prayer for Absolution	
		Comfortable Words	Comfortable Words	Comfortable Words	Comfortable Words
					Words of Institution

Sursum Corda	*Sursum Corda*	*Sursum Corda*	*Sursum Corda*	*Sursum Corda*	*Sursum Corda*
Preface	Preface	Preface	Preface	Preface	Preface
Sanctus	*Sanctus*	*Sanctus*	*Sanctus*	*Sanctus*	*Sanctus*
			Prayer of Humble Access	Lord's Prayer	
					Commemoration of the Living
	Consecration	Consecration	Consecration	Words of Institution	Consecration
Oblation		Oblation			Oblation
Invocation		Invocation			
					Commemoration of the Dead
Lord's Prayer	Prayer of Humble Access	Lord's Prayer	Communion		Lord's Prayer
		Prayer of Humble Access	Lord's Prayer		
Consecration					
Agnus Dei				*Agnus Dei*	*Agnus Dei*
Communion	Communion	Communion		Communion	Communion

ROMAN	LUTHERAN	CHURCH OF ENGLAND	AMERICAN EPISCOPAL	AMERICAN METHODIST	AMERICAN PRESBYTERIAN
	Nunc Dimittis				
Prayers (Communion and Postcommunion)	Thanksgiving	Oblation or Thanksgiving	Thanksgiving	Oblation	Thanksgiving
		Gloria in Excelsis	*Gloria in Excelsis*	*Gloria in Excelsis*	
Blessing	Benediction	Blessing	Blessing	Blessing	Blessing
Last Gospel					

In the American Episcopal service the "Summary of the Law" (St. Matthew 22:37–40) may be substituted for the Decalogue. This permission is included also in the Methodist service. While the *Agnus Dei* does not appear in the American *Book of Common Prayer*, it is very generally used under the rubric permitting the use of a hymn after the Prayer of Humble Access. The Methodist *Ritual* makes no provision for the use of the *Agnus Dei*, but *The Methodist Hymnal* includes two choral settings for it (Palestrina and Merbecke) under the heading of "The Holy Communion." "Order II" in the Methodist *Ritual* of 1944 begins with the Offertory. It omits the Comfortable Words, substituting the Collect for Purity at this point. The Prayer of Humble Access stands before the Consecration, as in the English service, and the Lord's Prayer after the minister's Communion but before the people's. Both the Consecration and the Prayer of Humble Access have been returned to the full text of 1552.

What is called "Another Order" in the Presbyterian *Book of Common Worship* of 1946 is closely similar to that set forth in 1932. The sequence is: Address to Congregation, Hymn, Words of Institution, Collect for Purity (adapted), *Sursum Corda*, Preface, *Sanctus*, Oblation of Ourselves (adapted), Communion, a combined Invocation and Thanksgiving, Hymn, and Hebrews 13:20f. as the Benediction.

The "Longer Form" in the Unitarian *Services of Religion* (1937) includes Sentences, a brief Exhortation, Collect for Purity, a Confession based upon the Prayer of Humble Access, Hymn, Scripture, Sermon, Offertory, *Sursum Corda*, Preface (with Proper Prefaces provided), *Sanctus*, a "Communion Prayer" akin to the Prayer for the Church, Communion, Lord's Prayer, Hymn, and Benediction.

Appendix G

SERVICE LEAFLETS OF THE MILLS COLLEGE CHAPEL

The leaflets whose contents are quoted below are those of the two Sunday-morning services immediately preceding the completion of this manuscript. They are typical respectively for Morning Prayer and for the Holy Communion.

Physically the leaflets are mimeographed on standard-size typewriter paper, folded once, and so measuring 5½ by 8½ inches. The material for Morning Prayer occupies one inside sheet, making four folded pages. Two sheets, running to about seven folded pages of type, are required for the Communion.

The cover is in the color of the day: green, white, purple, or red, as the case may be. The front outside cover carries a (variable) decorative design and the date. The inside-cover material first reproduced below appears regularly when the service is Morning Prayer. The back outside cover is used to list service personnel and to provide the week's announcements.

INSIDE-COVER MATERIAL

The regular Sunday morning service of the Mills College Chapel follows the general pattern of "Morning Prayer," which with the exception of the Holy Communion is the earliest type of worship developed by the universal Christian Church. Derived from the services of the ancient Jewish synagogues, and the parent of most of the forms used by the various Christian denominations in their Sunday worship, it represents the entire and widely varied heritage of members of the Mills community.

The services are conducted without announcement. You are asked to join cordially in all hymns, chants, responses, and congregational prayers, as indicated in the order of service for the day.

The *Hymnal* used is that of the Presbyterian Church in the United States of America, and the prayer book is the *Book of Common Prayer* of the Protestant Episcopal Church. It happens that the Episcopal and Presbyterian Churches have the largest numbers of members in the Mills student body; but that is not the primary reason for the choice of these materials. They were selected on the ground that each in its own field seemed best to meet the general needs of Christian worship, and also our specific requirements on the campus.

The service begins for each worshiper when he or she enters the Church. Many will find it helpful to kneel or bow in silent prayer for some minutes immediately after entering. Our custom is to stand for singing, and for the responsive reading and the Creed. The historic attitude of prayer is that of kneeling; this is invited, but not required. The essential consideration is that all of us shall be sharing truly in the spirit of prayer.

The first half of the *Gloria Patri* is said or sung with the head bowed in reverence, the second half with head lifted in consecration. All worshipers turn toward the altar each time the *Gloria* is used.

The Creed is to be understood as only marginally an expression of opinion. Basically it is a symbol of our unity with the historic Church, in the quest of truth and in loyalty to Christian values.

Most of the prayers used are ancient, because the ancient prayers are those which have stood the test of time as expressing the needs and aspirations of men and women through many years. New prayers are used occasionally, some of them written by religious leaders of our own time, and some prepared directly for special occasions in our College life.

Attention is called to the fact that each service is at once a unity and a continuity. The unity is determined by the theme of the day, which controls the selection of all variable parts of the service. The sermon never should be regarded as the sole reason for going to Church, nor even as the most important part of the hour. It is part of an organic whole, and it is best understood in relation to all that surrounds it.

The continuity of the service is one from confession through meditation (the lessons) and affirmation (the Creed) to specific prayer, and then to the directed meditation of the sermon and the personal consecration of the closing moments.

It is requested that after the recessional hymn all members of the congregation kneel or sit for the final prayer and the benediction, and remain thus until the candles have been extinguished and the ushers have withdrawn.

SERVICE OF 23 NOVEMBER 1952
(The Sunday next before Advent)

ORGAN PRELUDE   Fantasia in A minor
A composition for small organ by Johann Sebastian Bach, 1685–1750.

PROCESSIONAL HYMN No. 64   "Let us with a gladsome mind"
                                        Choir and Congregation, standing
A paraphrase of Psalm 136 by John Milton, 1624; tune, "Monkland," arranged
in 1861 by John Bernard Wilkes from a tune in *Hymns of the United Brethren*,
published in Manchester in 1824.

CALL TO WORSHIP   Isaiah 56:7, Psalm 65:2

THE GENERAL CONFESSION (*Prayer Book*, p. 6)   The Congregation,
                                                    kneeling or seated
Second Prayer Book of Edward VI, 1552.

THE PETITION OF ABSOLUTION
Sacramentary of Pope Gregory I, 590; introduced at this point in the service
by John Wesley, for use by lay leaders in American Methodism, 1784.

THE LORD'S PRAYER   Choir and Congregation
St. Matthew 6:9–13, as translated in *The King's Book*, 1543; a Gregorian setting,
adapted.

PRECES (*Prayer Book*, pp. 7f)
Psalm 51:15; introduced into the service by St. Benedict of Nursia, 480–544;
settings as in William Boyce's *Cathedral Music*, London, 1760.

VENITE, EXULTEMUS DOMINO (*Prayer Book*, p. 9)   Choir and Congre-
                                                    gation, standing
Words from Psalms 95f; a plainsong setting.

RESPONSIVE READING   from Psalm 145, *Exaltabo te, Deus*
                                Reader and Congregation, standing
Reader: I will magnify thee, O God, my King;
Congregation: And I will praise thy Name for ever and ever.
R: Great is the Lord, and greatly to be praised;
C: There is no end of his greatness.
R: One generation shall praise thy works unto another,
C: And shall declare thy power.
R: The memorial of thine abundant kindness shall be showed;
C: And men shall sing of thy righteousness.
R: The Lord is gracious and merciful;
C: Long-suffering, and of great goodness.
R: The Lord is loving unto every man;
C: And his mercy is over all his works.
R: The Lord is nigh unto all them that call upon him;
C: Yea, all such as call upon him faithfully.

GLORIA PATRI   Choir and Congregation, standing
Used in the Eastern Churches from the second century; plainsong setting,
as for the *Venite*.

THE FIRST LESSON   II Chronicles 6:12–21
Solomon's prayer at the dedication of the Temple in Jerusalem.

ANTHEM   Thanksgiving Hymn
Words and music composed for this service by Marilyn Feller '53, director
of the Chapel Choir.

THE SECOND LESSON
From Archbishop Cranmer's preface to the First Prayer Book of Edward
VI, 1549.

SILENT PRAYER

JUBILATE DEO (*Prayer Book*, p. 15)   Choir and Congregation, standing
Words from Psalm 100; setting by Henry Aldrich, Vice-Chancellor of Oxford
University, about 1692.

THE APOSTLES' CREED (*Prayer Book*, p. 16) The Congregation, standing
The "Symbol" of the faith of the early Churches of Western Europe, developed into this form and generally accepted by about the sixth century.

SUFFRAGES (*Prayer Book*, p. 16)
Ruth 2:4; Psalms 85:7, 51:10f; settings as in William Boyce, *Cathedral Music*,
London, 1760.

PRAYERS (the Congregation kneeling, or seated)
  Collect for the Sunday next before Advent (Sacramentary of Pope Gregory I,
    590)
  Collect for Thanksgiving Day (American Prayer Book of 1789)
  Collect for Peace (Sacramentary of Pope Gelasius, 494)
  Collect for Grace (from the same source)
  A Thanksgiving for God's Mercies (the first of the "Eighteen Benedictions"
    in the traditional service of the Jewish synagogues, dating from the first
    century of our era)
  The General Thanksgiving (*Prayer Book*, p. 19; said by the Congregation;
    Edward Reynolds, Bishop of Norwich, for the Prayer Book of 1662)
  A Prayer of St. Chrysostom (Bishop of Constantinople in the fourth century)
  The Grace (II Corinthians 13:14)

SERMON HYMN No. 93   "There's a wideness in God's mercy"
                              Choir and Congregation, standing
Words by Frederick William Faber, a Roman Catholic priest in London,
1862; tune, *In Babilone*, a traditional Dutch melody first published in 1710;
in its present form published in *The English Hymnal*, 1906, whose musical
editor was Ralph Vaughan Williams.

SERMON   How We Got Our Prayer Books

SILENT PRAYER

RECESSIONAL HYMN No. 82   "The Lord is rich and merciful"
Choir and Congregation, standing
Words by Thomas Toke Lynch, an Independent minister in England, in *The Rivulet*, 1868; tune, "Petersham," by Clement William Poole, a clerk in the Audit Office in London, 1875.

A PRAYER FOR THE SPIRIT OF PRAYER
William Bright, Regius Professor of Ecclesiastical History in Oxford University, 1861.

THE BENEDICTION
II Thessalonians 1:11f.

ORGAN POSTLUDE   *Vater unser in Himmelreich*
A setting for the Lord's Prayer published in *Geistliche Lieder*, Leipzig, 1539; harmonization by Philip Telemann, 1681–1767, choirmaster at the Katharinenkirche, Hamburg.

The only variation in the actual conduct of the service, from the order shown above, was the addition, after the Collect for Grace, of a memorial prayer for a former student killed in an accident during the week, and of a prayer for the healing of the sister of a sailor whom the chaplain had met on a train, and who asked that prayers be offered on her behalf.

The total duration of this service was fifty-seven minutes.

SERVICE OF 30 NOVEMBER 1952
(The First Sunday in Advent)

The musical settings for today's service constitute the Communion Service composed by Miss Barbara Browning, our Chapel organist, and today used for the first time in the celebration of the Holy Communion.

The congregation will not be able to join this time in the singing of these parts: *Kyrie, Credo, Sanctus, Benedictus Qui Venit, Agnus Dei,* and *Gloria;* but as we hear the choir, all of us may, if we will, worship with them in our hearts. And the hymns and the familiar setting of the Lord's Prayer will give us opportunity to sing with our voices too.

ORGAN PRELUDE   Larghetto
This movement, which itself is in C minor, is from a Pastorale in F by J. S. Bach, 1685–1750, composed for small organ.

PROCESSIONAL HYMN No. 354   "Jesus, thou joy of loving hearts"
Choir and Congregation, standing
Five stanzas of the fifty-quatrain Latin hymn, *Jesu dulcis memoria*, by an unidentified author of the eleventh century; translation by Ray Palmer, Corresponding Secretary of the American Congregational Union, 1858; tune, "Quebec," by Henry Baker, a civil engineer in India, 1862.

THE COMMUNION COLLECT
From the Sacramentary of Alcuin, religious adviser to the Emperor Charlemagne, ninth century A.D.

THE SUMMARY OF THE LAW
St. Matthew 22:37–40; first introduced into the service in the English Non-Jurors' Communion Office, 1718, and included as an alternate for the Ten Commandments in the first American *Book of Common Prayer*, 1789.

KYRIE ELEISON
Used in the Greek Churches from the earliest times, and today the only Greek language survival in the Latin Mass. Setting by Miss Browning.

COLLECT FOR DIVINE DIRECTION
From the Sarum Missal, the service book of the Diocese of Salisbury, 1085.

SALUTATION (*Prayer Book*, p. 70)
From Ruth 2:4; the original greeting with which the liturgy opened in ancient times.

COLLECT FOR THE FIRST SUNDAY IN ADVENT
First Prayer Book of Edward VI, 1549.

THE EPISTLE   Romans 13:8–14
"Love is the fulfilling of the law."

ANTHEM   "Come with us, O blessed Jesus"
A chorale of Johann Schop, organist at St. James' Church, Hamburg, Germany, published in his *Himmlische Lieder*, 1642, and best known to us as "Jesu, joy of man's desiring." The harmonization is from Cantata 147 of Johann Sebastian Bach, for the Feast of the Visitation of the Blessed Virgin Mary, 2 July 1716.

THE GRADUAL   Psalms 25:3f, 85:7
The transition from Epistle to Gospel, as appointed for this day in the Roman Missal.

THE GOSPEL   St. Matthew 21:1–13
                                    (the Congregation standing)
"Blessed is he that cometh in the Name of the Lord."

THE NICENE CREED   (the Congregation standing)
The Creed adopted at the Council of Nicea, 325, as expanded at that of Constantinople, 381. Setting and metrical recitation by Miss Browning.

SERMON HYMN No. 399   "Lord, speak to me"
                              Choir and Congregation, standing
Words by Frances Ridley Havergal, a minor English poet, 1872, originally titled "A Worker's Prayer"; tune, "Canonbury," arranged from Robert Schumann's *Nachtstück*, Opus 23, No. 4, 1839.

SERMON   How We Got Our Communion Service

SILENT PRAYER

HYMN No. 459   "Now thank we all our God"
Words by Martin Rinkart, a Lutheran minister in Eilenburg, Germany, translated by Catherine Winkworth in *Lyra Germanica*, 1858; tune, *Nun danket
alle Gott*, by Johann Crüger, organist of St. Nicholas' Cathedral in Berlin, 1648.

THE OFFERTORY   I Chronicles 29:11
It should be noted that the "offertory" is the presentation of the sacred elements
on the altar, and has no relevance in itself to the taking of a collection, despite
the fact that in many churches both take place at this point in the service.

PRAYER FOR THE WHOLE STATE OF CHRIST'S CHURCH
First Prayer Book of Edward VI, 1549.

THE INVITATION
The Order of Communion, 1548.

THE GENERAL CONFESSION (*Prayer Book*, p. 75)   The Congregation,
                                                  kneeling or seated
From the same source.

THE DECLARATION OF ABSOLUTION
From the Sarum Missal, 1085, and the *Consultatio* of Hermann von Wied,
Archbishop of Cologne, 1543.

THE COMFORTABLE WORDS
St. Matthew 11:28; St. John 3:16; I Timothy 1:15; I St. John 2:1; as translated
in the "Great Bible" of 1539.

SURSUM CORDA (*Prayer Book*, p. 75)
Used in Western liturgies from the third century.

PREFACE
Also from the ancient Western liturgies, based upon even earlier Jewish usage.

SANCTUS and *BENEDICTUS QUI VENIT*
Respectively from Isaiah 6:3 and Psalm 118:26f = St. Matthew 21:9; used at
this point in the service from the fourth century; settings by Miss Browning.

A PREFACE TO THE PEOPLE
Written by President White for use at celebrations of the Holy Communion,
and included in each Sunday and high festival celebration since January of
1947.

THE PRAYER OF CONSECRATION
Adapted from the Canon of the Latin Mass in the Prayer Book of 1549; the
precise form used this morning is that of the *Ritual* of the Methodist Church,
which follows the English usage of 1552.

THE LORD'S PRAYER   Choir and Congregation
St. Matthew 6:9–13, as translated in *The King's Book*, 1543; a Gregorian setting,
adapted.

THE PRAYER OF HUMBLE ACCESS
The Order of Communion, 1548; based in part upon the ninth century Greek
liturgy of St. Basil.

AGNUS DEI
A part of the *Gloria in Excelsis*, used at Rome from the seventh century as
a devotion to be sung during the consecration of the elements; setting by Miss
Browning.

A PRAYER FOR PEACE AND UNITY
A medieval prayer regularly used at this point in the Latin Mass, as the
priest's devotion immediately before his own Communion.

THE COMMUNION
There is no denominational nor doctrinal test for participation in this symbol
of Christian fellowship. The sole demand is for the spirit of genuine fellowship in the quest for truth, in the joy of faith, and in the consecration of life.

Members of the congregation remain in their places to receive the elements.
If it is desired the bread may be retained until the chalice is passed, and may
be dipped therein; or the wine may be drunk from the chalice.

THE OBLATION OF OURSELVES
Prayer Book of 1549, based on the Sarum use of 1085. In the American Episcopal service, which follows Scottish custom, this paragraph of self-consecration
is attached to the Prayer of Consecration before the Communion. The Methodist ritual follows what still is the English usage, in placing it after the
distribution.

GLORIA IN EXCELSIS DEO
Developed from St. Luke 2:14; used in the Eastern Churches from the fourth
century; the setting is by Miss Browning.

THE COLLECT FOR ST. ANDREW'S DAY
Second Prayer Book of Edward VI, 1552. This is the only one of our Collects
which was composed for that book. St. Andrew's Day, normally 30 November,
will be celebrated tomorrow, 1 December, because Advent Sunday takes
precedence.

THE BLESSING
Based upon Philippians 4:7, and on the Roman Bishop's blessing of the faithful;
in the present form first in *The Order of Communion*, 1548.

RECESSIONAL HYMN No. 83 "Through all the changing scenes of life"
                              Choir and Congregation, standing
A paraphrase of Psalm 34 in *The New Version of Psalms*, 1696, by Nahum
Tate, Poet Laureate, and Nicholas Brady, a London clergyman; tune, "Wilt-

shire," by Sir George T. Smart, organist and composer at the Chapel Royal, in his *Divine Amusement*, published about 1795.

COLLECT FOR THANKSGIVING DAY
First American Prayer Book, 1789.

THE BENEDICTION
II Thessalonians 2:16f.

ORGAN POSTLUDE   *Komm, heiliger Geist*
A chorale adapted from a fifteenth-century setting for the *Veni sancte Spiritus*, first published in chorale form in Johann Walther's *Geystliche gesangk Buchleyn*, 1524. The harmonization is by Philipp Telemann, 1681–1767, director of music for the city of Hamburg.

In addition to the above, there were inserted before the Prayer for the Church a prayer for a baby baptized the previous Sunday afternoon, and one for a couple married on the intervening Saturday.

The total duration of this service was sixty-eight minutes.

Appendix H

BENEDICTIONS AND ASCRIPTIONS

There are reproduced here only Benedictions and Ascriptions which are not commonly presented as such in our service books, nor frequently used as such in our churches. It will be noted that in some cases the words have been adjusted slightly to fit them for use in the service.

All of the following have been used in the services of the Mills College Chapel in the four years 1948–1952, some of them once only, and some several times. In each case a familiar Blessing had place in the service also: the Grace (II Corinthians 13:14) at the close of Morning Prayer, and the Communion Blessing ("The Peace of God, which passeth all understanding . . .") before the Recessional Hymn after the Holy Communion.

Many other possibilities will suggest themselves to one who looks through the Scriptures and the Liturgies for words appropriate to the close of worship, and to the varying themes of services.

BIBLICAL

Let mount Zion rejoice, let the daughters of Judah be glad, because of thy judgments. For this God is our God for ever and ever: he will be our guide even unto death. Amen.—Psalm 48:11, 14.

God be merciful unto us, and bless us, and cause his face to shine upon us: that his way may be known upon earth, his saving health among all nations. Amen.—Psalm 67:1f.

Be glad then, ye children of Zion, and rejoice in the Lord your God: for in mount Zion and in Jerusalem shall be deliverance, as the Lord hath said. Amen.— Joel 2:23, 32.

The Lord leave peace with you, the Lord give his peace unto you: not the peace that the world giveth, but the peace that is his. Amen.—St. John 14:27.

The Lord sanctify you through his truth, whose Word is truth. Amen.— St. John 17:17.

May God, who commanded the light to shine out of darkness, shine evermore in your hearts, to give the light of the knowledge of the glory of God in the face of Jesus Christ. Amen.—II Corinthians 4:6.

May the Lord approve you as the ministers of God, by the word of truth and by the power of God, by the armour of righteousness on the right hand and on the left. Amen.—II Corinthians 6:4, 7.

286

In Christ Jesus neither circumcision availeth any thing, nor uncircumcision, but a new creature. And as many as walk according to this rule, peace be on them, and mercy, and upon the Israel of God. The grace of the Lord Jesus Christ be with your spirits. Amen.—Galatians 6:15f., 18.

The God of our Lord Jesus Christ, the Father of glory, give unto you the spirit of wisdom and revelation in the knowledge of him: the eyes of your understanding being enlightened; that ye may know what is the hope of his calling, and what the riches of the glory of his inheritance in the saints.—Ephesians 1:17f.

May we all come in the unity of the faith, and of the knowledge of the Son of God, unto a perfect man, unto the measure of the stature of the fulness of Christ; may we grow up into him in all things, which is the head, even Christ. Amen.—Ephesians 4:13, 15.

Peace be to you, and love with faith, from God the Father and the Lord Jesus Christ. Grace be with all them that love our Lord Jesus Christ in sincerity. Amen.—Ephesians 6:23f.

May God supply all your need according to his riches in glory by Christ Jesus. Now unto God and our Father be glory for ever and ever. The grace of our Lord Jesus Christ be with you all. Amen.—Philippians 4:20f., 23.

The very God of peace sanctify you wholly; that your whole spirit and soul and body be preserved blameless unto the coming of our Lord Jesus Christ. The grace of our Lord Jesus Christ be with you. Amen.—I Thessalonians 5:23, 28.

May the name of our Lord Jesus Christ be glorified in you, and ye in him, according to the grace of our God and the Lord Jesus Christ. Amen.—II Thessalonians 1:11f.

Now our Lord Jesus Christ himself, and God, even our Father, which hath loved us, and hath given us everlasting consolation and good hope through grace, comfort your hearts, and stablish you in every good word and work. Amen.—II Thessalonians 2:16f.

Now the Lord of peace himself give you peace at all times in all ways. The Lord be with you all. Amen.—II Thessalonians 3:16.

Now unto the blessed and only Potentate, the King of kings, and Lord of lords; who only hath immortality; dwelling in the light which no man can approach unto; whom no man hath seen or can see: to him be honour and power everlasting. Amen.—I Timothy 6:15f.

May ye study to show yourselves approved unto God, workmen that need not to be ashamed, rightly dividing the word of truth. The Lord Jesus Christ be with your spirits. Grace be with you. Amen.—II Timothy 2:15, 4:22.

And now may ye come unto the city of the living God, the heavenly Jerusalem, and to an innumerable company of angels; to the general assembly and church of the firstborn, which are written in heaven, and to God the judge of all, and to the spirits of just men made perfect. Amen.—Hebrews 12:22f.

May ye rejoice in Christ with joy unspeakable and full of glory: receiving the end of your faith, even the salvation of your souls. Amen.—I St. Peter 1:8f.

The Lord through the Spirit purify your souls in obeying the truth, unto unfeigned love of the brethren; and that ye love one another with a pure heart fervently; through him who loved us and gave himself for us, Christ Jesus our Lord. Amen.—I St. Peter 1:22.

The God of all grace, who hath called us unto his eternal glory by Christ Jesus, after that ye have suffered a while, make you perfect, stablish, strengthen, settle you. To him be glory and dominion for ever and ever. Peace be with you all that are in Christ Jesus. Amen.—I St. Peter 5:10f., 14.

The Lord grant that we, keeping his commandments, may dwell evermore in him. And may we know that he abideth in us, by the Spirit which he hath given us. Amen.—I St. John 3:24.

For the truth's sake, which dwelleth in us, and shall be with us for ever: Grace be with you, mercy, and peace, from God the Father, and from the Lord Jesus Christ, the Son of the Father, in truth and love. Amen.—II St. John 2f.

EXTRA-BIBLICAL

Let the earth bless the Lord: yea, let it praise him, and magnify him for ever. Let us bless the Father, and the Son, and the Holy Ghost: praise him, and magnify him for ever. Amen.—*Benedicite, omnia opera.*

Extolled and hallowed be the Name of God throughout the world; and may he speedily establish his kingdom of righteousness on earth. Amen.—*Union Prayer Book for Jewish Worship.*

Eternal God, thou hast shown us what is good and what thou dost require of us: to do justly, to love mercy, and to walk humbly with thee. Great peace have they who love thy Law, and nothing can offend them. Lord, give strength unto thy people; O God, bless thy people with peace. Amen.—*Union Prayer Book for Jewish Worship.*

Blessed be the Name of the Lord for ever. Peace be with you all. In the peace of Christ let us depart. Lord, bless us. Amen.—*Liturgy of St. James.*

Depart in peace in the Name of the Lord. The love of God and the Father, the grace of the Son and our Lord Jesus Christ, the communion and gift of the Holy Ghost, be with us all, now and ever, and to ages of ages. Blessed be the Name of the Lord. Amen.—*Liturgy of St. Mark.*

Be blessed by the grace of the Holy Spirit. Go in peace, and may the Lord be with you all. Amen.—*Liturgy of the Armenians.*

The Mystery of thy dispensation, O Christ our God, is accomplished and perfected, so far as lies in our power. For we have the memorial of thy death, we have seen the figure of thy resurrection, we have been filled with thine unending life. We have enjoyed thine inexhaustible pleasure, of which vouchsafe to count us all worthy in the world to come; Through the grace of thine eternal Father, and thy holy, and good, and quickening Spirit, now and ever, and to ages of ages. Amen.—*Liturgy of St. Basil.*

May our Lord Jesus Christ be near you to defend you, within you to refresh you, around you to preserve you, before you to guide you, behind you to justify you, above you to bless you; Who liveth and reigneth with the Father and the Holy Ghost, God for evermore. Amen.—*Latin, tenth century.*

Almighty God, the Father, and the Son, and the Holy Ghost, bless you. The Lord be with you, unto the ages of the ages. Amen.—*Roman Missal.*

The Lord go forth with you from this his holy house; and send down upon you his love and light and calm, wherein ye may continually dwell and worship with him for evermore. Amen.—*William Ewart Gladstone, 1809-1898.*

May God the Father, the Son, and the Holy Spirit, give light to guide us, courage to support us, and love to unite us, now and for evermore. Amen.—*Forward, Lent 1938.*

May the life that is God animate our frames. May the truth that is God illumine our minds. And may the love that is God fill our hearts and govern our lives. Amen.—*Robert French Leavens, 1939.*

INDEX OF SUBJECTS AND NAMES

(Principal discussions are indicated by the use of *italics*.)

289